RGA

Where is the Eagle?

Where is the Eagle?

William E. Coffer
(Koi Hosh)

VNR VAN NOSTRAND REINHOLD COMPANY
NEW YORK   CINCINNATI   ATLANTA   DALLAS   SAN FRANCISCO
LONDON   TORONTO   MELBOURNE

Van Nostrand Reinhold Company Regional Offices:
New York   Cincinnati   Atlanta   Dallas   San Francisco

Van Nostrand Reinhold Company International Offices:
London   Toronto   Melbourne

Copyright © 1981 by Litton Educational Publishing, Inc.

Library of Congress Catalog Card Number: 80-24178
ISBN: 0-442-26163-2

Manufactured in the United States of America.

Published by Van Nostrand Reinhold Company
135 West 50th Street, New York, N.Y. 10020

Published simultaneously in Canada by Van Nostrand Reinhold Ltd.

15   14   13   12   11   10   9   8   7   6   5   4   3   2   1

Library of Congress Cataloging in Publication Data
Coffer, William E
  Where is the eagle?

  Includes index.
  1. Indians of North America—Religion and mythology.
2. Indians of North America—Legends.   I. Title.
E98.R3C67   299'.793   80-24178
ISBN 0-442-26163-2

To

An Ohoyo Aiukli
(*My Beautiful Woman*)

Preface
Where is the Eagle?

We know that the white man does not understand our ways. One portion of the land is the same to him as the next, for he is a stranger who comes in the night and takes from the land whatever he needs. The earth is not his brother but his enemy, and when he has conquered it he moves on. He leaves his fathers' graves and his children's birthright is forgotten.

There is no quiet place in the white man's cities—no place to hear the leaves of spring or the rustle of insect wings. But perhaps because I am a savage and do not understand, the clatter only seems to insult the ears. And what is there to life if a man cannot hear the lovely cry of the whippoorwill or the argument of frogs around the pond at night?

The whites too shall pass—perhaps sooner than other tribes. Continue to contaminate your bed and you will one night suffocate in your own waste. When the buffalo are all slaughtered, the wild horses all tamed, the secret corners of the forest heavy with the scent of many men, and the view of the ripe hills blotted by talking wires. Where is the thicket—gone! Where is the eagle—gone! And what is it to say goodby to the swift and the hunt—the end of living and the beginning of survival.

These were comments by Chief Seattle of the Dwamish Nation in a message to President Franklin Pierce in 1855. His concern was that the white invaders would continue their constant pressure against the Indian for land until they would destroy even themselves. He warns the whites of their impending doom in his analogous statement concerning suffocating in their own waste.

We are beginning to recognize the accuracy of his predictions with smog, pollution of rivers and lakes, and the constant threat of atomic or nuclear annihilation. Measures are beginning to be taken to forestall Seattle's predictions. Stringent pollution control standards are being formulated and enforced, conservation of energy has become a household slogan, treaties with countries who pose a nuclear threat are being implemented, wilderness areas are being set aside to preserve nature, and many other activities are being pursued in the attempt to preserve mankind.

What happens, though, to the sacred oral traditions of a people when the steamroller of "civilization" crushes them? How can the ghosts of the people perpetuate the stories which were traditionally passed from the elders to the children in the quiet hours of evening or in the calm of dawn? Must they, like the eagle, disappear and be gone?

Mankind has begun to realize the loss of the obvious, the physical things about them, and has initiated recovery programs and policies. What has not been recognized is the loss of an even more important facet of life, the philosophical and spiritual ability of the Indian to live in harmony with and complete comprehension of the powers of the universe. The rationale applied to the great mysteries of life enabled the Indian to consciously and pragmatically construct the lifestyle for which "modern" man is striving. The great complexity of current technological civilization has prevented it from recognizing the solutions to its own survival problems.

So, just as the Old World cultures trampled the Indian people in the frantic rush for acquisition of the material world, they also have nearly exterminated those esthetic attributes which sustained the native Americans.

Through forced educational processes which denigrated the traditional and glorified the new, the introduction of Christianity and compulsory adherance to its doctrines, and the outright suppression of native religions by the most heinous methods, many of the beautiful narratives have been lost. And once they have gone, there is no method of recovery. They are lost forever.

If Seattle were alive today he would be compelled to add to his prophecy, "Where are the stories—gone!"

All are not gone, however, and some do remain to continue to provide an anchor for today's Indian people. While many of these oral traditions have been diluted by the influence of the invading societies, and some are tinged with a European or Christian flavor, most still tell the basic stories, unchanged over the centuries.

This author has diligently searched over a long period of time, traveling many thousands of miles, visiting Indian communities and listening to the elders and the children from Alaska to Florida, to learn as many of these oral traditions as possible. The first publication of these was in *Spirits of the Sacred Mountains: Creation Stories of the American Indian.* This book, although it does contain a few creation versions not found in *Spirits of the Sacred Mountains,* provides a record of other tales which give logic to many facets of life for the Indian. Even those told in a humorous manner, or those which, in the concept of the non-Indian would be considered "fairy tales," contain logical explanations which satisfy the curiosity of an Indian child concerning the world in which he or she lives. These presentations provide and perpetuate "Indianness" in America and allow the native people to retain their sanity while the world around them seems to be mad.

Koi Hosh

Introduction

In their relationship to the world, the difference between the white man and the Indian is that the white man wishes to be dominant upon the landscape. The Indian considers himself but one of the many living creatures within a universe of living things. The white man is moved by nature as is the Indian, but when the wind blows through a forest, the Indian does not hear only its sound, he hears the voice of a Spirit which speaks to him.

When the white man views a mountain, he ponders, "Mountain, how can I conquer you?" An Indian, looking at the same mountain, asks, "Mountain, how can I live with you?"

The purpose of this book is to help create an awareness of the special feelings that the North American Indian has for the universe and how they influence his life. A great conflict between the white man and the American Indian originated in their understandings of the natural world. For the Indian, the earth is his mother, the ground the womb which held him. Like all living things, he is but a part of nature, one with his surroundings. It is his greatest desire to live in harmony with all things. His special commandment, given by the Great Spirit who endowed man with the tools to carry out the mandate, is that he be the caretaker of the Creation.

The white man views his role in nature in diametrical opposition to that of the Indian. According to the non-Indian, man has been created to conquer and subdue the world. He has been given special talents which set him above the other animals. Scientists and theologians have given such euphonious names to this gift as intellect, reasoning power, soul, etc., all of which have been devised to rationalize the greedy and capricious disregard for the environment.

This book is filled with the American Indian's relationship to the world around him. It contains mythical and spiritual examples of his explanations of his first, and his lasting, perceptions of the natural world.

These examples of customs, habits, and spiritual manifestations of the Indian are illustrated in a variety of settings. The reader will discover the Indian's dependence upon and his reverence for the natural world and should begin to comprehend the reasons why the natural world holds the meaning of life for the Indian people.

Translation of the oral traditions of the Indian people is not something new. Linguists, oral historians, bleeding-heart romanticists, and many others have written their versions of the stories told by Indians. It is imperative that the reader understand that such translations, however learned the translator, loses some of the important concepts. The Indian languages cannot, in many cases, be reduced to English and maintain their meaning. Therefore, we receive frivolous interpretations by writers lacking the acumen to comprehend the beauty of the Indian tongues and express them in English. They are generally presented, then, completely out of the context of the Indian cultural perspective.

We cannot appreciate fully the clarity of expression nor the grandeur nor the eloquence of these Indian languages. They are filled with drama, and they are clear, concise, and dignified in manner when spoken. How can that be captured on paper? There is also an ambiguous method of narration employed by some Indian storytellers which can only be understood in the native context. It is, therefore, complex to translate the Indian oral presentations to written English composition, and maintain fidelity.

Part of a speech of welcome made by the Delawares to the Cherokees, as the latter had sent ambassadors, indicates some of the eloquence which has been transferred from the native tongue to English.

It provides a subtle message of reproof and an offer to overlook past difficulties and establish amicable relations. With the following two paragraphs the leaders of the two great nations established a treaty which lasted until removal of the tribes rendered it useless many years later.

> We extract the thorns from your feet which you have got upon your journey. We take away the sand and gravel between your toes, and the wounds and bruises made by the briars and brushwood, we anoint with balsamic oil. We wipe the sweat off your faces, the dust off your eyes, and cleanse your ears, throats and hearts from all evil which you have seen or heard by the way or which has entered into your hearts.

The Cherokee responded in their attempt to re-establish peace between the two nations:

> We make a road extending above five hundred miles through the wood. We root out the thorns and bushes, remove all the trees, rocks and stones out of the way, transplant the mountains, strew the road with sand, and make everything so clear and light that one nation may look toward the other without any interception.*

In writing the following stories, this author has attempted to retain as much of the Indian eloquence and expression as possible while utilizing the English language to convey the meanings. It is his sincere hope that the reader receives the same spiritual uplift, and, in some cases, pure entertainment, that the writer has experienced in preparing the book.

Imola,
William E. Coffer
Koi Hosh

---

* John McLean, *The Indians: Their Manners and Customs* (Toronto: William Briggs, 1889). This oral presentation concluded a treaty between two powerful Indian nations in a clear, concise manner, yet used a manner of speech which could not be utilized by any two "white" nations in the world in comparable negotiations. Such a treaty by European logic would necessarily contain many pages of superfluous detail and bureaucratic jargon and be concluded only after numerous extended meetings by the participants.

Contents

Where is the Eagle?

One

The Southeast Indians

The Southeast area extends from the Atlantic Ocean to the lower Mississippi River Valley and from Tennessee to the Gulf of Mexico. This vast expanse is composed of a wide variety of terrain including coastal plains, inland plateaus, and wooded mountain regions. The area is generally characterized by a mild climate, abundant rainfall, and plenty of game and wild vegetation. The people who have lived in this area, from the earliest known habitation until now, have primarily been agriculturalists.

When the first Europeans arrived, many of the nations of the Southeast lived in agricultural villages and had elaborate social and ceremonial structures. There were great nations with populations exceeding twenty-five to thirty thousand which necessitated a rather sophisticated governmental system to cohere the small scattered village units into a unified political entity. Confederacies, some quite large, were formed from small nations of extremely diverse cultures. Some of these, such as the Creek and Powhattan Confederacies, played an important part in the history of the United States.

Nations such as the Choctaw and Cherokee controlled millions of acres of land which the Americans coveted as the expansion of the original thirteen colonies began. Millions of immigrants from the Old

1

World moving inland from the coast required much land for the development of farms and plantations. Deposits of valuable minerals discovered on Indian land helped establish a rationale for removing the original inhabitants. Although the Choctaw, Creek, Chickasaw, and Cherokee adopted much of the European cultural perspective in their political institutions, their social structures, their economics, and changed their ways of living to conform to the pattern set by the white man, they were called savages. They attempted to live in harmony with these strangers from the East, but there was no way this could be.

Every European power which exercised any interest in the New World and every American administration from that of George Washington onwards, subscribed to the same philosophy in the treatment of Indians and their problems—remove them to the West. Finally in 1830, Andrew Jackson mustered enough political clout to force the passage of the infamous Removal Act. This legislative action provided the president with authority only to negotiate treaties with the various Indian nations for removal. Jackson and his successor Martin Van Buren, assumed much more power than the law provided, using a wide variety of nefarious tactics against the Indian nations. The result was the insidious "Trail of Tears" and "Trail of Death."*

After the removal of these duped and defeated people to Indian Territory, the duplicity of the Federal government's dealings with them continued. In spite of myriad treaties securing their lands "in perpetuity," by 1907 when Oklahoma became a state, a provision specifically prohibited in many of the treaties, these nations vanished and the citizens became "Americans," or more specifically, "Okies."

In spite of the fraudulent treatment by the government, and in spite of the coercion and suppression of Indian culture by the dominant society, much of the Indian cultural perspective survives. It is the author's hope that the readers will empathize with him as his heart breaks in the writing of the following section. The spirits of his ancestors cry out in anguish as these stories unfold.

CADDO

Along the northwestern area of the Southeastern Indians, in northern Louisiana, southern Arkansas and eastern Texas, lived a unique group

---

* For a detailed explanation, see William E. Coffer, *Phoenix: The Decline and Rebirth of the Indian People* (New York: Van Nostrand Reinhold Co., 1979.)

of Indian people called the Caddo. Living west of the Mississippi River, they were like the other southeastern tribes in many ways, with a mixed agricultural and hunting economy, but for them the buffalo was the most important game animal. This formed a subsistence pattern which was intermediate between the Southeast and the Plains.

The Caddoan language family consists of four major components: Caddo, Pawnee, Wichita, and Kitsai. The Caddo dialect was the most divergent, probably because it was spoken by the tribal units more closely affiliated with the southeastern tribes while the other three dialects were spoken by the groups associating more with Plains cultures.

A rather populous nation in prewhite times with about eight thousand members, the Caddos have been reduced by various causes to between five hundred and one thousand people today. Most of the survivors are located in Oklahoma and are generally not full-blood.

Although their population is small and their tribal traditions have been seriously eroded, the Caddo still tell some of the stories which have survived for centuries. The following is an example:

How Death Came to the People

When the Creator made the world He did not make death and everyone lived forever. Soon there were so many people on earth that there was no room for any more. A great council was held to determine what should be done.

One man proposed that people should die and be gone for a while and then return. When he had finished and sat down, Coyote arose and said he thought that people should stay dead forever. He said the world was too small to hold everyone if those who died were allowed to return. Soon there would not be enough food for everyone and they would all be hungry.

All the others at the council objected for they wanted their friends and relatives who died to come back and live with them. Otherwise, the people would grieve and there would be much unhappiness in the world. Everyone except Coyote agreed it would be better to have the people die and be gone for a little while, and then return back to life.

The elders then built a large grass house with its doorway facing the rising sun. They then called everyone together and told them they had decided to have the ones who died come to the medicine house to be restored to life. The chief medicine man would sing a song to call the spirit of the dead and when it came into the grass house it would live again. Everyone was happy for they were anxious to have their friends and loved ones come back to life and live with them.

When the first man died, the medicine men gathered and their leader began to sing the song to attract the spirit. After about seven days* a whirlwind blew in from the west and began to circle about the grass house. Coyote saw it, and as the whirlwind was about to enter the house, he slammed the door. The spirit, not being able to enter, left and went on beyond the western horizon.** Death forever had been introduced and, from that time on, people grieved over their dead and were unhappy.

Now, whenever a person sees a whirlwind or hears the wind howl, they know it is someone's spirit wandering about looking for entry to the grass house. Ever since Coyote shut the door, the spirits of the dead wander over the land trying to find someplace to go, until they finally find the road to the Land of Spirits.

When Coyote realized what he had done, he ran away and never returned. Ever since that time he runs from place to place, looking over one shoulder and then the other to see if anyone is after him. He became an outcast, and, until this day, has no friends and is always restless and on the move.——Caddo.

CHOCTAW

The Choctaws were the largest tribe belonging to the southern branch of the Muskogean language family. Divided into three geographic districts, each headed by its own leader, they covered most of the southern part of Mississippi, extending eastward into Alabama and westward across the Mississippi River into Louisiana.

The first contact with Europeans came when Hernando de Soto, the Spanish explorer, invaded their country in October 1540. This meeting brought on an horrendous battle as the Choctaws attempted to repel the Spaniards who had left a trail of murder, rape, and pillage across Flor-

---

* The number "seven" is quite important to many Indian groups. It represents the seven cardinal elements which make up the universe, the number of days the spirits of the dead remain before going on the the Spirit Land, and other important facets within the cultures of many nations.
** Many tribal groups have only vague concepts of life after death but believe that the Spirit Land, or whatever name it may be called, lies beyond the western horizon.

ida and Alabama. The Indian leader Tuskaloosa (Black Warrior) and his Choctaw army inflicted heavy losses on the Spanish before succumbing to the superior weaponry and armor of de Soto's infantry and cavalry. Eighty-two of the invaders perished but the natives suffered a tremendous number of casualties as well as the incineration of their town, Mabila (Mobile). After the battle de Soto remained in the area quite a while, sending out foraging parties to rob the natives of provisions and to kidnap females for use by the troops. Finally on November 18, 1540 his soldiers had recovered enough for de Soto to leave Choctaw territory.

After this introduction, the Choctaws were wary of any European alliance and only accepted French overtures in the eighteenth century. Spain and England failed in their attempts to ally with the Choctaws. Throughout the history of the United States, however, there has never been warfare with the Choctaw Nation.

In 1830 most of the Choctaw people moved west of the Mississippi River and relocated in Oklahoma where they re-established themselves as a prosperous nation. The Indians who remained in the Mississippi homeland were isolated from the other inhabitants and were able to maintain their cultural traditions relatively undisturbed until the mid-1960s. Language, dress, religion, ceremonies, and other cultural entities were retained. Oral tradition is very much in evidence among the Mississippi Band.

Oklahoma Choctaws, having been forcibly assimilated when Oklahoma became a state in 1907, some twenty thousand Choctaws were forced into the mainstream of American society. There is no reservation but many rural communities in southeastern Oklahoma are principally populated by members of the tribe. In these areas the traditions are carried on but in a diluted form.

The following stories were selected by the author from the many he has heard in Oklahoma and Mississippi.*

How Tibih Lake Became Haunted

Many years ago, long before the coming of the white man, a Chickasaw hunter and his wife along with two little children were camped in

---

* It is only natural that the author, being Choctaw, would include a rather large sampling of the rich tradition of his own people.

the Tibih Swamp near a little hole of water formed by the roots of a fallen tree. One morning the hunter and his wife went in search of game and, as was their custom, left the children to play in camp. They hunted all day with little success and started to return to their camp about sundown.

When they reached their camp, they were shocked and horrified at what they found. Their campsite had been swallowed up by the earth and in its place was a lake. While they were looking at the scene in fear and awe, they saw two enormous snakes swimming toward them across the newly formed lake. They turned and fled in terror for the same power which had formed the lake had transformed their children into gigantic water snakes. The hunter and his wife returned to their people and told what had happened.

Even to this day, no Chickasaw or Choctaw will go near the lake. The entire area is shunned by them and no one will live or approach anywhere near the area. The story has several variations, being changed slightly as it is told and retold, but it is generally believed by both tribes. All agree the lake was brought into existence by the wrath of the Great Spirit and it has been the home of evil spirits ever since.——Choctaw

Why the Possum Grins

One day Wolf was very hungry. He hunted everywhere but could find nothing to eat. He went down to the creek and drank a lot of water but that didn't help his hunger a bit. His stomach was so empty that it growled and growled.

As he wandered about, he looked up in a persimmon tree and saw Possum. Now Possum didn't worry much about going hungry for he would eat anything. This day he was filling his belly with sweet, ripe persimmons and this made Wolf even hungrier. He asked Possum how he got up in the tree and Possum answered, "I climbed up to get the persimmons. Sometimes though the persimmons just fall off the tree to the ground."

As Wolf watched Possum enjoying his meal, he became even hungrier. He said, "I sure wish I had some of those persimmons."

Now Possum, remembering that Wolf had made a meal out of other possums on many occasions, decided this would be a good time to get even. He said to Wolf, "Well, you just go way off yonder and run with all your might and butt your head against the persimmon tree and shake some down."

Wolf did as he was directed. He came running at the tree as fast as he could and hit it with his head. This broke his neck and he died. Possum was so tickled at Wolf's death that he has never stopped laughing. He laughs and grins yet.——Choctaw

The Origin of Corn

In the beginning Choctaw people were hungry. "We have nothing to feed our little ones and our old people are starving," they lamented. "We do not have strength enough to chase the deer."

Then one day birds came from the south. They flew over the place where the Choctaws were camped, and the people noticed they carried something truly remarkable in their claws and beaks. They dropped this thing into the Choctaw fields and soon a beautiful and mysterious plant began to grow. Because of the long stalks, the green coating, and the silken covering, the Wise Men knew it was corn, a gift of the Spirit brought on the wings of the birds.

Before long the Choctaws had a new life, and they were no longer hungry. Their journey was over and they could now live in the place where the Choctaw Spirits had brought them. The sacred corn would enable them to survive.——Choctaw

The Black Squirrel Eats the Sun

The Black Squirrel is full of mischief. He is always getting into trouble by poking his nose into everyone's business. He even attempts at times to eat the sun, thereby causing a great darkness to come over the earth.

When the Black Squirrel gets hungry for the sun, he starts nibbling away at it. As he eats more and more, it gets darker and darker. The white man calls this an eclipse but the Choctaw knows what it is. Therefore, as soon as the Black Squirrel starts eating the sun, the cry goes out, "Fani lusa hushi umpa! Fani lusa hushi umpa!" (The Black Squirrel is eating the sun.)

As if by command, all the people begin to make all the noise possible in order to frighten the squirrel away. Women and children ring bells, beat on pots and pans, and shout as loudly as they can. Even the dogs join in with yelping, howling, and barking as they run excitedly around the area. The men load and fire their rifles as fast as they can, careful not to shoot the sun itself. All the people and animals work together to make so much noise that Fani Lusa will be fightened away for a long time.

Invariably, the shrieking of the women and children, the yapping of the dogs, the beating of the pans, and the shooting of the rifles produce the desired results. Admittedly, as in a total eclipse, the exorcism takes longer at times, and it is necessary to strain every vocal organ to the utmost, and the beating and shooting have to be extended for the Black Squirrel can be very stubborn.

Eventually though, as the disk of the sun begins to reappear, a joyful shout of "Fani lusa hosh muhlata," (The Black Squirrel is frightened.) will be heard above the mighty din. "Fani lusa hosh muhlata," usually sends the noise to even a higher pitch as the people make sure the Black Squirrel will not return. It is only after the sun totally reappears and nature resumes its normal course that the people also begin their natural operations, grateful to the Great Spirit who has given them the victory.——Choctaw

How the Choctaws Got Corn
or
Ohoyo Osh Chisba (The Unknown Woman)

Many years ago, two hunters were camped in a swamp at the bend of the Alabama River. They had been hunting for several days without success and on this particular night were very hungry. They had killed no game and the food that they had brought from home was long since gone. One of the hunters was able to shoot a black hawk just at sundown, and they were getting ready to eat their poor and scanty supper when they heard a strange noise. From out of the swamp came a soft and plaintive sound such as the melancholy cooing of the dove. However, neither of the men had ever heard anything just like it and they could not imagine what was making the sounds. They looked up and down the river but could not find anything.

Suddenly, they saw a beautiful woman standing on a mound a few yards away. She appeared all at once for there was nothing there a few minutes earlier. She was dressed in a flowing snow-white robe and held

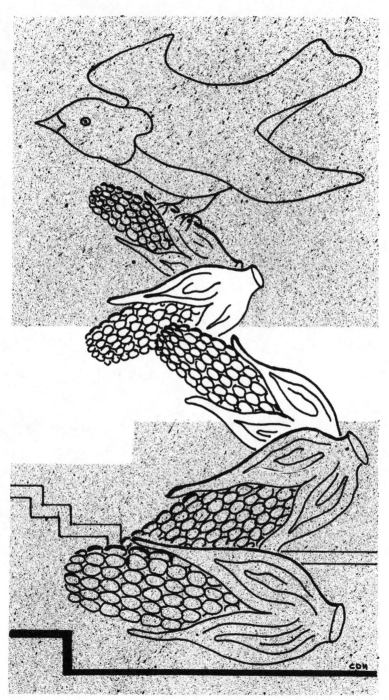

How the Choctaws Got Corn
Choctaw

a wreath of fragrant flowers in her hand. As she beckoned the two hunters to approach, she seemed to be surrounded by a halo of light which gave her a supernatural appearance. The men thought her to be the Great Spirit and the flowers she carried to be the spirits of their loved ones who had passed to the Spirit Land beyond the horizon.

As they approached her, the mystery was solved. The beautiful woman said she was hungry and asked if the men would share their food with her. Although they only had the small black hawk and that was not very good food, they freely offered it to her. She accepted it with much gratitude, and after eating only a small portion, handed it back to them. She told the young men she would remember their kindness when she returned to the home of he father Chittokaka, the Great Spirit.

Then she left the men with instructions to meet her in exactly one year at the mound on which she was standing. She was then borne away on a gentle breeze and disappeared as mysteriously as she had come. The hunters stood there for a while, dumbfounded by what had happened. Finally, when morning came, they broke camp and returned to their homes.

At exactly the same time a year later, the two hunters returned to the mound where they had seen the lovely lady. The found that, instead of the beautiful woman, the mound was covered with a strange plant. They had never seen anything like it, but, upon trying it, they found it to be an excellent food. Ever after, the plant was cultivated by the Choctaws and was given the name, Tanchi (corn).——Choctaw

The Liver Sacrifice

When a deer or bear is killed on a hunting expedition, the liver is divided into as many pieces as there are fires. A boy is then sent with a piece to each man who has a fire so he may burn it as a sacrifice to the Great Spirit. Since women do not hunt, fires belonging to them are excluded from this ritual. If more than one animal is killed, the livers of all are treated in the same way.——Choctaw

Dreams or Spirit Leaving

At night when a person is asleep and all is quiet, the spirit steals away from the body and wanders about the country. During this time, it sees many people and things which are known to the individual when he awakes. Therefore, dreams are actually a reality and should be studied seriously. If during its wanderings the spirit meets large animals of any sort, the person will suffer misfortune before many days have passed.——Choctaws

Violent Death Precludes Heaven

Persons dying by violent means, especially if it entails the shedding of blood, even a few drops, do not pass into Aba (Heaven), regardless of how good they were or what status of life they held. Violent death automatically excluded one's spirit from enjoying the happiness in the "land of spirits."

The spirits of those who do not die violently, with the exception of those who murder or attempt to murder their fellow Choctaws, go to Aba to spend eternity in that happy place. There it is always Spring with abundant sunshine and flowers, and there are always plentiful fruits, birds, and game. There the Choctaw always sing and dance and trouble is unknown and all who enter become virtuous, regardless of their state while on earth.

The unhappy spirits who fail to reach Aba remain on earth near where they died. But Nanukpulo (Bad Spirit or Devil) is never able to gain possession of the spirit of a Choctaw.*——Choctaw

Life After Death

In the Choctaw traditional belief, there is another state of existence to which the soul goes after death. Somewhere in the universe, we know not just where it is, there is a land called "shilup i yakni," the land of the spirits. To this land of delight, where the sun shines and it is warm every day, the soul goes as soon as it is released from the body.

Death, to Choctaws, is not the end of life but merely another step in living. It is a transition from one state to another; the throwing off or shedding of the external covering of the shilup, or soul, as the snake sheds its skin. So the shilup having cast off its envelope and left its im-

* This version of Heaven and Hell is traditional with some of the isolated groups of Choctaws, especially those located west of the Mississippi River in Louisiana.

perfections behind, retaining its human shape, enters this land of happiness. When it arrives there it experiences no more the trials and sorrows of this earthly life. The aged exchange the gray head and the decrepitude of old age for the beauty and vigor of youth. Those who die young are preserved in a state of perpetual youth and know no fear of the encroachments of time.

Here the shilup regales itself with melons and other fruits and feasts on all the products of the earth. Here is a continuous succession of games, dances, and good times so the time passes in an atmosphere of mirth and happiness. The spirits are able to participate in any activity they choose, especially those which brought joy and contentment in their earthly sojourn. If great satisfaction is obtained from plying one's skill as a craftsman, tools and equipment are available. If it be the stickball game which has provided pleasure, kapuchas and toli (sticks and ball) are provided. Whatever one wants is freely available.

To enter this land of delight and happiness, no spiritual qualifications. no purification of the heart, no rigorous adherance to a set of rules in life is necessary. No one is excluded from participation in the pleasures of this existence except those who have committed murder of the most aggravated kind. All others, however evil and debased they may have been, find pleasures suited to their taste and capacity.

Close to the borders of this happy land, and within sight of it, is the place where the spirits of murderers go after death. By some odd reason they are unable to find the correct path which leads to the land of pleasure and happiness, and are compelled to take the road which leads to their destination. Here, though they can clearly see the happy land, they cannot share in the pleasures and enjoyment. Since they cannot participate in these joyous activities, they are, of course, very unhappy. Being a prey to their ungovernable passions in their earthly life, they are naturally miserable in their new home.

The misery which the ghosts of murderers suffer is not considered a punishment inflicted on them by some vindictive God; nor is the happiness and contentment enjoyed by those who reach the good land a reward for their obedience to a set of rules. Both situations are considered as matters of natural consequence, taking place in the order of nature, with no interposition of a superior power.

It is the ancient belief of the Choctaws that every man has shilombish, the outside shadow which always follows him, and shilup, the inside shadow, or ghost which at death goes to shilup i yakni, the land of ghosts. The shilombish remains on earth and wanders restlessly about its former place of life. Often, especially at night, it utters pitiful moans intended to frighten its surviving friends to make them leave the spot and seek another place to live. Many times the shilombish assumes the form of a fox or an owl, and by barking like a fox or screeching like an owl, causes great concern among the living who interpret the sounds as omens of ill. The people know it is shilombish because when a fox barks or an owl screeches, another fox or owl replies. When shilombish imitates the sound of either animal, there is no response.——Choctaw

How the Bear Lost His Tail

A long time ago when the animals were here and there were no people, the bear had the most beautiful tail of all the creatures of the forest. He would strut through the woods and boast how lovely he looked with his long colorful tail. The other animals grew tired with his boasting and tried many ways to overcome his attitude, with no result.

One cold winter day, Bear went hunting for food. All the nuts, berries, and animals were covered with the deep snow or well hidden deep in their dens and old Bear was really hungry. He traveled to the lake and walked out on the ice. He could see the fish unde the frozen surface so he broke the ice with blows from his powerful paws. Now he could get to the water but he could not catch the fish. Finally he figured a way to get himself a fine fish dinner. He would stick his long colorful tail in the water and hope the fish would grab onto it. He sat down on the ice and dropped his tail in the icy-cold water and waited.

All this time Coyote was watching Bear and thought he was crazy. He called the other animals to look at the weird thing at the lake.

Bear continued to sit there without one bite on his tail and he was getting colder and colder and his tail was beginning to freeze in the ice.

Coyote saw this and figured this would be a good time to get even with Bear for all his boasting about his beautiful tail. He slipped out of the woods and started throwing rocks and sticks at the bear and taunted him with insults. Bear became very angry and decided to teach Coyote a lesson. He tried to get up to chase Coyote but his tail was stuck in the ice.

He struggled and tugged at the tail and pulled as hard as he could.

Finally, he felt the tail come loose and he started after Coyote. By this time many of the other animals had gathered to see what was making all the commotion. When Bear got loose and started to run, he was amazed at what he saw. The other animals were rolling on the ground, holding their sides, and roaring with laughter. He realized then that they were laughing at him.

Looking back he saw his beautiful tail still stuck in the ice and in its place he had only a short stub. He was deeply ashamed, and very angry. And that is why bears today have short tails and short tempers.——Choctaw

How Medicine Was Given

There was a time, long long ago, when only the animals lived on the earth. They were happy and lived in peace with each other and there was no sickness, no anger, and no fighting. One day the Great Spirit made Man and put him on the earth to be the caretaker of everything and the brother to all the plants and animals. Each lived in his own way and nobody interfered with the other. Things were so peaceful that all the animals and the plants and man could speak and understand the others' languages.

But some greedy people began to take advantage of the gifts of the Great Spirit and started stealing and lying, and even killing the animals in order to sell their fur. As a result, the numbers of animals became smaller and smaller. It was necessary for them to hold a council to decide what must be done.

The bear called the meeting and presided over it because he was the largest and the strongest of all the creatures. For days the group discussed how best to deal with the people and punish them for their misdeeds.

Mountain Lion thought they should attack the people and kill them all, but Owl, the Wise One, explained that they were no match for the bows and arrows. The birds wanted to carry away the houses and the beavers suggested gnawing holes in the bottoms of the boats. Even the flies buzzed and argued over how to punish the humans. No one could come up with a solution for the problem.

Finally, Grandfather Fly came up with an acceptable idea. He said, "Let's ask the spirits to send down a disease upon all the men who are harming us. We flies will carry it and spread it all over the land." All the animals agreed to this and the meeting was over.

Soon sickness came to the villages of the people and they began to die. Everyone was ill and the innocent suffered along with the guilty. No one could go out for food so those who were not sick began to starve. Little children and old women were affected along with the rest, and this disturbed the animals.

They had only meant for the guilty and wicked humans to be punished. This way was not at all fair. So another council was called to decide how to remedy the situation.

The animals and birds and plants all started asking how this could be brought under control. Finally, the healing herbs and grasses whispered their advice to the others. "We have marvelous healing powers," they said, "and if Man will let us, we can help." So the people were told the healing remedies and which plants were useful in healing certain illnesses.

The people gathered the plantain, the mullen, wild beets, and the other herbs. They used them as the little spirits, who are concealed in the plants, told them. They told the humans what to use and how to prepare the medicine.

This is the way medicine was given to Man and how the Indians learned to use all the plants and herbs for healing. They learned a great lesson from the other children of the Great Spirit.——Choctaw

The Choctaw Migration Story

Many years ago in the land beyond the place where the sun sets, lived a group of people who were the ancestors of the Choctaw. They had been conquered by a much stronger nation and were greatly oppressed.

A great council was called by the spiritual leaders in order to ascertain what should be done to alleviate their situation. Many days were spent listening to suggestions and it was finally decided that they should leave their homeland and seek a new place to live where they could be happy and free. They agreed on a departure date and spent the intervening time preparing for the journey.

At the appointed time, all the people came together and camped for the last time on their native soil. That night, a fabussa (pole) was firmly set in the ground by the chief medicine man and it pointed straight toward the heavens. The people had no idea where their "promised land" was or even what direction they should march. They placed their trust in the Great Spirit to show them the way, and the next morning the fabussa was leaning toward the east. This was interpreted as a sign indicating that they should travel eastward, so they set out to find their new home.

At the front marched the great prophet carrying the sacred fabussa and every evening he would solemnly place it upright in the center of the camp so it might direct their next day's march. This ceremony took place day after day, month after month and each morning the fabussa leaned to the east and the people continued their march.

Babies were born and old people died but the people only stopped long enough to observe the ceremonies accorded these events before continuing on. Scaffolds were erected to allow the flesh of the dead to decay. The bones were then packaged in skins, for the flesh is temporal but the bones of the dead are sacred and last forever. The bone packages were then given to the young men to carry for they could only be placed in the earth when the new homeland was reached.

After a time, the burden of carrying the bones became a gigantic task and the young folks began to moan and complain because so many had died on the trail. Yet, each morning the fabussa leaned to the east and the march continued. Each night the people would think that perhaps the journey was over and that they could stop, but the fabussa always leaned to the east.

One day the caravan came to a huge river across which they could hardly see. They called this huge body of water "Mishasipokni" (one beyond time), and they felt sure they had at last reached their goal. Anxiously everyone awaited the coming of the first morning light, and when they could see, a great wail arose for the fabussa pointed beyond the great river. The people dutifully constructed rafts and built canoes and ferried the entire congregation to the east bank and the next day continued their pilgrimage.

At last they came to a lush, verdant area with an abundance of water and game. In the center rose a large mound which leaned slightly so the people called it Nanih Waiya (leaning mountain). They were quite excited and thought that their journey was at last over. As they arose the next morning, they were overjoyed for the fabussa stood as erect and straight as it had the night before. They joyously cried, "Fohah hupishno Yak!" (Here is where we rest.)

By this time the group had grown so large the area could not accommodate everyone. The leaders, two brothers called Chahta and Chickasah, met to decide what should be done. They played a game of chance with the understanding that the loser would take his followers and find a new home. Chahta won and Chickasah moved to the north and established his nation there. The followers of Chahta settled near Nanih Waiya and built the great Choctaw Nation.——Choctaw

Why the Possum's Tail Is Bare

One day long ago Coon and Possum met on the road and sat down to have a talk. They chatted for a while about everyday happenings, about fishing and tola (ball games). All the time they talked, Possum couldn't keep his eyes off Coon's beautiful striped tail and he became very envious. Finally, he could stand it no longer and, although it was not very courteous, he asked Coon where he had gotten his tail.

Now Coon, feeling a bit perturbed at Possum for his ill-mannered action, decided to play a trick. He told possum he had wrapped his tail in hickory bark and set fire to it. This created the different-colored rings around his tail and made it look so beautiful.

When they parted, Possum could hardly wait to try the hickory bark for he was very anxious to have his tail become beautiful like Coon's. He wrapped it around and around with bark from the hickory nut tree and then set the bark on fire. Now the hickory bark burns with a very hot fire and before Possum knew what was happening, the blaze burned all the hair from his tail. Ever since that time possums have had bare tails and have traveled at night because they are ashamed. That is why possums are shunned by all other animals.——Choctaw

How The Tribes Came to Be

In the distant past, the Great Spirit (Chittokaka), created many people, all of whom spoke the Choctaw language (Chahta anumpa). All these people came from under the surface of the earth and were made from yellow clay. These were the first people and there were none who lived before them.

Why the Possum's Tail Is Bare
Choctaw

One day they gathered together and began to wonder what the clouds and the blue sky above them might be. After much discussion, their curiosity became so great they decided to see what was there. They determined to build a mound, for they were mound builders, so high that they could climb to the sky. They brought rocks and piled them together and started their mound which would reach the heavens.

After working hard all day, they were very tired and went to sleep soon after sundown. They slept so soundly they didn't hear the strong wind which blew during the night. However, in the morning they found the rocks had been blown from the mound.

The second day the people again piled their rocks on the mound, and again that night the wind scattered them once more.

The third day the people worked hard to raise their mound to the sky and that night the wind destroyed their work.

The fourth day was spent piling rocks on the mound, and when night came the people slept close to the rock pile so they might protect it. However, the wind howled once more and this time the rocks came rolling down on the people.

They were not killed, but when daylight came and they crawled from under the stones, they became greatly alarmed. As they talked the people found the spoke various languages and could not understand one another. Some continued to speak their original Choctaw language, and from these sprang the Choctaw Nation. The others, who could not understand this language, began to fight among themselves, and finally they moved away in different directions. The Choctaws remained the original people and the others scattered throughout the world and became the various other peoples.——Choctaw

The Choctaws and the Birds

In the far distant past, the people, whom the Great Spirit* had created, became so wicked that He decided to destroy them and the world He had made for them to enjoy. There was one man, Oklatabashih, who was a good man, so the Great Spirit devised a plan whereby he and his family would be saved. He told Oklatabashih to build a large boat and to take on board a male and a female of every animal on earth. These

* Chittokaka is translated as Great Spirit. Aba is another name for God, Jehovah, or Heavenly Father.

would be saved and be the procreators of all living inhabitants for His new world.

Oklatabashih did as he was instructed and caught pairs of every type of creature. He was unable, however, to catch three kinds of woodpeckers for they were too quick for him. They hopped and fluttered so rapidly that they constantly eluded Oklatabashih; therefore he gave up the chase and closed the openings of the boat.

Then it began to rain and it continued for many days and nights. The rain fell in torrents such as had never been seen before. Gradually the waters rose and the entire earth became covered with water. People drowned and the survivors began climbing to higher ground only to find that even the tops of the mountains began to be inundated. All the earth was at last overwhelmed by the flood and all its inhabitants except those in Oklatabashih's boat perished. This craft floated over the vast sea of waters for many months.

Finally Oklatabashih sent out a dove to try to find some dry land. Soon she returned with some grass in her beak and Oklatabashih knew the water had at last started to recede. He rewarded the dove for her accomplishment with a little salt mixed in her food. Soon the water subsided and the new earth appeared and all the inhabitants left the boat to begin their lives as they were created to do. The dove, having acquired a taste for salt, returned to the area where Oklatabashih and his family settled to get her daily ration of salt. This habit was handed down to her descendants, generation after generation, and doves always ate a little salt after each meal. One day, however, after a fine meal of grass seed, a dove forgot to eat some salt. For this neglect, the Great Spirit punished her and her descendants by forbidding them forever the use of salt. When she returned home that evening her children and grandchildren began to coo, asking for their salt. From this day on, doves all over the world continue their cooing for salt which they will never be permitted to eat again.

The three birds which Oklatabashih had not been able to capture, the bishinik (sapsucker), the fitukhak (yellowhammer), and the bakbak (red-headed woodpecker), flew high in the air at the approach of the flood. As the waters rose they flew higher and higher until they reached the sky, on which they lit. While they were sitting on the edge of the sky, their tails hung down and were constantly drenched by the spray of the surging waters below. This spray notched and forked the ends off their tails which remain that way even today.

Because of their agility in escaping Oklatabashih and their wisdom in surviving the flood, these birds, especially the bishinik, were made the guardians of the Choctaw people. On the eve of the ball game, the favorite sport of the Choctaws, they would come to the villages and excitedly flit and flutter around the trees in anticipation of the event. In times of war, the bishinik were always around camp to warn the Cochtaw of any approaching enemy. In many ways these birds proved their love and friendship for the Choctaws, and they in turn, have always cherished these birds. They remember the gift of the Great Spirit in the days of the great flood.——Choctaw

The Footlog to Heaven

Choctaws believe that the spirit lives on after death. After spending three days around the body, the spirit departs for a land in the west, beyond the horizon. To reach that faraway place it is necessary to cross a deep and rapid stream which is hemmed in on both sides by high and rugged bluffs. Across the stream, from bluff to bluff, is a slippery pine log, with the bark peeled off, over which the dead (spirit) must pass to reach the land of spirits (shilup i yakni). On the far side of the steam are six personages who throw rocks at the spirit attempting to cross the chasm on the log.

If the spirit makes it across the treacherous log, it finds a land of enchantment. There is one continual day, and the trees are always green. The sky has no clouds and there is always a cooling breeze. It is a land of feasting, dancing, and rejoicing where there is no pain and people never grow old but live forever in youth enjoying the pleasures of young living.

As the wicked attempt to cross the footlog, they see the stones coming and try to dodge them and fall to the raging waters below. There they are dashed against rocks by the roaring water which stinks of the dead fish and animals. The evil spirits are carried around by whirlpools which bring them back to the same place over and over again. It is a land of desolation where the trees are all dead and the waters are full of toads, lizards, and snakes. The dead are always hungry and have nothing to eat, always thirsty but with only putrid water to drink. They are always sick but never obtain the relief of dying. The sun never shines and the wicked are continually climbing up by the thousands on the side of a high rock from which they can look over to the happy land but are forever unable to reach it.——Choctaw

The Eclipse

Since the sun works hard every day to provide heat and light, he becomes very dirty and smoked from the great fire within. It is necessary for him to rest and clean himself every so often. After doing so, he shines even brighter. During the eclipse he is removing the accumulated dirt. A similar explanation applies to the dark of the moon. The solar eclipse is known as "Sun dark or dirty" and the lunar eclipse as "Moon cleaning itself."——Choctaw

Thunder, Lightning, and Comet

Thunder and lightning are two great birds. Thunder (Heloha) is the female, and Lightning (Melatha) is the male. When there is a great noise in the clouds, Heloha is laying an egg, just like a bird, in the cloud which is her nest. When a tree is shattered as a result, it is said to have been caused by Melatha, the male, since he is the stronger. If the tree is only slightly damaged, it is said to be caused by Heloha, the weaker.

Great trouble, or even war, follows when a comet is sighted in the nighttime sky.——Choctaw

How the Choctaw Got Corn

A long time ago a child was playing around the house. A large crow (fala chitta) flew over and dropped a grain of corn. The child found it and asked his mother what it was. "It is tanchi," said the mother. The child planted it in the yard and the corn grew up and matured. So the child was the finder of corn. In this way the forefathers of the Choctaws got their seed corn.

Another version of how the Choctaw people got corn says:

In the beginning, many years ago, a crow got a kernel of corn from beyond the Great Waters and brought it to this country. He gave it to a child who was playing in a yard. The child named it tanchi (corn) and planted it in the yard. When the corn grew up high the child's parents ignored it and wanted to cut it down. The child, however, cared for the plant and hoed it, hilled it up, and laid it by. When this single grain matured, it made two ears of corn, and it was really in this way that the Choctaw discovered corn.——Choctaw

The Nameless Choctaw

Many years ago there lived the only son of a great Choctaw chieftain. He was a fine-looking young man and the leaders of his village knew he would be a great warrior someday. True to Choctaw tradition though, he had not earned his name by some deed so he was merely called "Chahtah Hosh Ochiffo Iksho" which means "The Nameless Choctaw."

In the same village lived a beautiful maiden who loved the young nameless one. However, since the young man had not earned a name, they were forbidden by custom to marry. Time passed slowly for the young people until it was the day for the young man to go with a raiding party to the land of the Osage.

The Choctaw party made their way far to the west to find their traditional enemies so the young men could distinguish themselves in battle. They found a large cave and stopped there to decide on their plans. They sent The Nameless Choctaw and another warrior to examine the surrounding countryside and locate the Osage.

While the two scouts were away, an Osage war party found the cave which housed the Choctaws and killed them all. When the one scout returned to the cave and found his comrades dead, he returned home with the sad story. Since The Nameless Choctaw was not seen and did not come home, he too was considered to have perished. The promised wife of "The Nameless Choctaw" grieved his death so heavily that it was not long before she died. The people buried her at the spot where she and her lover had said goodbye.

The supposition that The Nameless Choctaw had died was incorrect for he was able to escape. The Osage chased him for days before giving up and the young man found himself hopelessly lost. He had run so far and switched directions so many times that he was thoroughly confused. The sun seemed to be rising in the west and setting in the east and all nature was out of order. He wandered for many months before, through much meditation and with the help of the Great Spirit, he found his way home.

He had been gone so long and since he was thought dead, no one in his village recognized this stranger. He did not tell anyone who he was, but immediately sought his loved one. He found her lonely grave and grieved greatly. Standing beside the burial place he called to the Great Spirit to take him to the Land of Spirits so he could be with his lover. He then fell on the grave and died.

The people of the village found him there and recognized him as the long-lost Chahtah Hosh Ochiffo Iksho. They buried him beside her and for three nights thereafter the howling of a solitary wolf was heard and then never heard again. However, this same wail was taken up by the pine forest surrounding the place where the lovers were buried and can still be heard to this day.—Choctaw

The Great Flood

In ancient time, after many generations of Choctaw had lived and died, the people became so corrupt and wicked they displeased the Great Spirit (Chittokaka). He determined to destroy the earth and its inhabitants and to start over again to populate it with a people who would do good to one another and live in peace. First, however, he decided to give them one more chance, so he sent a prophet among them to try to redeem them. This messenger went to all the villages and told of Chittokaka's displeasure. He warned the people of the fearful consequences if they did not turn from their wicked ways but no one paid any attention to him. They continued living as they had, as if they did not even care.

The Great Spirit then sent clouds which obscured the sun by day and the moon by night. The people lived in darkness and had to use torches to see even during the middle of the day. The Prophet went again to all the villages and to all the tribes telling of what was to come and, even then, the people refused to change. The animals sensed something dreadful was about to take place and huddled around the campfires in the villages, completely unafraid of the humans.

Suddenly, a crash of thunder, louder than anyone had ever heard, rolled over the land. The winds began to scream through the trees and the people became exceedingly fearful. They fled from place to place seeking refuge from the great noise, but there was no escape. All at once they saw a bright light in the north and thought the sun was returning. They were wrong though, for they saw the gleam of mighty waters rushing down on them. Wave after wave it came as it rolled over the earth destroying everything in its path.

Stretching from horizon to horizon the massive waves poured on and on until the entire earth was covered. Nothing could withstand the mighty power of the waters which swept away all the humans and animals and left the earth a desolate place. All of mankind, except the Prophet who had been sent by the Great Spirit to warn the people, was destroyed. He had saved himself by following the instructions of Chittokaka and making a large raft of sassafras logs which floated upon the great waters. He was able to see the dead bodies of the men and animals as they rose and fell on the heaving billows.

After many weeks of aimlessly floating, a large black bird came to the raft flying in circles above the head of the Prophet. He called out for assistance, but the bird only replied in loud croaking tones and flew away. A few days later a bird of bluish color with red eyes and beak came and hovered over the raft. The Prophet called to the bird and asked if there was any dry land anywhere in the world. The bird fluttered around the raft a few moments, uttering a mournful cry, and then flew away toward where the sun was sinking into the water.

Immediately a strong breeze came up and began to blow the raft in the direction in which the bird had flown. Soon night came on and the moon and stars came out. Still the Prophet's raft continued its westerly journey, and as the sun arose the next morning, the Prophet saw an island in the distance. Before the day was over the raft had washed up on the beach and the Prophet was safe. Looking around his island home, he found it inhabited with all the animals of the old world except the mammoth. All the birds and fowls of every kind were there. He discovered a black bird, identical to the one that ignored his cry for help, and he regarded it as a cruel bird. He named it Fulushto (Raven)—a bird of ill omen to the Choctaws to this day.

He also found the bluish bird which had caused the breezes to blow his raft to safety. Because of its kindness and its great beauty he called it Puchi Yushubah (Lost Pigeon) and it has been respected and loved by the Choctaws ever since.

After many days the waters receded and plants began once more to grow. In time Puchi Yushubah became a beautiful woman with whom the Prophet fell in love. They married and from them the world was again peopled. This is how the Choctaws came to be.——Choctaw

The Choctaw Lovers

Once, a long time ago, the Choctaws had a bountiful harvest and came together in a great council to celebrate. Speeches were made, ball games were played, and everyone had a happy time. One day the conversation turned to things of nature and someone posed a question as to where the sun, the giver of heat and light, went when it passed the western hills. It was decided that someone should make the journey to find where the sun slept. One young Choctaw named Oklanowah (Walking People) volunteered for the mission. Before he left, he bade goodbye to all his friends and gave his loved one a string of shells to keep as a reminder while he was gone.

Oklanowah traveled far to the west and was gone for many years. When he returned home he found he was a stranger among his people. He finally found one old, decrepit woman who remembered the young man who went in search of the sun's sleeping place. Oklanowah knew this old woman was his loved one for she still had the string of shells and spoke of the love she had for the young man. No amount of argument, however, could convince her that the old man she saw before her was her lover of the past.

Oklanowah spent his few remaining days telling his people of his adventures in the west. He told of the plains and the huge mountains and of the strange men and animals he saw. He told how the sun goes to sleep in the big blue water every night. Still, after hearing all these stories, the old woman would not accept the old man and lived out her life waiting for her young lover to return.

In the spring, Oklanowah lived out his time and was buried near the sacred mound, Nanih Waiya. Before the time for corn planting had come, the old woman also died, and she too was buried near Nanih Waiya by the side of her unrecognized yet ever faithful Oklanowah. Unable to be together in life, their love united them after death.——
Choctaw

A Choctaw Creation Story

Soon after the earth was made, men and grasshoppers came to the surface through a long passageway that led from a large cavern in the interior of the earth, to the summit of a high hill, Nane Chaha. There, deep down in the earth, in the great cavern, man and grasshoppers had been created by Aba, the Great Spirit, having been formed of the yellow clay.

For a time the men and the grasshoppers continued to reach the surface together, and as they emerged from the long passageway they would scatter in all directions, some going north, others south, east, or west.

But at last the mother of the grasshoppers, who had remained in the cavern, was killed by the men and, as a consequence, there were no more grasshoppers to reach the surface, and ever after, those who lived on the earth were known to the Choctaw as "eske ilay," (mother dead). However men continued to reach the surface of the earth through the long passageway that led to the summit of Nane Chaha, and, as they moved about from place to place, they trampled upon many grasshoppers in the high grass, killing many and hurting others.

The grasshoppers became alarmed as they feared that all would be killed if men became more numerous and continued to come from the cavern in the earth. They spoke to Aba, who heard them and soon caused the passageway to be closed and no more men were allowed to reach the surface. But as there were many men remaining in the cavern, he changed them to ants. Ever since that time the small ants have come forth from holes in the ground.——Choctaw

CHEROKEE

The Cherokee have a migration story which tells of travel from the northeastern portion of the United States to their homeland in the southeast. Ethnologists, historians, and anthropologists, generally agree on the exodus and set the time at about one thousand years ago. Since the Cherokee speak a dialect of the Iroquoian language family, it is easy to validate the oral tradition with acceptable linguistic evidence.

The first contact with whites was in 1540 when Hernando de Soto reached the edge of Cherokee land. Continuous association commenced when Virginia began to be settled. Traders from the first towns moved inland toward the Appalachian Mountains to exchange manufactured goods for agricultural products and skins. The relationship between the European invaders and the Cherokees vacillated between friendship and bitter enmity. In 1730 the natives aided the English in a war against the Tuscaroras, and in 1730 a number of Cherokees accompanied Sir Edward Cuming on a trip to England. By 1759, however, the Cherokee and the British were at war. During the Revolutionary War the Cherokees were again on good terms with the English and allied with them against the Americans, continuing the fighting even after the cessation of hostilities by the two major combatants. The Nation finally made peace with the United States government in 1794.

After passage of the Removal Act in 1830, pressures were increased on the Cherokees to relocate their nation west of the Mississippi River. Some bands of Cherokees had already succumbed to the inevitable and moved to Arkansas, Missouri, and Texas. On December 29, 1835, the United States, utilizing insidious methods of bribery, coercion, and fraud, prevailed on a small group of Cherokees to sign a treaty which was then ratified by Congress as an instrument accepted by the entire Cherokee Nation. The Treaty of New Echota brought an end to the Nation in their homeland and initiated the "Trail of Tears." The major portion of the people removed during the winter of 1838–39, suffering extreme hardships and losing about one-quarter of their total population on the trail.

To keep from leaving their sacred homeland, several hundred Cherokees escaped to the mountains where they lived off the land until 1842 when, through the efforts of William H. Thomas, a white trader, they received permission to remain on land acquired by Thomas for their use. Eventually the Qualla Reservation was established and set aside for the Eastern Cherokee.

Although, like the Choctaws, the Cherokee were acculturated by the "dominant society" early in the history of this country, much of their cultural heritage has survived. The stories are still alive and still satisfy the questions concerning natural phenomena and provide a spiritual identity for the Cherokee people. A few examples are given on the following pages.

How the Moon Was Made

Long ago during a ball game between two villages, a player from the losing side angrily picked up the ball with his hand and threw it toward the goal. This was an act which violated the rules of the game and everyone was astonished. The ball stuck against the vault of the sky and remained there where we can see it today. It reminds all other ball players never to cheat by touching the ball with their hands.

When the moon looks small and pale the old folks say that someone handled the ball. Therefore ball games were never scheduled except during a full moon.——Cherokee

How Fire Was Made

In the beginning there was no fire and the world was very cold. One day Thunder, who lived in the other world above the great arch of the sky, sent his lightning and started a fire in the bottom of a huge syca-more stump which grew on an island in a great lake. All the animals knew it was there for they could see the smoke coming out of the top of the stump. However, they couldn't get the fire because of the water, so they held a council to decide what to do.

Every animal who could fly or swim was anxious to go for the fire. The first to volunteer was Raven and everyone thought he could do it because he was so big and strong. So off he flew, high and far across the water. He lit on the sycamore stump to study the situation and got his feathers all scorched black from the heat. He became frightened and flew back without the fire. This is why Raven has such black feathers today.

The next volunteer was the little Screech Owl. He flew over the water to the island, but as he was looking down into the stump a blast of hot air came up and nearly burned out his eyes. He managed to make it back home but he was nearly blind and even to this day his eyes are red.

Next the Hooting Owl and the Horned Owl flew over to the island to try to bring back some fire. By the time they made the trip, the fire was so big and hot that the smoke nearly blinded them and the ashes carried up by the heat made white rings form around their eyes. They tried to rub the rings from around their eyes but with no success and they are there yet.

Since the birds were having no success, Little Black Snake decided to try. He swam to the island and glided up to the stump. Seeing a small hole at the base, he went inside. The heat was terrible and there was much smoke and the little snake was nearly overcome. After much darting around, he found the opening he had entered and escaped the blaze. He was, however, scorched black by the fire, and, to this day, has the habit of darting about as if he were trying to escape.

Next to try to get the fire was the great black snake. He swam to the island and climbed up the outside of the stump. However, upon reaching the top, he fell inside and he, too, was burned black.

The animals held council to try to decide what to do. Everyone was afraid to venture near the island and its burning sycamore stump. Yet, it was so cold that something had to be done.

At last the Water Spider said she would go for the fire. Everyone laughed for she was so small. How could she bring back fire when the other larger creatures had failed. Not discouraged, Water Spider ran across the water to the island and approached the stump. She spun a fine, silver thread from her body and wove it into a tusti (carrying) bowl, which she attached to her back. She then placed one small coal of fire in the bowl and quickly ran across the water to where the other animals were waiting. They started a large fire and warmed up their land. Ever since that time the world has had fire and the little Water Spider still has her tusti bowl.——Cherokee

The Pretty Little Snake

Long ago there was a famous hunter in the tribe who always brought home a lot of game when he went hunting. One day as he was returning home with some quails he had shot, he saw a little snake beside the trail. It was a pretty snake with many pretty colors on it, and it looked friendly. After watching for a while, the hunter thought it might be hungry, so he threw it one of his birds to eat.

On the next hunting trip the hunter passed the same place with some rabbits he had shot. He saw the snake again and it was still friendly but it seemed to have grown quite a bit. He watched it some more and left it a rabbit to eat and went home.

A few weeks later the hunter was again passing the same place with some turkeys he had killed in the woods. The snake had grown to be very large, and, although it was still friendly, it seemed quite hungry. The hunter stopped and watched the snake for a while, then he gave it a turkey to eat and went on his way.

On the next hunting trip the hunter killed two buck deer, and, as he was going home, he again came to the place where he had seen the little snake. By this time, although he still seemed friendly, the snake had grown huge in size and seemed very hungry. The hunter again shared his game and gave the snake an entire deer to eat. He watched as the snake swallowed the buck, and then he went home.

One night the people decided to have a stomp-dance and invited all the neighbors to the festivities. They were all dancing around the fire, singing the old songs when all at once the huge snake appeared. It began to circle the people until they were completely penned up by the serpent. It still seemed to be friendly and was still quite beautiful, but it also looked quite hungry. It began to eat some of the people and the young men got their bows and arrows and started shooting. The snake was hurt but by this time it had grown so large that the people couldn't kill it. Instead, as it thrashed about the campfire, hurting because of the arrows, it killed a lot of the people.

They say the snake was just like the white man.——Cherokee

Cherokee Monster

In ancient times the Cherokee had moved to this land they called "The Island" and became a large and prosperous nation. The men were excellent hunters and farmers and the women were fine homemakers. Everything they wanted and needed was available and there was no shortage of food or shelter.

The Cherokee hunters observed a sacred custom which was very important in their lives. Since they believed all living creatures possessed a soul, they always offered a prayer for any animal which was killed for food. In this way the spirit of the animal, which continued to live after physical death, would understand the necessity of giving its life.

As time passed, some of the young men grew fat and lazy and ceased to offer these prayers to the souls of the slain animals. They became rather complacent and forgot the teachings of the elders concerning respect for their animal brothers. Some of the young hunters even began to ridicule the corpses and boast of their prowess as killers. This was extremely foolish for it not only insulted the spirit of the animal who had given up his body for food but it indicated the hunter had forgotten about the Creator who still ruled the world and had made all his children equal.

Finally, the animals called a council to consider what was happening and to discuss what should be done about their cruel human brothers. Some had witnessed the acts of the humans and told the council about the outrages. The wolf told of one hunter who had been filled with hatred when he saw a great buck deer proudly walking through the woods. He told of the hunter's heart, black and filled with spite, as he proclaimed that he was the ruler of the forest, and how he had laughed at the deer as he killed it.

Each of the animals related similar stories of the cruelty of man and of their astonishment that one of the Creator's children would become so boastful and consider himself better than the others. The forest creatures all agreed that man should be punished for his evil ways, but each was afraid to attempt the punishment. Man had become so expert in hunting and killing that they feared for their lives.

Finally, one of the feathered beings hopped down to a branch and asked to speak. He claimed he had a solution to the problem. This was rather amusing to the other creatures for Bird was one of the smallest and most harmless of them all. A chuckle spread through the crowd but Bird continued to speak, "In my many travels, I have flown all over this whole Island we call the world. I have seen one being who might be able to punish the two-legged if he would be willing to do it."

The council members discussed this possibility at great length and finally Bear stood up and made a formal request that Bird ask this brother to help them. The bird flew off in search of the creature and left the council to discuss their fate.

Meanwhile, with the humans, nothing had changed. Some of the elders would from time to time warn the young hunters and remind them of their responsibilities as caretakers of the earth, but they would just laugh at the gray-haired ones. The hunters thought they were invincible with their new bows and arrows and spears. They called the old ones "superstitious" and made fun of their fears. The elders, however, talked among themselves and were frightened by what the young ones were doing. They knew the Creator had established a pattern of life and the young hunters were destroying it. Surely, this would not go unpunished.

One day, a peculiar noise was heard by some of the villagers with good hearing. It was as if the wind was rustling the leaves in the trees. It came from the North and only a slight westerly breeze was blowing. The people were quite puzzled and a bit fearful.

The next day the noise was louder and all the villagers heard it. Some thought it was the wind and others claimed it was the earth shaking and making the trees talk. They all agreed it was coming from the North and was getting louder all the time. Toward evening the people began to be more alarmed and the children thought it was an approaching storm.

Few people slept that night as the noise became louder. No one knew what it was but everyone was afraid.

As dawn broke, everyone in the village was up and listening to the fearful roaring. The earth shook at even intervals as if some giant was approaching the village with heavy footsteps. Sounds of trees breaking and being uprooted were mixed with the roar as if a great storm was ripping apart the forest. The women and children cried and waited with fright and the men held their weapons with trembling hands realizing how useless they would be against any creature which could be so loud.

Suddenly the trees at the edge of the forest split apart and a huge beast burst into the clearing. No one had ever seen anything like it. It was huge, many times larger than the largest animal they had ever seen. When it saw the people it screamed so loudly it nearly deafened them. It was covered with long hair, had huge fangs curling out from its mouth, and had a long arm growing from the center of its massive head. Everyone was terrified and tried to escape. Some ran but were trampled by the massive feet; some sought refuge in the trees but these were caught by the great arm growing out of the monster's head; and those who climbed the larger trees too high to be reached were shaken out as if they were apples as the great beast shook the trunks.

After crushing all the houses as if they were eggs and killing all the people it could catch, the great hairy beast turned and crashed off through the woods towards the North, from whence it had come. Those who were left alive were petrified with fear and would never forget what they had seen. The noise became less loud and finally stopped as the monster got farther and farther away, but for years the people would quake with fear every time a gentle wind rustled the leaves on the trees. Those who had been so haughty were as meek as field mice and no one boasted of his power any more.

Those who survived this great catastrophy had learned their lesson and passed the story of the great hairy creature along to their children. If nature is misused, and the order of things that the Creator has established is warped, and sacred customs are ignored, something will happen to set things right again.

Long ago, things were set right by the great hairy beast which came out of the North, a beast so rare that the people no longer even remember what it was, and perhaps it was the last of its kind. There are those who wonder what will be sent next time things need to be set right. The time is near.——Cherokee

The Origin of Hope Flowers, or the Trailing Arbutus

Once, long ago, an old man sat in his lodge thinking of the long trail of years he had traveled. His tired eyes had seen many snows come and go and most of his friends had already gone to the land of the spirits. He knew that the time was close when he would join them.

As he meditated he wondered what he could leave his people so they would remember him. He wanted to leave something which would be of use or of great beauty so his people would always speak kindly of him. To aid him in deciding what gift to bestow, he called all the good spirits to his lodge.

One of these was a young maiden who was beautiful in appearance and always spoke softly to the old man and was always pleasant. Her dress was quite unusual and her hair was covered with white moss. On her feet were soft moccasins made of pussy willows. Her cheeks were of a delicate pink and white, partly shielded by a spray of green which she wore around her shoulders.

As soon as she entered the lodge a sweet fragrance filled the place. Her presence so gladdened the heart and revived the spirit of the old man that he thought, "If only I could impart as much cheer to my people as she has brought into my lodge, I could then die happy."

"Who are you?" he asked of the maiden.

"My name is Hope," she replied. "I am the spirit who cheers your people through the long winter months and keeps them happy. I have come to aid you in your wish to leave your people something to help them. The Great Spirit has read your heart and knows your desire, and He has sent me."

"And what will you do to assist me?" inquired the old man eagerly.

"I will be the promise of Spring," the young maiden replied.

The old man smiled and was happy for he was satisfied with her pro-

The Origin of Hope Flowers, or the Trailing Arbutus
Cherokee

posal. He knew the need of such cheer as she would impart to his people during the cold winter weather.

He arose and made his way feebly to the door of his lodge where he fell to the ground, all the life breath gone from him.

The maiden drew near to his prostrate form, covered him over with leaves and moss, and then among them tucked some tiny, pink blossoms which she had kept hidden in the folds of her garments. They were so sweet they filled the air with their fragrance.

Today when the snow melts and the first signs of Spring are apparent, these tiny pink flowers cover the hillsides and lake shores. The Indians call them "Hope Flowers" for they know they were left by the good spirit maiden as a promise of Spring. White folks call them "Trailing Arbutus."——Cherokee

The Spirit Defenders of Nikwasi

Long ago a powerful unknown tribe invaded the country from the southeast, killing people and destroying settlements wherever they went. No leader could stand against them and in a little while they had wasted all the lower settlements and advanced into the mountains. The warriors of the old town of Nikwasi, on the head waters of the Little Tennessee, gathered their wives and children into the townhouse and kept scouts constantly on the lookout for the presence of danger. One morning just before daybreak the spies saw the enemy approaching and at once gave the alarm. The Nikwasi men seized their arms and rushed out to meet the attack; but after a long, hard fight they found themselves overpowered and began to retreat, when suddenly a stranger stood among them and shouted to the chief to call off his men and he himself would drive back the enemy. From the dress and language of the stranger, the Nikwasi people thought him a chief who had come with reinforcements from the Overhill settlements in Tennessee. They fell back along the trail, and as they came near the townhouse they saw a great company of warriors coming out from the side of the mound as through an open doorway. Then they knew who their friends were—the Immortals, although no one had ever heard before that they lived under Nikwasi mound.

The Immortals poured out by the hundreds, armed and painted for the fight, and the most curious thing about it all was that they became invisible as soon as they were fairly outside the settlement, so that although the enemy saw the glancing arrow or the rushing tomahawk, and felt the stroke, they could not see who sent it. Before such invisible foes the invader soon had to retreat, going first south along the ridge to where it joins the main ridge which separates the French Broad from the Tuckasegee, and then turning with it to the northeast. As they retreated they tried to shield themselves behind rocks and trees, but the Immortals' arrows went around the rocks and killed them from the other side, and they could find no hiding place. Along the ridge they fell, until when they reached the head of the Tuckasegee not more than half-a-dozen were left alive, and in despair they sat down and cried out for mercy. Ever since then the Cherokee have called the place "Dayulsunyi" (Where They Cried). Then the Immortals' chief told them they had deserved their punishment for attacking a peaceful tribe, and he spared their lives and told them to go home and take the news to their people. This was the Indian custom, always to spare a few to carry back the news of defeat. They went home toward the north and the Immortals went back to the mound.

And they are still there, because, in the last war (i.e., the Civil War), when a strong party of Federal troops came to surprise a handful of Confederates posted there, they saw so many soldiers guarding the town that they were afraid and went away without making an attack.——Cherokee

How the Buzzard Became So Ugly

A long time ago, the most beautiful of all the birds was the great buzzard. He was the ruler of all the birds and was loved because of his beauty and his courage. As time passed, Buzzard, like many people even today, became overly impressed with his own importance. He began to press his authority on everyone and in everything. He became rude and had no feeling for any of his brother birds.

At feasts, he was the first to eat and no one else could touch the food until he came and gave his permission. He created such ill-will among the other birds, they held council to decide what to do about him. Some wanted to banish him and others, especially Eagle and Hawk, wanted to kill him. Some of the birds wanted to change him into something ugly to humiliate him. After much discussion and many suggestions, the decision was made.

A great feast and celebration was arranged in his honor. The day arrived and all the preparations had been made for the occasion. All the food was placed next to a trap which had been prepared for Buzzard and it was arranged so he must go into the trap in order to get the food.

Buzzard arrived, and, without any thought of a trick, began to gobble up the food. The other birds watched in amusement, waiting for just the right time to spring their trap. After he had nearly finished his gorging on the food, Owl sprang the trap and the fun was on. Buzzard found his head was caught and began to fight desperately to release it.

He pulled and tugged for a very long time and finally succeeded in freeing his head. All the other birds burst out laughing and pointed at Buzzard. In his violent fight to free his head he had worn off all the beautiful feathers and his head and neck were bald and red. He attempted to hide his head under his wing but found the underfeathers had been worn off there too. He sneaked off amid the scorn and ridicule of the other birds, never to be allowed to associate with them again.

The bird council then decided that he and his descendants would thereafter lead the life of scavengers and would only be allowed to eat carrion. They would always be shunned by other animals and would have to fly high in the sky looking for the dead carcasses on which to feed. And that is the way it is even today.——Cherokee

CREEK

Stretching from the Atlantic Ocean in Georgia to the area around the Savannah River in Alabama, the Creek Confederacy was composed of many diverse groups of indigenous people. Never a cohesive unit, they were divided into the Upper Creeks and Lower Creeks according to geographic location and, especially after the formation of the United States, by political affiliation. This division at times became so acute that civil war existed between the two factions.

Located in a central position between the English, French, and Spanish colonies, the Creeks were affected by the constant bickering of all three European powers. Each courted the natives and used their in-

fluence on the Indians close to their colonial boundaries, thus foment-
ing divisive feelings within the Confederacy. This political agitation
carried on after the United States entered the picture until March 27,
1814 when Andrew Jackson broke the back of the Creek Confederacy.
His decisive victory at Horseshoe Bend on the Tallapoosa River sig-
naled the end of Creek resistance to invading forces.

Population estimates of the Creeks have always shown disagree-
ment, varying greatly according to conditions of the census. For example, in 1792 the American estimate was two thousand eight hundred
and fifty Creeks and yet in 1832, the same group had increased to sev-
enteen thousand nine hundred and thirty-nine in spite of great losses
in several military encounters during the forty-year interim. According
to the census of 1930, there were 9083 Creeks, including the Alabama-
Coushatta Reservation in Texas and individuals scattered over various
other states.

During the "Removal Period" of 1832–33, the Confederacy lost
forty-five percent of their population and many more died after reset-
tlement in Oklahoma. The former factional troubles were still in evidence for many years and the relationship between the Upper Creeks
and Lower Creeks was strained. Eventually they were adjusted and an
elected government with a chief, a second chief, and a representative
assembly of two houses was established. This structure functioned
until the Creek Nation was incorporated into the State of Oklahoma.

Throughout the years of hardship, the Creeks held onto many of
their traditions and maintained the practice of passing stories orally
from generation to generation. Although these tales have been eroded
and in many cases lost because of the assimilation process imposed by
the dominant society, many still exist in contemporary Creek culture.
The story of the Origin of Tobacco is an example.

The Origin of Tobacco

A long time ago, a young man and a girl were walking together in the
woods. They fell in love and before long they had intercourse. This
was such a happy and pleasing experience that they decided to marry
and live together the rest of their lives.

Later, while on a hunting trip, the man returned to the place where
they first made love. He found a beautiful flower with fragrant leaves

growing on that spot. When he returned to his people, he took along the pretty flower and told the complete story. The people said, "We will dry the leaves and smoke them and then we can give this wonderful plant a name." They called it "Where We Came Together" or, as we call it today, "Tobacco." The elders said that since man and woman were so completely happy and at peace when the plant was made, it would be smoked at councils for promoting peace and friendship from that time.——Creek

NATCHEZ

According to Natchez tradition, they migrated from Mexico where they had lived for centuries. They followed the rising sun, continuing their wanderings for many years until they reached the great Mississippi River. They crossed and settled at a point on the river where the city of Natchez now stands. They were a numerous people, estimated at about five thousand people, and occupied a large territory.

The Natchez were Temple Mound people who lived under a theocratic form of government. The leader was called the "Sun" and was believed to be the literal brother of the sun, the giver of life. Each morning the Natchez ruler would ascend to the highest point of land and with a greeting and a sweep of his arm would direct his brother, the sun, on his journey across the sky from east to west.

The temples of the Natchez were holy places and they utilized them as places of worship. Within them was kept a perpetual fire which was never permitted to be extinguished. It was thought that if the fire was allowed to go out, the great Natchez empire would be destroyed. Their leader was more than a political official and was considered to be a deity. The chiefdom was inherited through the lineage of a ruling class, and the social divisions among the people were very well defined. A person could not rise above the caste to which he was born regardless of deeds of valor or even marriage. These Muskogean-speaking people were indeed unique among all the nations of Indians in America.

In the mid-1700s the French, with their Choctaw allies, attacked the Natchez in their fortified city and killed, captured, or drove away nearly every member of that group of people. They, for all practical purposes, forcibly ended the existence of a great nation. A few escapees made their way to friendly neighbors, but in the passing of time, they lost their identity and became integral parts of their benefactors' tribal entity.

Although genocide was perpetrated on the Natchez Nation, some of their culture has been kept alive. Some examples of their cultural heritage are provided in the following presentations.

The Lawgiver from the Sun

In ancient times a man and a woman descended from the sun and lived among the people here on earth. They were so dazzling bright that mere humans could not look on them. The man told the people that he had seen how wretched they were and how they couldn't even govern themselves, so he had left his beautiful home above to come down to teach them how to live happily on earth. He then gave them moral laws by which they must live. First, never kill a man except in self-defense; second, only have one living wife; third, always be truthful; fourth, be strictly honest; fifth, drink no intoxicants; sixth, be generous and share your possessions; seventh, be charitable to those less fortunate; and eighth, always help the poor in their distress.

The stranger and his admonishments greatly impressed the people, and after a council was called and much deliberation had occurred, they decided to request that the sun-man become their chief. The next morning, with all the pomp and ceremony they could manage, the people proceeded to the sun-couple's house and begged the man to become their chief. At first he refused for he knew they would not obey his teachings. He told them that their willful ways would eventually bring about their destruction. The people were very insistent and pleaded earnestly for his leadership. At last, moved by their supplications, he agreed to be their chief only if they accepted certain provisions.

He said they must migrate to a distant country, to which he would lead them, where they would become prosperous and happy. He also demanded that the people strictly obey the laws he would establish and, finally, that all future chiefs would be from his descendants. The people loudly acclaimed him as their chief and agreed to comply with all his regulations.

The sun-man then called down some fire from the sun and commanded the people to keep the fires burning in the two temples which were to be built at the northern and southern ends of their country. The fuel to feed the perpetual flame would only be walnut wood which had been stripped of its bark. He then selected eight men for each temple to serve as priests and to guard the sacred fires so they would burn forever. Death was assigned as punishment for any priest on duty if a fire was extinguished on his watch. If the fires in both temples were ever allowed to go out at the same time, great calamities would come upon all the people. If the fire in one temple were to go out, the priests must relight it only with fire from the other temple and from nowhere else.

To obtain fire to relight one of the temple fires, it was imperative that blood atonement be made to pacify the offended spirits. Therefore great fighting was always present at the transfer of temple fire and an atoning sacrifice of the erring priest was usually in order.

The sun-chief lived to be very old and the people obeyed him implicitly and he was considered the founder of their laws and institutions. After his death, they gave his descendants the title of Suns in honor of the origin of the great law-giver. These Suns had absolute rule over the people with no opposition in the inherited and promised right of their great progenitor.——Natchez

The Natchez Ceremonial Calendar

The first moon (march) is that of the Deer. The renewal of the year spreads universal joy. In order to render this feast more distinguished it represents an event of historic interest to the tribe the memory of which they guard preciously.

The second moon (April) is that of the Strawberries. The women and children gather them in great quantities.

The third moon (May) is that of Old Corn. This month is always awaited with impatience. The corn from the previous year is usually gone or, if not gone, very hard and tasteless.

The fourth moon (June) is that of Watermelons. This is a month of great feasting.

The fifth moon (July) is Peaches. This month is also the month for harvesting the wild grapes.

The sixth moon (August) is that of Blackberries. At this feast birds are also brought to the great Sun.

The seventh moon (September) is that of Maize or New Corn. It is during this time that the hardened field corn is gathered for storage.

The eighth moon (October) is that of Turkeys. It is at this time of the year that the great bird comes out of the thick woods to eat on the nettle seeds of which it is very fond.

The ninth moon is that of Buffalo and corresponds to our month of November. It was during this time when the men went on the hunt. The women and children also went along for there was much hard work for everyone. Skins must be prepared and meat must be dried for use during the rest of the year.

The tenth moon (December) is that of Bears. During this month the feasts are not large for many of the people, men, women, and children, are away on the hunt.

The eleventh moon (January) is that of Geese. At this time ducks, geese, and other birds of this type are plentiful.

The twelfth moon (February) is that of Chestnuts. Although these nuts have been gathered a long time, this month bears their name.

Finally, the thirteenth moon is that of Nuts. It has been added to complete the year.* It is at this time the nuts are broken in order to make nut bread by mixing the nut meats with corn meal.——Natchez

PASCAGOULA

This small Muskogean-speaking tribe was closely associated with the Siouan Biloxi people because of their geographic proximity along the Mississippi gulf coast. Never a large group, perhaps with a maximum population of around five hundred, they are now extinct as an identifiable tribal entity. Along with many autonomous tribal units in the southeastern part of the country, the Pascagoulas became absorbed by their larger neighbors as the European powers began their land acquisition and military depredation. They became fewer and fewer in numbers and by the time of the removal of the Southeastern Indians in the 1830s, they had disappeared.

* Since a moon consists of four weeks or twenty-eight days, twelve moons would only be forty-eight weeks. A year consists of fifty-two weeks so the Natchez, and most other Indians who reckoned time by the moon, added the thirteenth moon to make their year consist of thirteen equal parts. This seems much more logical than dividing the year into twelve parts of varying and unequal portions as introduced by the Europeans.

Like many of their contemporaries, the Pascagoulas had a rich oral tradition. The stories of these small nations have been preserved to some extent, primarily by the larger units which absorbed them. The following story relates one version of how the Pascagoulas disappeared.

How the People Disappeared

Many years ago, a small tribe of Indians of a light complexion and with different customs and manners lived in the country near the mouth of the Pascagoula River. They were called the Puskaoklas, the Bread People. According to their tradition, they emerged from the sea to live in that beautiful land. They were a kind and peaceful people and spent most of their time enjoying life to its fullest, participating in many festivals and celebrations. These Bread People were also a very religious people and built a great temple, where they worshipped their Sea God. Every night, when the moon was changing from dark to full moon, they would gather in their temple to sing and dance and play their musical instruments to honor their deity.

One day, a stranger appeared among them. He was a white man with a long, gray beard and was dressed in long, flowing, white garments. In his right hand he carried a large cross which he kissed over and over again. He also carried a book and read to the Puskaoklas, explaining what they should do. He told them they must forget their Sea God and follow his teachings. Many of the people were beginning to believe this white stranger and were being converted to his way of life.

One night when the moon was full, there came a great catastrophe which ended this whole affair. All of a sudden, a rising of the water took place and it rolled over all the land. At last a giant wave came rolling along the channel of the river and on the crest of the foaming waters sat a woman. This was no ordinary female for she had magnetic eyes and sang a song in such a sweet voice that everyone was drawn toward her. The entire tribe of Puskaoklas, as well as the white stranger, ran to the river bank. The strange woman began singing even louder and in more fascinating tones, repeating the chorus over and over, "Come to me. Come to me children of the sea. Neither book nor cross shall keep you from your queen."

Soon the entire tribe was entranced by the undulating tones of the song, and one by one, they leaped into the raging waters. As soon as they touched the water, they disappeared. As the last Puskaokla entered the water, a loud and exultant laugh was heard and the waters immediately returned to their normal course, leaving no trace of the flood. The bearded white man soon died of grief and loneliness and the land of the Puskaoklas was once again at peace.*——Pascagoulas

SEMINOLE

Members of the Creek Confederacy living in Spanish Florida became known as Seminoles, a Muskogean word meaning "those who are camped away." As pressures from the southern colonies increased and, after the formation of the United States, from the states themselves, this territory became a haven for refugees from various Indian nations as well as runaway slaves. All were welcomed and the conglomerate society became known as the Seminole Nation.

After the acquisition of Florida, the United States was involved in two bloody wars with the Seminoles, the first in 1817–18 and the second in 1835–42. These wars were long and bitter contests in which the Indians demonstrated to their fullest capacity the possibilities of guerrilla warfare in a swampy semitropical country. This contest is particularly noteworthy because of the personality of Osceola, the great Seminole leader who directed the activities of his people's resistance. His capture by treachery is an abominable stain on the pages of American history.

Diplomacy, coupled with the trickery of Osceola's capture, finally accomplished what the military might of the United States could not. Most of the Indians surrendered and were included in President Andrew Jackson's removal operation. The Seminoles suffered tremendous losses of life during their "Trail of Tears" but were finally relocated in Oklahoma in the western portion of Creek country.

The remnants of this group who stayed behind in Florida were allowed small reservation areas in the southern part of the state where they still live. Never a large group, by 1930 the population of Okla-

---

* Anthropologists have placed this occurrence according to chronological evidence, shortly after the destruction of Mabila in 1540 by Hernan de Soto. The time has been established according to oral tradition. However, belief among anthropologists concerning the authenticity of the event has been less than universal.

homa and Florida Seminoles numbered only two thousand and forty-eight. Currently, there are approximately eleven hundred of these indomitable people living on three small reservations near Hollywood, Florida.

Although they were decimated by warfare the Seminoles have maintained a rather conservative attitude toward outside forces. They live much as they wish and accept "white society's" encroachment only to the degree necessary for survival. They are, as they have always been, extremely resolute and independent people.

Throughout their rocky history, the Seminole have retained and perpetuated their oral traditions along with many other facets of their culture. Their explanation of "How The Three Races Were Made" is typical of the stories still told by the elders of the tribe.

How the Three Races Were Made

When the Great Spirit made the Earth, he created three men at the same time. All of the men were fair-complexioned, and one day the Great Spirit took them to a lake and ordered them to jump into the water. One immediately obeyed the command and, when he came out of the water, he was fairer than before. The second hesitated and when he jumped, the water was a bit muddy because of the first man's agitation of the water. When he climbed out, his skin had become copper-colored. The third, having waited until the water was quite disturbed and muddy, came from the water with his complexion changed to black.*

The Great Spirit then placed before the men three sealed packages. He wanted to compensate the black man, so he gave him first choice as to which package he wanted. He took each package and tested its weight, and figuring the heaviest would have the most valuable contents, chose it. The copper-colored man chose the next heaviest, and the lightest was left for the white man. When the packages were opened, the first contained spades, hoes, and other implements used in manual labor, thus the black man has been relegated to this type of existence.

---

* This story was undoubtedly created after the appearance on the North American continent of white and black men. Indians needed an explanation for every unusual feature in nature, which of course, the strangers were.

The second package, the one chosen by the red man, was opened next. It contained fishing tackle and weapons for hunting and war. The red man, or Indian, was designated by the Great Spirit to live close to nature and gain his livelihood from hunting and fishing.

The white man was the last to open his package and in it he found pens, ink, and paper. He was given the implements to make books and to write the stories of his people.

Each was given a place on the earth to occupy and carry on the particular life-style he had chosen.——Seminole

Two

The Southwest Indians

The states of Arizona, New Mexico, and parts of California, Nevada, Utah, Colorado, and Texas make up the area which is generally considered when dealing with Southwestern Indians. The geography of this region is extremely diverse and the people who inhabit these states have cultures which vary greatly. Because of the extremes in temperature and the general harshness of the terrain, the Indians in the southwest have been allowed to follow their traditional way of life more than in any other area of the country. Consequently, lifestyles and culture have remained relatively unchanged and the acculturation process, although it has been utilized, has not had the erosive effect on these native people that it has on many of their peers.

The huge expanses of the Navajo and Papago Reservations held little attraction for non-Indian America until recent mineral discoveries were made. The forbidding mountain homes of the various Apache groups were not coveted until the last decade or two, and the desolate areas of the Great Basin tribes contained little that the white man wanted. Where there were pockets of desirable land in the southwest, these were taken over by the invaders and either developed into permanent settlements or stripped of anything of value and abandoned.

45

Throughout the immense territory, evidence of this rape is obvious. Any productive areas are under the control of elements of the dominant society, while barren wastelands are assigned to Indian habitation.

Since the California natives are discussed in a separate chapter, this portion of the book will focus on the balance of the great Southwest, primarily on New Mexico and Arizona. When the first Europeans entered this area, there were perhaps one hundred thousand inhabitants from twenty or thirty tribes. Most of the ancestors of these tribes can be identified and the lineal descent is known. The Pueblo Indians are mostly representatives of the Anasazi and can trace their people back to the inhabitants of the great ruins found at Mesa Verde, Chaco Canyon, Aztec, Canyon de Chelley and other ancient cities. The Zuni and perhaps the Acoma people are descended from the Mogollon and Anasazi after the two archaic cultures merged in the thirteenth and fourteenth centuries. Along the Colorado River, the Yuma, Mojave, Yavapai, Havasupai, and Walapai Indians came from the Patayan culture, and in the southern Arizona desert, the Pima and Papago are descendants of the Hohokam people.*

The diverse backgrounds also are apparent in the diversity of the languages represented in the Southwest. There are six major language families, dialects of which are spoken by these tribal units: Athapascan, Keresan, Tanoan, Uto-Aztecan, Yuman, and Zuñian.

Although the Pueblo Indians share a similar cultural pattern and live close together, they are quite diverse in language. The Hopi speak a Shoshonean language of the Uto-Aztecan family and the Zuñi speak a unique language, totally unrelated to any other in the world. The Keresan speakers of Cochiti, Santo Domingo, San Felipe, Santa Ana, Zia, Laguna, and Acoma have only minor dialectal differences between their pueblos. The rest of the Pueblos speak one or another of three related languages belonging to the Tanoan linguistic family— Tiwa, Tewa, and Towa. The people of the pueblos of Isleta, Picuris, Sandia, and Taos speak dialects of the Tiwa language, and the people of San Juan, San Ildefonso, Santa Clara, Nambe, Pojuaque, and Tesuque speak the Tewa language. The only Indians speaking the third Tanoan language, Towa, are those living in the Jemez Pueblo.

* For more information read William E. Coffer, *Phoenix: The Decline and Rebirth of the Indian People* (New York: Van Nostrand Reinhold Co., 1979).

In the desert country of southern Arizona, the Pima, Papago, and Yaqui—refugees from Mexico—speak closely related dialects of the Uto-Aztecan language family. Many tribes in northern Mexico also speak dialects of this language. Also, many other tribes in the Southwest speak variations of the Uto-Aztecan language family. Included in these are the Shoshonean-speaking tribes of Colorado, Utah, Nevada, and southern California.

Along the Colorado River Valley of western Arizona and eastern California, seven Indian tribes speak dialects of the Yuman language. These are the Yuma, Cocopa, Mojave, Maricopa, Walapai, Yavapai, and Havasupai. Many of these people cannot understand or converse with members of other tribes using the Yuman language, though, for the dialects are quite different.

The last language family represented in the Southwest is Athapaskan. The well-known Navajo and the various bands of Apaches belong to this family and, although they speak the same basic language, they are not all able to converse with the others.

Since the southwestern Indians have not been the unwilling recipients of forced acculturation as have so many other groups, their traditions have survived to a greater degree. Religious ceremonies, housing, food patterns, oral traditions, and general cultural continuity have been maintained and many southwestern Indians have been relatively untouched by the outside world. Some of the stories which have been handed down for generations are provided here.

ACOMA

No one is sure just how long Acoma, the Sky City, has been in existence. The elders of the tribe claim that the word "Acoma" means "a place that always was." Archeologists, while differences do exist even among them as to the actual age, agree that Old Acoma was inhabited at least from A.D. 1200 to the present. One archeological excavation made on Acoma Mesa in the 1940s near the mission church tended to support tribal claims that Acoma was inhabited before the time of Christ. Even though controversy still exists, everyone agrees that it is an extremely old city.

The pueblo is located on a rock mesa or penal, three hundred and fifty-seven feet above the plain, about fifty miles west of the Rio

Grande in New Mexico. Coronado's men, under the leadership of Vicente de Zaldivár, laid waste to the city in January, 1599 and decimated the population.*

In 1680 the Pueblo Revolt left the Acomans in control of their own destinies but, as the Spanish reoccupied the area in the latter years of the seventeenth century, they were once again subjugated.

In the two hundred and eighty years that followed, the Acoma people were to be subjected to two more ruling powers—Mexico and the United States. During this time and, although Catholicism affected their lives drastically, the people of the Sky City maintained much of their original culture and perpetuated their oral traditions. The hunting rituals are an example of the ancient training the young men of the pueblo are given by the elders. These rules are still strictly observed by traditional Acomans. There are still approximately two thousand of these puebloans living atop the high mesa in their centuries-old, apartment-style homes.

Hunting Rituals

As soon as a hunting party settled into camp, each of the hunters went off in a different direction to solicit aid in the venture. They prayed to the best hunters: the cougar, the hawk, the eagle, and the wolf. Then they buried their prayer sticks, picked up a piece of wood, and sprinkled it with sacred cornmeal. They then told the wood that it was the deer they were going to kill. The surrogate deer would then be brought back to camp and thrown into the campfire with more cornmeal. This respectful action would assure success in the hunt.

When the hunter actually killed a deer, he performed an additional ceremony which was designed to calm the spirit of the slain animal. This would allow that spirit to be led back to camp so the hunting would continue to be good.

Yellow pollen would be dropped on the deer's mouth, then rubbed on the mouth of the hunter, and finally shaken out toward camp. The hunter would then place his little flint animal fetish on the deer to symbolically feed it. This would restore the hunting power the fetish had loaned the hunter for his kill. During the entire ceremony, the hunter

* Coffer, Ibid.

talked to the dead animal in a gentle voice, asking forgiveness for taking his life and explaining the necessity for the act.——Acoma

APACHE

The Apache are perhaps the most misunderstood of all the Indian people of America. Because of their love of freedom and their fierce defense of their homeland, they have been vilified by historians, anthropologists, novelists, and almost everyone else who has had the occasion to refer to them. The very attributes which Americans have glorified, such as love of country, resistance to oppression, love of freedom, etc., have been condemned when commenting on these same attributes as exemplified by the Apache people.

Together with the Navajo, the Apache constitute the western group of the southern division of the Athapascan linguistic family. They inhabited much of the area in southern New Mexico and Arizona, western Texas, and southeastern Colorado, also ranging over much of northern Mexico.

The Apache tribes evidently drifted down from the north long before the whites began their invasion of this hemisphere, probably along the eastern edge of the Rocky Mountains. When the Spanish first encountered them, they called them Querechos, and they were living in eastern New Mexico and western Texas and apparently did not move into Arizona until after the 1540s. They were first called Apache by Onate in 1598, this name being derived from the Zuñi word "apachu," meaning enemy. The Apache call themselves "Inde" or "Nde" which means "The People."

There are six groups of these independent people—Lipan, Jicarilla, Kiowa-Apache, Mescalero, Chiricahua, and Western Apache—plus the Navajo. Throughout history these seven bands were always autonomous and never united in any endeavor. If they had been a cohesive entity, the history of westward expansion of the Americas would have been written quite differently.

There were never a lot of Apaches in the Southwest, although many who felt the brunt of their savage warfare would probably claim that there were tremendous numbers of them. A reliable estimate of five thousand in 1680 is given and the census of 1930 enumerates six thousand five hundred and thirty-seven. The Department of Commerce's booklet, *We, The First Americans,* published in June, 1973, gives the current total Apache population as twenty-two thousand nine hundred and ninety-three, making them the eighth largest tribe in the United States. Since the slaughter of these people ceased and they have been allowed to live a more independent, undisturbed life in their remote reservations, their population has increased dramatically.

The Apache Indians have always been deeply religious people believing in a supreme being, a giver of life, and a host of other supernatural beings, with the sun, moon, and winds playing important roles. They have elaborate stories telling of their origin, culture heroes, and gods. The elders also explain natural phenomena by the use of tales which have been handed down through untold generations. "The Legend of the Salt" and "Life After Death" are examples of these stories.

Legend of the Salt*

His eyes burned, crusted from sand and heat. He had forgotten when it rained last. All of his land was parched.

Sand whipped across deep furrows, and dust devils, that rose high into the blue sky above, twisted along the dried-out riverbed.

"It's time now," he said, and turned toward his camp. The hot, dry winds had deposited more sand on the few remaining pit houses. The walls of others lay crumbling below their thatched roofs, becoming buried ever deeper each time the winds blew.

The night before, all the headmen of the tribe had gathered to decide on moving the camp. The final decision of when to move was left to him. He was their chief.

"It's time to go," he said softly, reaching the campsite. His people quietly rose to follow him. They had done it several times before, each time the new site promised water, food, and comfortable shelter. And each time the fire came, or the wind and the drought. Disease came, killing the people and killing their stock, and again they had to move on, just as they were doing today.

They had walked a long time. The abandoned camp was far behind

* Used by special permission from Brigitta G. Ludgate. This story appeared in the July, 1979 edition of *Arizona Highways* magazine and corresponds almost completely with versions heard by this author on the Arizona reservations.

now, even though they moved slowly. Their blistered feet ached in the hot sand, and the burdens on their backs grew heavier in the wind and heat. Suddenly one of the headmen motioned to stop.

"Where is the large jar?" he asked. He could not see it among the sparse possessions of his family. It was very special.

When his family first made it, they used materials from the earth but only enough to complete the container. They did not want to rob the land, and had asked their resources for forgiveness, promising that no part would be wasted. Now, the jar was left behind at the old camp, left there against their promise, to be forgotten in the dust and heat.

"The drought has punished us long enough, for what we are not sure. If we leave the jar where it is, we will anger the spirits of the earth and the plants even more. How much more can we bring upon ourselves?"

A little girl of a headman's family was chosen to return for the old container. She knew the importance of her mission and fearlessly hurried along, her little dog following close behind her.

It was late in the day when she came at last to the abandoned camp and found the jar. Knowing that night came quickly, she could not linger in her steps but must hurry back to the people of her band or she would be lost. But, the jar was large and awkward, and she quickly grew weary. Many times she had to stop to rest.

Now the sun was sinking fast, and she hurried on. Finally, she reached the spot where she had parted from her band earlier that day. But she could not see any of them.

He dark eyes filled with fear. Had she returned to the correct place? Had they moved on without her? She hurried on for a distance. But still she could not see them. Ahead, boulders blocker her view of the horizon. She hurried toward them as the sun was about to disappear, then she stared out along the empty horizon.

"They have left without me," she cried. "I won't catch up with them before it's dark."

As she walked on, the land around her rapidly changed from that of the open plateau. The empty river bed fell deeper into a valley and with it the trail.

The little girl followed it. On both sides now high buttes hovered above her. Their silhouettes in the night sky threatened her every step. She was terrified. She groped around the boulders for the shelter of an overhang. At last an opening appeared in one of the rocky walls, and she went inside with her little dog.

It was a small cave, cold and dark, its floor covered with rocks. Her feet ached from the long walk, and her arms were weak from carrying the big container. She set the jar down and shivered. She felt alone and hungry. The dog whimpered and pressed against her. She reached down toward him and held him tight. Her trembling hands stroked his bristly coat.

Nights until now had always been comforting to her at the camp. All the people she knew were always there, around the crackling fire. But here, the night was different. There were no familiar sounds, no chanting and shuffling of dancing feet. There were no rattling gourds, no crackling bonfires spreading warmth. There were no low whispers by the men sitting on warm blankets. There was no muffled talking by the women as they ground the corn.

There were only the eerie sounds of the cave. Many she had never heard before. It seemed as if the land around her had suddenly awakened with shrieks and howls. There were creaking sounds, moaning trees and weeping rocks. There were rustling wings in the air, and black night birds flying low.

The little girl held her dog tighter. The unfamiliar sounds grew louder and louder. Tears filled her dark eyes. More followed, pushing the first onto her cheeks. Trembling she clutched her dog.

Then from somewhere came the sound of her father's voice, speaking gently to her, as he had done many times before, "An Indian girl is strong and does not cry," the voice said.

"Father," she called, halting her tears. He did not answer.

"Father," she called again. And still no answer came. He was not there. There was no one there. She cried again. This time harder than before. She cried unhaltingly, wiping her eyes with her hands. The tears pearled onto them, soaking them. When they were too wet to hold any more, she wiped them on the rocky wall. One by one the salty tears rolled down the rocks and into a crevice. They rolled on from there, tumbling and gathering.

She cried for a long time. Eventually, her tears reached the ancient river bed, deep below its sandy surface. And when the rains came to once again soak the land and fill the river bed, the girl's tears mixed with the fresh water miraculously turning it salty.

From then on, with each seasonal rain, the river returned and its water was again made salty. And with time, the Indians of the land came to call the watercourse the Salt River, and it is still known by that name today.——Apache

Life After Death

When a person dies, he goes underground to the world there. There is an opening in the ground and someone leads the dead person to it so they will not miss it. The hole is surrounded by tall grass to hide it and make it look natural.

When this hole opens, there is a great conical pile of sand below it. It is very far from the top to the bottom, and once a person is down there, it is almost impossible to get out. Once a person who is really dead goes through the hole he cannot come back to life. If, however, he is just very sick and near death, he might recover and come back to tell about the underworld. But it is almost impossible. Many have tried, but they get so far up and the sand makes them slide back down.

The lifestyles we have here are carried on under the ground also. Those who live there eat, and sleep, and dance and can actually feel the flesh of the others. People remain the same age they were when they died and there is no sickness, death, pain, or sorrow there. Those who were good and those who were bad are all down there together and they still live the same way. The same places, the same sacred mountains, and the same ceremonies exist there as do here. It is just as though everything is transferred from here to there.

There is no hunger and there is plenty for everyone to eat. Everyone goes on living except in a much better way. Life seems much fuller and more meaningful than before and all are happy. There are the good things of the former life like hunting and raiding, and the same puberty rites, masked dances, and sacred mountain spirits.

In the underworld it is like one big village with everyone divided into their clans and families as before. Each is with his own and each does the same things he did on earth. With all pleasant things from above still existing below, it is understandable why death does not frighten the people.——Apache

COCHITI

Cochiti is one of the nineteen pueblos affiliated with the All-Pueblo Council of New Mexico. It is situated on the west bank of the Rio Grande 27 miles southwest of Santa Fe. Like the other Pueblo people, the Cochiti trace their ancestry to those beings who had their origin in the underworld. They emerged into this world through an opening called Shipapu. They then drifted south slowly to the Rio Grande where they took up residence in Frijoles Canyon along with other Puebloans. They constructed the cliff dwellings found there today and lived in them for many years. Long before the coming of the Europeans, they abandoned the canyon and moved farther south, separating into a number of autonomous village communities. When the Spanish found them in the 1540s, they called them "Pueblos," a Spanish word meaning "villages."

Missions were established in most of the towns and the people converted to Catholicism to some degree. Perhaps "converted" is not exactly the correct description; "toleration" would better explain the relationship between the Catholic Church and most Pueblos. In 1680, partly because of pressure applied for more control of the natives' lives by the church, the Pueblos revolted and drove the Spaniards out of their country and returned to their traditional religious practices.

By the end of the eighteenth century, Spain had once again gained mastery over the Pueblo country and again established their national church in the villages. This time, however, realizing the determination of the people to maintain their religions, the missionary work was done as more a harmonious activitiy and the Puebloans allowed the Catholic churches to remain. Many of the people even became "token" Catholics, attending services and outwardly aligning themselves with the church. The missionary effort was for the most part however, a failure, for these independent people maintained their kivas and conducted their spiritual lives according to the centuries-old native religions. Even today, the ceremonies and Pueblo life rotates around their traditions.

All of the Pueblos experience a rich ceremonial life and Cochiti is a typical example of how the traditional religious activity remains very much alive today. Cochiti ceremonial has retained its aboriginal emphasis upon curing, fertility, and weather control. As with other Indian

Why Coyote Is Restless
Cochiti

groups, their stories, handed down generation after generation, help rationalize and give explanation to natural phenomena in their environment. The following version of "Why Coyote is Restless" is an example.

Why Coyote Is Restless

Many years ago, Man came from the underground world to dwell here on top. With him he brought all the animals, great and small. He brought the bear, the cougar, the fox, the mouse. He also brought the quail, the dove, the hawk, the eagle, and all other birds and animals. They found here on earth all the things they needed to sustain their lives.

One day Man called a council and every kind of animal was invited. They met to decide what could be done to make the world an even better place to live. One thing which was decided was to place stars in the sky to give light to the night when the moon was asleep.

The task of placing the stars in their proper places was assigned to one person who was called Star Man. He positioned many stars and found it was very hard work. Growing tired he decided to rest and take a short nap. Placing the rest of the stars in a jar, he prepared for his sleep. Noticing Coyote and remembering how curious he was, Star Man warned Coyote not to touch the jar which contained the rest of the stars.

Now, before Star Man slept, he took seven stars out of the jar and placed them in the sky so the animals could see to get around while he rested. He arranged the seven stars in the form of a great dipper which we can see in its beauty today if we get out of bed early enough.

Coyote, not wanting to be outdone and not able to contain his curiosity, sneaked over to the star jar to take a peek. "What if I do sneak a look?" he thought, "I won't hurt anything and no one will even know." He slowly lifted up one edge of the jar's lid, and all the stars jumped out. They scattered all over the sky and began to multiply until they stretched from one end to the other. This is why today there are so many stars in the sky.

The council was very upset at what Coyote had done and assigned him a punishment to fit his crime. They told him that, since he had caused so much concern, he would be disliked by everyone and that wherever he traveled he would not be trusted. Wherever he would go he would always be hungry and discontented and never be happy. The council gave all other animals a feeling of pride and worth which Coyote could never know.

Even to this day, all animals except Coyote roam free and are content while he continues to find mischief wherever he goes and is forced to roam from one place to another.——Cochiti

HAVASUPAI

In Cataract Canyon, some three thousand feet below the surrounding land, lives a tribe of Indians called Havasupai. Their small reservation lies totally within the boundaries of Grand Canyon National Park. Hemmed in by towering walls of red sandstone and inaccessible except by a narrow winding trail or by helicopter, this fertile canyon is a place of beauty and tranquility.

Originally the Havasupai utilized a reservation about five miles wide and twelve miles long. In 1882, the Federal government reduced their holdings to an irregular strip of canyon bottom-land, a mere 518.6 acres. Due to strong advocacy by Arizona Congressmen and litigations, congressional hearings, and political maneuvering, recently the usurped land was returned to the tribe.

For many years the Havasupai were fairly isolated and ignored by tourists and government agents and were able to live relatively traditional lives. Generations of Havasupai have carried on trade with the Navajo and Hopi, obtaining blankets, wool, and silverwork in exchange for dressed animal skins and agricultural products. The Walapai traded raw deer hides to the Havasupai for the Navajo and Hopi goods in addition to fruits and vegetables. Thus the "people of the blue-green water" were able to obtain needed outside materials without the drastic acculturation process suffered by many of their neighbors.

Many stories of these unique people have survived over the centuries because of their isolation. One example, "How the World Got Its People," is provided here.

How the World Got Its People

In the Beginning, there were two gods of the Universe. The good god was called Tochopa and he was kind and loving. But the other god, called Hokomata was very bad and only thought evil. Tochopa had a beautiful daughter* named Pukeheh, whom he had planned to be the mother of the human race which would inhabit the earth. Hokomata, the evil one, seemed to possess the most magic and boasted that he would flood the earth and destroy everything.

The good god, Tochopa, fearing he (Hokomata) would carry out his threat, made a large boat from a hollow piñon log in which he hoped to save his daughter. He placed food and other articles necessary for survival inside the log and made a window in it so Pukeheh could see out. He then called his daughter to the log and, after explaining what was to take place, sealed her inside and waited for Hokomata to destroy the world.

Before long, the great floods began to descend, not just rain, but huge cataracts, rivers, and deluges came and covered the whole earth with water. The piñon log floated and protected Pukeheh while the water rose higher and higher until it covered the highest mountain.

Finally, the flood ceased and the water began to rush into the great sea. As it roared down, it cut through the rocky plateaus and made the deep canyons of the Colorado River. Soon all the water had drained away and the earth began to dry. Then the log came to rest on the ground and Pukeheh looked out through the window. Although it was misty and almost dark, she could see in the east the distant outlines of the San Francisco Mountains. Looking to the north, she saw the Canyon of the Colorado and, to the west, the Canyon of the Havasu.

Seeing the water gone, she came out of the log and, since she had grown into a woman, began to weave baskets and make pottery as her father had taught her to do. She was very lonely for her father, but she had to live alone a long time in the dark, dismal world.

Many months of darkness had passed when one morning the darkness began to disappear and in the east a faint brightness appeared. The young woman knew that the Sun was coming to conquer the long night and bring light into the world. During the time of waiting for the

---

* There is no explanation provided as to who was the mother of Pukeheh.

coming of light, Pukeheh had a great longing for a child but there was not a man in the world to father a child.

When the Sun rose in the east, she decided he should be the father of her child. She conceived and when the time was fulfilled, bore a son whom she called Son of the Sun.

As time passed Pukeheh longed for another child and gave birth to a daughter. When these two children grew up they became the progenitors of the human race. The Havasupai were created first, then the Apache, the Walapai, the Hopi, the Paiute, and all the other tribes. Tochopa showed each tribe where they were to live and gave them their language. The Havasupai were to live in Cataract Canyon where you find them to this day.——Havasupai

Havasupai Traditions

During the last few months of pregnancy, a pregnant woman must scratch with a stick if she has an itch, never with her fingers.

The souls of twins were in such close sympathy that whatever happened to one, must happen to the other. Therefore, the weaker twin, or the girl baby if it were a boy/girl combination, would generally be killed to protect the other.

If a parent kills a snake before the child learns to walk, it might never walk. When a snake is killed, it loses its spirit; and where else can it go but into the child?

Young boys must get up at first light and run toward the rising sun. This prepares them for the hunt and makes them swift in capturing the enemy.

MOJAVE

Mojave comes from a native word meaning "three mountains" and is the name given to a group of Yuman-speaking natives who lived in the Colorado River Valley on both sides of the river. Alarcón, the Spanish explorer, reached Mojave territory in 1540, followed by Oñate in 1604. In 1775–76, Father Garces established missions in the villages of the Mojave and, for a time, experienced friendly relations with them.

The Mojaves were great travelers and frequently made trips down the Colorado to visit and trade with their allies, the Yumas. The Yavapai neighbors and the Chemehuevis were considered friends but the Pima, Papago, and Maricopa were enemies. The Mojaves frequently traveled to the Pacific Ocean to visit and trade with the Chumash Indians who lived near present-day Santa Barbara, California, and spoke a dialect of the same language as the Mojave. Evidently, from artifacts found in their villages, these large, stalwart warriors, moving in a steady trot, covered most of southern California to trade, visit, and exploit the land. Stories relate that the Mojave men could run across the desert for as long as four days without food.

The Colorado River Reservation was established in 1865 for the Mojave and some of their neighbors. Since until fairly recent times there was not much in the area to interest the whites, the Mojave people were generally insulated from the acculturation process until the twentieth century. Consequently, much of the spiritual life and their oral tradition remained. The story of "The Fox and the Quail" typifies Mojave legends.

The Fox and the Quail

Many years ago, a Fox and his wife lived in the Mojave Valley of the Colorado River. After breakfast one morning, the old man decided to go out and gather some firewood. He told his wife he would be gone until afternoon, so she said she would cook something so he could eat when he returned after mid-day.

The Fox started out and after he had traveled about a half a mile, he met a quail. He grabbed the quail and pulled all his feathers out so he couldn't fly anymore. Then he ordered the quail to walk back to the Fox's house by following the Fox's tracks. When the quail got there he was to tell the Fox's wife she was to cook him so Fox could have quail soup when he got back. So the quail did as he was told and went to Fox's home and told the woman he had a special message from her husband. "He said you were not to question it, but you should cook his new sandals so he can have sandal soup when he get home." And the little quail went on its way.

The Fox kept thinking of the quail soup he would have when he got home so he gathered the wood as fast as he could. He got a big load of wood and hurried home, arriving a little after noon. The first thing he did was grab a large spoon and start eating the soup. He said, "Wife, you sure know how to make delicious quail soup." "What quail soup?" she asked. "That soup was made from your new sandals just as the quail told me you wanted."

This made the Fox very angry and he started out after the quail. Now the little quail had a half-day's head start but he couldn't fly and had to walk or run. He knew that without his feathers he would be easy prey for the Fox. He ran to a waterhole he knew, but it was dry. He went to another and another, but they were all dry. Finally, after sundown, he found a waterhole that still had plenty of water in it. He was sore, tired, and thirsty, so when he had all the water he could drink, he climbed a nearby tree to sleep and recuperate from his injuries the Fox gave him when he pulled his feathers out.

The Fox followed the tracks of the quail to the first waterhole, which was dry, and ran around and around it looking for Quail's tracks so he could follow him. It was so dark by this time that Fox headed back home. He vowed the next day he would catch the quail and eat him without even cooking him. When he arrived home, he ate the rest of his sandals and went to bed.

Early the next morning, he was on Quail's trail again. Although the tracks were hard to follow by this time, Fox stayed with it and caught up about noon. The quail was sitting on a limb by the waterhole, out of reach of the Fox. The Fox looked down into the water and saw the quail's image. He was so mad he didn't even stop to think. The Fox jumped into the pool after the quail, and he drowned.——Mojave

NAVAJO

The Navajo Nation with its huge land area of over twelve million acres and its one hundred and fifty thousand people is the largest reservation in size and population in the United States. It is located in northeastern Arizona, northwestern New Mexico, and southeastern Utah, the "Four Corners" area, with scattered, small units detached from the main reservation, mostly in west-central New Mexico. The history of this determined people is fraught with abuse and mistreatment but, in spite of this, they have displayed a remarkable resilience. After being starved into submission in 1863 by Kit Carson and the United States Army, marched to Bosque Redondo over hundreds of miles of desolate, desert country on the infamous "Long Walk," and being reduced to barely ten thousand persons, the Navajo bounced back.

Although in many ways the Navajos are very progressive, even dealing with the OPEC nations for possible oil transactions, they are as a whole very traditional in their spiritual perspectives. Medicine men are given an honored place in Navajo society and "sings" are used to return ill Navajos to harmony with the universe. Elders tell stories at night in the hogans, and Spider Woman and the Hero Twins are integral parts of Navajo culture even today. Canyon de Chelly remains as sacred ground and the center of the Navajo universe.

Some Navajo men and women drive pick-up trucks, work in offices, live in urban settings, and are a functioning part of mainstream America. Yet these same Navajos must return home for certain occasions and must participate in many traditional activities or they fail to fill the proper place in their world. They then become dysfunctional and are lost.

Books have been filled with stories the Navajo people have perpetuated for generations. It is impossible to offer more than a few examples in this book. The following five tales are illustrative of the many Navajo stories.

The Story of the Twins

Once long ago, twins were born to a young girl. They had been fathered by a god but this was kept secret from everyone. One of the children was afflicted with blindness and the other was lame and could not walk. Their relatives were too poor to keep them so they wandered from place to place, living on whatever they could beg and always searching for a cure for their handicaps. The blind boy carried the lame and the lame boy supplied the vision for the blind one.

They wandered from one habitat of the gods to another, but each of the deities demanded jewels or other valuables from the boys, and when they found the children had nothing, they sent them away with ridicule. Finally, their father, still keeping his anonymity, secretly began to leave food in various places for them and eventually gave them a cup of ever-replenishing cornmeal.

After twice making the rounds of the sacred places, the identity of the father was discovered and the gods took the twins into the sweat house to cure them. The boys were instructed not to say a word during the ceremony. However, as the blind one became aware of light he cried joyously, "Brother, I see, I see!" When the lame one felt strength in his legs, he cried, "Oh, Brother, I can walk!" By speaking, the boys had undone the magic of the gods and returned to their former condition and were sent out to get a fee with which they could buy the healing.

The gods aided them by supplying magic and the boys tricked the wealthy Pueblo people into giving them the needed treasure. Provided with this, they returned to the gods and in an elaborate, nine-day ceremony, were at last made perfect. They took the ritual back to their people and then returned to live with the gods. The boy who had been blind became the keeper of the rains, and the boy who had been lame became the guardian of the animals. They maintain these duties to this day.——Navajo

The Coyote and the Badger

Badger was hunting prairie dogs and had killed a bunch when he met Coyote. Now Coyote was hunting, too, but he hadn't caught any prairie dogs. When he saw all the ones Badger had, he tried to figure out how to get them. He said to Badger, "Let's have a race around the mesa, and the one who wins will get to eat all the prairie dogs." Badger said, "Okay, but let's put them in the ashes of the fire to cook so they will be ready to eat when the race is over."

So they built a fire and put the prairie dogs in the ashes with just their tails sticking out, and then they started the race. Well, Coyote was pretty fast, and in no time at all, he was out of sight. Badger knew he could not outrun Coyote, so when Coyote went around the end of the mesa, Badger ran back to the fire and pulled the prairie dogs out by the tails, and ate them all. Then he put the tails back sticking out of the ashes, and ran off and hid in some bushes.

Pretty soon Coyote came running around the mesa all tired and panting, and he figured he had won the race since Badger was no where in sight. He ran over to the fire, laughing about how he had tricked Badger, and grabbed the prairie dog tails and pulled them out. He was amazed when he saw he had nothing but tails and the prairie dogs were gone. Badger laughed and laughed because he had fooled old Coyote, the trickster.

And that is why prairie dogs are still cooked the same way Coyote and Badger cooked them.——Navajo

How Clans Were Created

After the monsters had all been killed and everything was peaceful within the area bounded by the sacred mountains,* Changing Woman's husband, the Sun, asked her to live with him in a beautiful home that he would build for her in the Western Ocean. At first, Changing Woman refused, but her husband and the Twins finally persuaded her to do it. A number of the people (animals) went with her.

However, after a while the people decided to return to their homes in the East. Because Changing Woman thought there should be more humans, she created the beginnings of the four original clans by rubbing off flakes of skin from various parts of her body. She also provided an animal guardian for each clan. For one she gave a bear to look out for it. Another received a lion, and the third was given the bullsnake. The fourth clan was assigned the porcupine as its protector.

Accompanied by Talking Gods, the four groups were taken by magic to a point near their homeland. Then, on foot, they visited what is now known as the Bill Williams Mountains, the Female Mountain, Corner of Mountain, what is now Tuba City, a place called Water-on-it, Black Mountain, a spot on the east side of Black Mountain, Tonalea, Thief Rock, El Capitan, Wooded Mesa, Beautiful Mountain, and the Lukachukai Mountains.

On this long trek the people (now Navajos) encountered many enemies and were attacked, but the animal guardians saved them. One by one, though, the guardians were left behind to fight the persuers or because they asked to leave. Later, when the people tired of the journey and tried to turn back, Changing Woman knew of their thoughts and ordered that the Blessing Way Ceremony be held for them at four places, and the people decided to stay in their homeland. These sacred ceremonies are still held today and are part of the power that guides the people.

Gradually, guided by the Holy People, the Navajos increased and prospered. Many additional clans developed and the result is the Navajo Nation we have today.——Navajo

---

* For an explanation of these four sacred mountains see *Spirits of the Sacred Mountains,* by William E. Coffer (Koi Hosh), published by Van Nostrand Reinhold, Co., New York, 1978.

Why We Have Day and Night

The moccasin (shoe) game is very popular among the Navajos today. It is, however, an ancient game which was given to the people by a mysterious being named One Walking Giant. He taught them how to play at the House Made of Banded Rock, near a cave in Red Rock Canyon on the eastern side of the Lukachukai Mountains. One Walking Giant had visited the people several times before he could persuade them to learn the game. At the Navajos' request, the Holy People and many animals, including Coyote, attended. The giant explained that those who traveled by day would play against those who traveled by night. In other words, day competed with night.

The giant laid out one hundred and two yucca counters and explained that the side which won all the counters would be the winner of the game. It was understood that if the day people won, there would always be daylight. On the other hand, if the night people won, there would always be darkness.

The large group—Holy People, Navajos, and animals—played all night long. When it was nearly dawn, the night people knew they must be home before the sunlight came or they would perish. Therefore, One Walking Giant called the game off with neither side wining. This is why the world now has half night and half day.——Navajo

Navajo Beliefs

If you are a hunter and a deer cries at you, something will go wrong.
If an owl comes to your house every night, you will have bad luck.
If you kill a frog, you will be crippled.
If you whip a snake to the ground, you will be struck by lightning.
Don't burn snakes or your body will swell.
If a boy shows off in front of girls, he will have bad luck.
If you break a hand tool or a weaving tool, you will be afflicted with aching bones, sores, or itching.
If you break a wooden spindle, you will get dizzy and have headaches.
If you put your hand in the loom, you will not think clearly.
If you crawl in the window of your house, you will start having problems in it and it might even burn.

If you are pregnant, you are not to do the edging or warping on a rug, because it is dangerous for your baby's umbilical cord. It might twist and the baby will become stupid.

When you are pregnant you are not to do the side edging cords or you will have twins.

Do not weave storm patterns, for it will cause bad weather, especially in the winter. Lightning may strike you or one of your friends.

If you weave a sand painting design before you have a special ceremony, you will live only a short time.

You must not weave a yei-bichei rug before having the yei-bichei ceremony. Some people die if they do. When you are young and are weaving this design, even after the ceremony, you must ask the yei-bichei for help occasionally or you may lose your hearing or go blind.

Do not lose your temper and curse your rug, for the rug knows and something bad will happen to you. If you can sing the song of your rug, it will be easier for you, but you must not sing too loudly or the witches will hear.

Wash in cool or cold water or you will get wrinkles in your face.

Don't burn ants or red spots will appear on your back.

Don't stand on high rocks or they will grow into the sky with you.

Never carry or touch a human bone or extremely bad things will happen to you.

The Twins Journey to the Sun

Long ago Begochiddie, the Navajo God of Creation, approached twin boys who were hunting to get food for their families. Begochiddie could not be seen in his natural state by the boys, so he appeared in the form of an eagle. He told them that they had been sired by the Sun and, as they were now becoming men, it was time for them to visit their father so they could find out their mission in life. He then gave them a ray of light and a rainbow to help them make the long journey into the heavens. Begochiddie also warned them that their father would offer them many gifts to bring back to the people, but they should only bring back the flint armor, the lightning arrows, the stone knife, big cyclones, big hail, and a magic firestick. Thus instructed, the twins started on their journey to visit their father, the Sun.

The boys rode the ray of light and the rainbow over deep canyons, rivers, and sky-piercing mountains. They passed swiftly under Day-break, the After-Glow of Sunset, the Dusk and Darkness until they reached the Turquoise House where the Spirit of the Sun lived with other heavenly spirits and his messenger, the Dragonfly.

To make sure the boys were really his and not imposters, the Sun put them through a series of severe trials. He threw them onto spikes of obsidian, smothered them with steam, and exposed them to violent storms and freezing nights. The boys endured all of these tortures which convinced the Sun that these were indeed his sons. He then informed the boys that they were to be the protectors of their people and presented them with the magic weapons which they were to use to kill man's enemies.

The twins then returned by rainbow and light to the earth where they still protect the people with their magic.——Navajo

PAIUTE

Pauite is not properly a tribe but rather a linguistic designation. The Northern Paiute constitute a dialectal group of the Shoshonean Branch of the Uto-Aztecan language family while the Southern Paiute belong to the Ute-Chemehuevi group of the Shoshonean Branch. These diverse people occupied a huge portion of the Great Basin area extending from southeastern Oregon into parts of eastern California, Utah, most of Nevada, and parts of northwestern Arizona.

Although the territory of the Paiute has been occupied by humans for a long period of time and cultural modification has occurred from time to time along its margins influenced by neighboring groups of people, there seem to be few changes in the fundamental culture of this area as a whole. Economic life has basically been formed around hunting and gathering.

Crises have from time to time occurred which temporarily effected drastic changes in the normal peaceful lifestyles of these people. One such incident was the discovery of the "Comstock Lode" at Virginia City, Nevada. For ten years following this, miners penetrated every part of the area and boom towns sprang up in the midst of sheer deserts. Introduction of livestock and destruction of native plant foods, along with physical depredations, had a drastic effect on the native population. Similar problems were encountered by the northwestern

Paiutes a few years earlier when gold was discovered in northern California.

Estimations of seven thousand five hundred were placed on the Paiute population in 1845 and the 1910 census enumerated three thousand and thirty-eight. The census of 1930 reported four thousand four hundred and twenty scattered on small reservations and colonies all over the vast territory. Considering the area covered and the many states in which these people live, it is nearly impossible to obtain an accurate figure today.

Many groups of Paiutes retain much of their tradition and stories are still passed from generation to generation. One of these, "The Stone Animals of Bryce Canyon" is presented in this collection.

The Stone Animals of Bryce Canyon

A long time ago, before man was put on this earth, it was inhabited only by the animals. One of the most beautiful places and one most loved by these creatures was a beautiful canyon known to us today as Bryce Canyon. It did not look as it does today and was filled with trees and all manner of wild flowers. Everything the animals needed was there and they were very happy.

At this time all the animals were physically much like people and also much like people in their psychological make-up. In this land of plenty where there was no want, eventually the animals began stealing and fighting among themselves, just like people. Coyote saw what was happening and became very angry. He decided to punish the ungrateful animals by turning them into stone.

Today, the colors and massive, bright shapes of the canyon are the painted faces and bodies of Coyote's wrath.——Paiute

PAPAGO

Archaeological excavations at Ventana Cave and along the Santa Cruz River in southern Arizona have indicated that man has been in this region for a very long time. Papago Indians, the desert people who now live in this area, are descendants of the Hohokam, "The Ancient Ones" whose cultural identity spans from about 300 B.C. to around A.D. 1450. These early Indians practiced irrigated farming along the river valleys and literally "made the desert bloom." Theirs was an extremely sophisticated civilization which, for some unknown reason declined sharply and disappeared shortly before the arrival of the Spanish in 1540.*

In the late 1600s the Papago economy underwent a great change due to the introduction of cattle and horses by Father Eusebio Kino, a Jesuit missionary and explorer. Along with the economic influence Kino and his contemporaries had on the Papagos, there was a change made in the religious activities also. Catholicism was introduced and partially accepted by the people.

The Papagos, even under pressures by the various Christian denominations, have always maintained a tenacity for their native religion. The Catholic Church, unable to convert the Indians totally, compromised and designed a special Catholicism for these fiercely independent people. Within the Sonoran Catholic Church, as it is called, there are no hymns in Latin, no mass, no confession, no marriage ceremony, baptism is performed by godparents, and the Papago bury their own dead. With this special, diluted form of religion, about eighty-five percent of the population now claim membership and are very loyal to the church.

Along with this imported religious organization, the Papago people adhere strongly to their native religion. Although assimilation has eroded these beliefs to some degree, especially in the areas where white infiltration has been the most active, the rural Papagos place great faith in their traditions. Ceremonies are conducted in the same way they have been for centuries and stories are still passed fom generation to generation. Most of the eight to ten thousand Papagos scattered over nearly three million acres of reservation still tell and retell the tales related by their forefathers.

Some of these stories are provided in the following pages.**

The Magic Deer

When the People first came from the underground world, E'Etoi created the deer for their food and clothing. However, He gave the deer special powers and it was more than just food and clothing. Deer

* See William E. Coffer, *Phoenix: The Decline and Rebirth of the Indian People*, p. 9.
** The author lived on the Papago Reservation and taught at Indian Oasis School at Sells, the Papago capital. Many of the stories were related to him by students in the classroom.

meat has special curative powers and the first deer of the season is cooked with great ceremony. Each person in the village is given some of the flesh to provide "abundant" life for the coming year.

The white tail of the deer also possesses great magical power and is used with reverence by the People in special events. It is given as an offering to enemies killed in battle. It is laid out reverently under the stars on the night the sacred wine must ferment and is worn by spiritual leaders during particular ceremonies.

In order to create the deer, E'Etoi first tried to make it from the squirrel. He slit the soft belly but the squirrel cried out, so He changed animals. Today the squirrel has a white underside to show where he was cut. E'Etoi then took the tiny desert mouse and slit its underparts. Although it was small, the mouse did not make a sound so E'Etoi made the deer from him.

He gave the wind to the deer as a friend to carry the scent of an enemy and give warning. He gave the deer sensitive ears to hear the rustling of a leaf and to feel the vibration of the earth if danger approaches. He left out the gall bladder so the deer feels no anger and He provided it with the knowledge of "when its time was come." At that time the deer voluntarily goes to the hunter and calmly sacrifices its life so the hunter may eat.

When the hunter kills a deer, he lays its head to the west and reverently makes his apology for taking the life. He explains to the deer the plan E'Etoi devised: that the deer was made so the People might eat and live. He then takes the tail home as his most cherished possession and distributes the meat among the villagers. He admonishes his neighbors to dispose of the bones in a proper manner and not let them lie around where the dogs might drag them off. They must be buried in the earth with proper dignity. The hunter then composes a song glorifying the deer.——Papago

The Children's Shrine

Many years ago, long before the coming of the white man, the Papago people freely traveled into present-day Mexico to visit friends and relatives. While on such a trip to the region around Magdalena, a group of Papagos came to a village which had been wiped out by a flash flood. The houses were demolished and all the people were drowned except three small children who had clung to a mesquite tree. They were found huddled together, very hungry and fightened, crying for their parents.

Now, the Papagos were a kindly people, so they took the children home with them when they returned to the north. Although the children were well-treated, they were extremely sad and cried constantly for their lost loved ones.

One day, out of the ground near Santa Rosa, a spring of water gushed. It was a great spring and soon all of Papago-land was being flooded. The situation grew worse each day until the elders called a council to discuss what to do. They met and talked for a long time, and finally decided the flood was a sign sent by the parents of the children that they wanted their children returned.

The children were then taken to the place where the water was gushing from the earth and dropped into the opening. The flood immediately ceased. The elders knew for sure then that they had been right and the flood was a sign from the parents. They erected a shrine at the place in honor of the children. It was surrounded by a fence of ocotillo branches with openings to the four primary directions, north, east, south, and west.

Today this shrine is still cared for by the Papagos. The stones which were the seats of the elders when they held council are still in place, and every few years, as the ocotillo branches age, new branches are cut and a new fence is built. The old branches are piled at the sides of the area. This practice has been taking place for so long that the branches at the bottom of the piles have long since decayed and returned to the earth, leaving ridges of dirt in their place.

Papagos leave small gifts, ribbons, combs, coins, or other small offerings at the shrine for the children. No one really knows what happens to these gifts, but overnight they disappear. The older Papagos believe the children come for them during the night and take them to their underground home where they now live with their parents. The elder Papagos also claim that if you visit the shrine on a quiet night, you can still hear the children laughing and playing below. They are very happy to be back with their families.——Papago

The Death of the Witch

Many years ago an evil witch lived in Papago-land and did all sorts of bad things to the people. She caused droughts and floods, brought sickness, made flies and gnats, and even ate children who wandered too far from their homes. The people were very frightened and called on E'Etoi, the Elder Brother, to help them.

Now E'Etoi lived in his cave where he had made the first people, in the huge granite peak of Baboquivre Mountain. He heard the pleas of the people, and, as he looked out over the valley below, he saw the deeds of the wicked witch. Although, like the Papagos, E'Etoi was quite peaceful until pushed too far, he became very angry and decided to kill the witch.

The witch, although she was extremely wicked, was also very powerful, so getting rid of her was no easy task. A great fight developed between E'Etoi and the witch in the valley below Baboquivre Mountain. As the two pulled and pushed, great ridges and valleys were formed as they strained against each other.

E'Etoi kicked at the witch and missed and to this day you can see where his big toe dug a hole in the side of the hill. At last he was successful in striking the witch a heavy blow which broke her back. She fell in a twisted heap and her remains formed a gnarled ridge southwest of Baboquivre. The people were joyful at the end of their tormenter and named the area where the toe print and the broken body of the witch lay, Há-ák Muerto, which is a Papago-Spanish mixture, meaning "The Death of the Witch."——Papago

How the World Was Started

In the beginning, Earthmaker and E'Etoi shaped and peopled the new world. They were followed everywhere by Coyote, who was not created, but just came to life. Coyote was very nosey from the beginning and started immediately to get into trouble. In this new world there was a great flood and the three agreed before they took refuge that whoever came out first after the water went down would be their leader and have the title of Elder Brother. Earthmaker, the creator, emerged first and E'Etoi came out second. E'Etoi, however, insisted that he should have the title of Elder Brother, and, after much argument, got his way.

E'Etoi, although he was killed by the People, had so much power that he came back to life. Then he invented war and went underground to get help to do away with the ones who had killed him. He found the

Papagos and brought them up from the underground. It is thus they explain their origin.

They lived in a land covered by ruins of the Hohokam, "the people who are gone." Archeologists still do not know what happened to these people, but the Papagos know. E'Etoi drove them from the land and they are now the other tribes found scattered throughout the southwest. Some went far to the north and became the Plains and Mountain tribes and others went south into Mexico and South America.

E'Etoi, having set things in place now lives, a little old man, in his cave in the top of Baboquivre Mountain.——Papago

The Creation and the Flood

The Great Spirit made the earth and all living things before He made man. He descended from heaven, and digging in the earth, he found clay such as the potters use. Ascending to the sky, He dropped this clay back into the hole He had dug. Immediately there came out Montezuma and, with his assistance, the rest of the Indian tribes in order. Last of all came the Apaches, wild from their hour of birth, running away as fast as they were created. Those first days of the world were happy and peaceful days. The sun was nearer the earth than he is now; his graceful rays made all the seasons equal and rendered garments unnecessary. Men and beasts talked together in a common language that made all brethren. But an awful destruction ended this happy age.

A great flood destroyed all flesh wherein there was the breath of life; Montezuma and his friend, Coyote, escaping.* Before the flood began, Coyote had prophesied its coming, and Montezuma took the warning and hollowed out a boat for himself, keeping it ready on the topmost summit of Santa Rosa Mountain. The Coyote also prepared an ark, gnawing down a great cane by the river bank, entering it, and stopping up the hole with a certain gum. When the waters rose these two saved themselves and met again on dry land when the flood has passed away.

Naturally, Montezuma was anxious to know how much dry land had been left, and he sent Coyote off on four successive journeys to find exactly where the sea lay, toward each of the four winds. From the

---

* This legendary Montezuma, whom we meet so often in the mythology of the Southwest, should not be confused with the two Mexican monarchs of the same name.

west and from the south the answer came quickly: The sea is at hand. A longer search was made towards the east, but at last the sea was found there too. On the north only was no water found though the faithful messenger almost wore himself out searching.

In the meantime the Great Spirit, aided by Montezuma, had again repeopled the world, and animals and men began to increase and multiply. To Montezuma had been allotted the care and government of the new race. He was so puffed up with pride and self-importance, however, that he neglected the most important duties of his position and allowed the most disgraceful wickedness to pass unnoticed among the people. The Great Spirit came down to earth and vainly remonstrated with His viceregent, who only scorned His laws and advice, and ended at last by breaking out into open rebellion.

Then indeed was the Great Spirit filled with anger, and He returned to heaven, pushing back the sun on His way to that remote part of the sky he now occupies. But Montezuma hardened his heart, and collecting all the tribes to aid him, set about building a house that should reach up to heaven itself. Already it had attained a great height and contained many apartments lined with gold, silver, and precious stones. The whole tower was making good the boasting of the power of its architect when the Great Spirit launched His thunder and laid its glory in ruins.

Still Montezuma hardened himself; proud and inflexible, he answered the Thunderer out of the haughty defiance of his heart. He ordered the temples to be desecrated and the holy images to be dragged in the dust. He made them a scoff and a byword for the very children in the village streets. Then the Great Spirit prepared His supreme punishment. He sent an insect flying away towards the east, towards an unknown land, to bring the Spaniards. When these came, they made war upon Montezuma and destroyed him, and utterly dissipated the idea of his divinity.*——Papago

The Story of the Man Eagle

Once, long ago, there was a man who turned into an eagle. No one knows how or why this happened, but it did. At first he did not know

* Hubert Howe Bancroft. *The Works of Hubert Howe Bancroft* (San Francisco: A. L. Bancroft & Company, 1883), Vol. III, pp. 75–77.

what to do so he flew to a tree and just sat there. Now he was such a big eagle that the tree broke and he flew to another tree. This tree also broke, so he flew to a rock but that broke, too. He finally had to fly to a huge stone mountain where he found a large cave. There he could keep cool, so he made the cave his home.

He was a very large eagle, as big as a man, so he could not live on mice and rabbits and birds as most eagles do. He had to live on large animals and, since the animals were scarce, on people. He would raid the villages every day and kill people and carry them off to his mountain cave. He killed so many people he could not eat them all so he just piled them up in one corner.

There was one woman the eagle did not kill. He liked her so he took her for his wife and carried her off to his rocky home. She lived with him and, after a while, she had a baby. It did not look like a real baby but looked half-child and half-eagle.

The woman was afraid of the eagle and the weird child and wanted to leave but she could not climb down from the cave. It was high on the side of the mountain and no one could get there except by flying.

The people were also afraid of the eagle and the baby so they went to E'Etoi, the Elder Brother, to seek his help. They thought that since E'Etoi was their Creator and had taught them how to live on the earth, He would know what to do. After hearing of their trouble, E'Etoi said He would come to help them.

E'Etoi made arrows from ironwood and flint and shot them into the side of the mountain, one above the other, and made a stairway to reach the eagle's cave. He climbed the stairs and reached the hideaway where He saw the woman and the eagle-baby. As He was looking over the situation, the huge eagle returned so E'Etoi turned Himself into a fly and hid in a crack in the roof of the cave.

Soon, after the eagle had eaten a few more people he brought home, he lay down and went to sleep. The eagle's wife sang songs to the eagle-baby until he, too, fell asleep beside his father. Then the little fly came out of the crack and turned back into E'Etoi, who took a stone ax and chopped off the eagle-child's head right where he lay. He then turned to the huge eagle and chopped off his head, too. The eagle, however, did not want to die and flopped around and his great wings knocked over everything in the cave. E'Etoi changed back to a fly and turned the woman to a fly and they both flew into the crack where they would be safe.

The eagle's body jumped around so much and so hard that it made an earthquake and great pieces of stone fell off the mountain and rolled down below. They rolled so that they made steps and, after that, anyone could climb up the mountain.

E'Etoi and the woman came out of the crack and assumed their natural shapes again. E'Etoi asked the woman to boil some water for Him, which she did. He then poured the water on the bodies which had not been dead very long. They came to life at once and began to jump around and shout. "You make too much noise," said E'Etoi, "and you jump around too much. I don't want you to live near me so you go across the mountains and be the Apache." This is why the Apaches live in the mountains far from E'Etoi and are always shouting and jumping around.

The next people did not come to life quite so soon, but, when they did, they were fine, healthy people who were quiet and worked hard and ran only when it was needed. "This is fine," said E'Etoi. "I want you to live near me and be my Desert People." And this is why the Papagos live in the desert around the sacred mountain called Baboquivre.

The next ones were near the bottom of the pile and they came to life very slowly. It seemed as though they could hardly move and they did not jump at all. In fact, they hardly talked. E'Etoi did not want them too near him so he sent them off to live by the river. That is why the Pimas, the River People, are so slow and do not work very hard.

The last people had been dead a very long time, so long, in fact, they had turned white. They did not know how to act and could not talk at all, so E'Etoi gave them something with which to write.

"Go far from me," he said. "Go to the far end of the world and stay there. You can spend your time writing since you do not know how to do anything else. You can be the White People."

So the people went to their places and E'Etoi and the woman walked down the steps from the cave and that is how the eagle-man was killed and how different people came to live where they do.——Papago

PIMA

In the valleys of the Gila and Salt Rivers near present-day Phoenix lived the Pima Indians. Closely related to the Papagos, these Uto-Aztecan-speaking people have been exposed to white influence since

1694 when Father Kino reached Casa Grande.* Since that time the Pimas have encountered missionaries, bandits, explorers, trappers, outlaws, border ruffians, and about every other type of "outsiders" found in the western portion of this country. One of the most precious commodities in the desert—water—has been the source of conflict between the Indians and the newcomers.

The eight to ten thousand Pimas located on the Gila River and the Salt River Reservations are still forced to contend with whites for the water in the two rivers. They are also engaged in the struggle for cultural survival, for the proximity of urban centers forces assimilation onto the Pimas more than any other group of Indians in the Southwest. Numerous religious organizations, close association with great numbers of whites, integrated education, and exposure to urbanization have finally had the effect of bringing about many cultural revivals in the tribe in self-defense against the alien influences, and one of the most effective facets of this movement is the perpetuation of the oral tradition. A few of these stories are provided on the following pages.

How the Earth was Made

In the beginning there was nothing but darkness. The darkness gathered over a long period of time and formed the spirit of Earth Doctor. Since he had no home and just floated on the breezes, Earth Doctor decided to try to build himself a place to live. He took a piece of dust and flattened it into a cake. Then he planted a seed in it and the creosote bush grew.

Next Earth Doctor made some insects and then he made Termite who immediately began to work as hard as he does today. Termite shaped the dust cake and it began to grow until it was the earth as we know it now.

Earth Doctor danced and sang on the earth and it began to develop so he made the sky to cover it. He then made a gray spider who spun a web around the disconnected earth and sky, and earth grew firm and solid.

Then Earth Doctor made the mountains, trees, grass, water and all the things we have about us today. He then made the sun and moon

* Casa Grande National Monument at Coolidge, Arizona.

and placed them in the sky and gave them their paths which they still follow. He then took some water in his mouth and sprayed it in the sky to make the stars and broke a magic crystal and threw it into the sky to make the larger stars. Next he took his walkingstick, and placing ashes on the tip, he drew it across the sky to make the Milky Way.

When the earth was finished, Earth Doctor made all the animals and birds and fishes. Then he formed images of clay and commanded them to become humans. They obeyed him and became the ancestors of the People we know today.——Pima

How the World Was Started

In the beginning, Earthmaker made the whole world out of a little ball of dirt. He danced on it until it spread and touched the edges of the sky. Then there was a great noise and out sprang another being whose name was E'Etoi. E'Etoi and Earthmaker together put the world into shape. Coyote, who had been in the world since the beginning, helped them. People came into the world, too, but they were not the right kind so the two gods decided to destroy them with a flood. They did so, and They and Coyote agreed that, when the waters went down, whichever one of them came out first from hiding should be the elder brother.

It was E'Etoi who gained this title and He has been the Elder Brother to the People ever since. He made new people out of clay and taught them all the things they do now. Earthermaker was angry that E'Etoi had gotten ahead of Him, so he sank through the earth and disappeared. E'Etoi lived with His people a long time and helped them in all their troubles.

But, at last, He changed his nature, so the people quarreled with Him and killed Him. These people, the elders say, were not the Papago and Pima. They were the ones who lived here earlier and the ones who built the great house, Casa Grande. They were the Hohokam, the Ancient Ones.

E'Etoi was angry with them and He went under the earth, looking for friends who would come and help Him drive the Hohokam away. Under the earth, He found the Pima and the Papago. They know this is true because they, like most other tribes, believe they came from under the earth. E'Etoi led His new people through the country and drove out the old ones, and this is why archeologists cannot find any trace of the

Hohokam; only the ruins of their homes are left. He then told the Pima and Papago to settle where they are now, and He showed them the feast they must hold to bring rain and to keep the world in happiness. The People, O'otam, still observe this celebration today and that's why they are always happy.——Pima

Why Bats Have No Feathers

A long time ago, Indians were very cold. They sent a young woman to the east where the sun is born, to get some fire. After being gone many days, she returned very tired and told the people she had walked as far as she could and could not get to the place of the fire. A boy was sent out but he returned and said he could not get any fire either. Next, an oriole was sent and he also came back empty-handed. Buzzard was the next to try and he found the fire. He flew too close though and the heat nearly got him. When he came back his face was burned and red and his feathers were burned black.

The Indians then decided they would send a night bird to bring back some fire. They called on Na-na-ku-muli, the Bat, and he took off to the east. He was gone a long time and the people feared he had been lost. Then, one cold dark night they saw a spark of fire flying through the black sky and knew Na-na-ku-muli had made it back with some fire. As the bat flew overhead, he dropped a glowing ember which the people fanned and put grass and sticks on until they had a great fire burning. It was the first time they had been really warm.

The next day everyone went out looking for Na-na-Ku-muli to thank him for bringing the fire. They found him hanging from a limb of a tree and all his feathers had been burned off. From then on, bats have had no feathers.——Pima

The Creation and the Flood*

In the beginning the earth was made by Chiowotmahke, the Earth-prophet, and it appeared as a great spider's web, stretching far and fragile across the nothingness that was. Then the Earth-prophet flew

* Hubert Howe Bancroft, *The Works of Hubert Howe Bancroft* (San Francisco: A. L. Bancroft & Company, 1883), Vol. III, pp. 77–80.

over all the land in the form of a butterfly, until He came to a place He thought was fit for His purpose, and there He made man. The Creator took clay in His hands, and mixing it with the sweat of His own body, kneaded it into a lump. Then He blew upon the lump until it was filled with life and began to move; and it became man and woman.

Chiowotmahka had a son called Szeukha who, after the world was peopled, lived in the Gila Valley. At the same time and in the same area lived a great prophet. One night as the prophet slept, he was awakened by a noise at his door and, when he looked out, a Great Eagle stood before him. The Eagle spoke to him saying, "Ayise thou that healest the sick, thou that shouldst know what is to come, behold a deluge is at hand!"

But the prophet just laughed and, gathering his robes about him, went back to bed. After a time the Eagle came again and warned him of the waters near at hand, but he gave no ear to the bird at all. Perhaps he would not listen because this Eagle had an exceedingly bad reputation among men, being reported as taking at times the form of an old woman who lured away children to a cliff so they were never seen again.

A third time the Eagle came to warn the prophet, and to say that all the valley of the Gila would be laid waste with water; but the prophet gave no heed.

Then, in the twinkling of an eye, and even as the flapping of the Eagle's wings died away into the night, there came a peal of thunder and an awful crash; and a green mound of water reared itself over the plain. It seemed to stand upright for a second. Then, cut incessantly by the lightning, goaded on like a great beast, it flung itself upon the prophet's house.

When the morning broke, there was nothing to be seen alive but one man—if he could be called a man; Szeukha, the son of the Creator, had saved himself by floating on a ball of gum, or resin, from the mesquite trees.

When the waters fell a little, he landed near the mouth of the Salt River upon a mountain where there is a cave that can be seen today. In it can still be found some of the tools and utensils Szeukha used when he lived there. Szeukha was very angry at the Great Eagle, who he thought had more to do with the bringing of the flood than he did.

At any rate, the general reputation of the bird was sufficiently bad, and Szeukha made a ladder from the tough bark of a tree and climbed the cliff where the Eagle lived and slew him.* Looking about him, he saw the mutilated and decaying bodies of those the Eagle had taken as prey. He restored them all to life and sent them out to repeople the earth. In the Eagle's nest he found a woman the monster had taken as a wife, and a child. These he also sent on their way and from these descended that great people called Hohokam, the Ancient Ones. These people were led in all their wanderings by a Great Eagle who eventually passed on into Mexico.

One of these Hohokam named Sivano built the Casa Grande on the Gila River. At the death of Sivano, his son led a branch of the Hohokam to the Salt River where they built certain edifices and dug large canals. At last it came about that a woman ruled the Hohokam, and her throne was cut from a blue stone and a certain bird was her constant attendant.

These Hohokam were at war with a people who lived to the east of them on the Verde River. One day, the bird warned her that the enemy was close at hand, but the warning was disregarded, or it came too late. The eastern people came down in three bands, destroyed the cities of the Hohokam and killed or drove away all the inhabitants.**——Pima

Origin of the Horse

Two brothers were the greatest deer hunters in the tribe. Day after day they followed the deer and antelope to supply meat to their families and neighbors. When they killed the animals, however, they had to carry them home on their backs, and this was extremely heavy work.

One day the elder brother told the younger that he had a plan to make it easier to transport their game. He instructed the younger brother to shoot an arrow through his body from front to back and another from side to side. He then said, "After that is done, cut my body

* For killing the Great Eagle, Szeukha had to do a sort of penance, which was never to scratch himself with his fingernails, but always with a small stick. This custom is still observed by some of the old traditional Pimas, and a bit of wood is carried in their long hair for this purpose.
** For another description of the Hohokam and their wanderings, read this author's account in William E. Coffer (Koi Hosh) *Phoenix: The Decline and Rebirth of the Indian People* (New York: Van Nostrand Reinhold Company, 1979), pp. 8–9.

in four sections and throw me in the lake. In four days you must come back and see what has happened."

The younger brother was hesitant to do this for he loved his brother, but after a while he agreed and performed the task. When he returned in four days, he found four strange animals which we call horses. Two were male and two were female, and they were colored black, white, bay, and buckskin. The brother made a bridle from a rope and rode one horse home, driving the others ahead of him.

Thereafter the horses multiplied and in time all the hunters had animals to ride and carry the game. If it were not for the sacrifice of the older brother, there would never have been any horses.——Pima

How Coyote Made the Stars

Long ago, Coyote lived in the heavens, far above the earth. One day, he was very hungry and could find nothing to eat. He looked for rabbits and young quail but could find neither. The longer he looked, the hungrier he got. Finally he noticed a house a short distance away. Since he saw no one around it, he sneaked over and peeked in a window. He could not see anybody so he went inside and began to look for something to eat.

In the pantry he found a bag of cornmeal and was about to eat it when he heard someone coming. Coyote dashed out of the house, carrying the sack in his mouth. The cornmeal that was scattered as he ran across the heavens is now visible as the stars.——Pima

SANTA CLARA PUEBLO

Located on the western bank of the Rio Grande, about thirty miles north of Santa Fe, is the Tewa pueblo of Santa Clara. The people of this village suffered during the Spanish occupation in the sixteenth and seventeenth centuries, as did all the Southwest, but like some of their contemporaries, they maintained much of their traditional lifestyle. Utilizing the best of the Spanish culture and incorporating it into their daily lives, the Pueblos synthesized a functional culture. Today, the six hundred residents of the Santa Clara Pueblo present a strange amalgamation of Spanish-Indian mixtures, extracting the best of the two groups.

The story of the Bear Paw Pottery is an example of the oral tradition retained by this small pueblo.

Bear Paw Pottery

Many years ago there came a great drought in the Rio Grande Valley of what is now the State of New Mexico. The Santa Clara Pueblo Indians were drastically hurt when the rains failed to come. The grass dried up, the rivers and streams disappeared, trees died and desolation was everywhere.

The men were too thirsty and weak to hunt for deer or other animals and the women could not make their beautiful pottery. The dogs were too dry to bark and even the children stopped their playing and just sat around and cried.

The elders and headmen met in council to decide what must be done. Even the wisest of these could offer no solution to the problem. The people and their animals brothers began to suffer, and, as the days passed with no rain, some became so weak they went to join the spirits. Meanwhile the sky remained cloudless and the Father Sun shone with terrible heat. It was as if it were a fiery ball in the vast blue sky.

At last, in the entire village there was only one young man who had strength enough to stand. He volunteered to use his last bit of power to go in search of water for his people.

All day long he hunted with no result. The only animals he saw had long been dead and no life was found anyplace. Suddenly he saw a big, fat, black bear lumbering through the woods. This bear was not thirsty and evidently had been drinking plenty of water. He was rolling fat and his coat was bright and shiny.

The young man knew the bear had found a supply of water so he decided to follow him. This was no easy task for the bear was strong and agile and the Indian was very thirsty and weak. Yet he stayed as close to the bear as possible, sometimes losing sight and having to depend on his skill as a tracker. All day long he stayed on the trail.

Finally, as the sun began to descend in the western sky, the bear entered a very heavy thicket. The young Indian boy crept silently and cautiously into the grove and, to his great surprise, saw the bear drinking from a cool, clear spring which bubbled up from the ground. The water only ran a short distance before the thirsty earth drank it all so it

Bear Paw Pottery
Santa Clara

was impossible to know the spring was there unless you happened to enter the thicket.

The boy ran to the spring and as soon as the bear left, threw himself into the cool water. He drank his fill and hurried to his village to inform his people of his find. Great joy was expressed by the Indians and, as they partook of the life-giving water, their strength returned. The men could again go hunting, the children once more began to play, and the women again could make their beautiful black pottery.

Finally, the autumn rains came and the streams ran with their pure water. The Santa Clara people gave thanks that they had been able to survive the terrible ordeal of the drought because the spring was discovered. They were so thankful to the black bear for leading them to the water that, to this day, they make the bear track which the young Indian followed a design on many of their exquisite pieces of pottery to demonstrate their appreciation.——Santa Clara

WALAPAI (HUALAPAI)

The Walapai (Pine Tree People) is a Yuman-speaking tribe which lives along the middle portion of the Colorado River. They are closely related with the Havasupai and the Yavapai. They were encounted by the Spanish perhaps as early as 1540 when Hernando de Alarcón explored the Colorado River attempting to meet and furnish supplies to the Coronado Expedition. Their treatment since that time has been much like that of the other tribes of the Southwest. They have been the recipients of misunderstanding, depredations, abuse, and exploitation.

Since the Walapai lived in an area which offered little to attract the white man and were rather passive in nature, the population has remained rather stable over many years. Today some twelve hundred tribespeople occupy the rather remote reservation with minimal contact with the outside world. Since they have been comparatively isolated, the Walapai have retained and perpetuated much of their oral tradition. Two of their stories are presented here.

The Great Flood

A long time ago, soon after the Creation, the People began to turn to evil ways. It was then that Kathatkanave decided to punish them, so he sent a great flood. Water covered the whole land and the people were frightened and didn't know how to save their lives. Not wanting to punish innocent ones, Kathatkanave turned the good people into fish so they could survive the flood. The others all perished.

There was one man, a giant, who was so big and strong he could move about in the water. He took his big flint knife, and his war club he used to crack the enemies' heads, and he walked about in the water until he found the deepest part. Then he stuck his knife in the ground and pushed it back and forth. Then he pounded it down with his war club until a great crack appeared under the water. The water roared into the crack and rushed off to a great sea. The water still runs through the huge crack in the earth which was made by the giant man. The Indians call it Hackataia, which means "roaring noise" but the white people call it the Colorado River and the Grand Canyon.

The descendants of the good people who were changed into fish still live in the great river and that is why the Walapai to this day do not eat fish.——Walapai

How the Races Were Made

The first being on earth was Kathatkanave and he lived in the mountains and liked to walk under the pine trees or sit by the running stream. For a while he was happy, but he began to be lonely and became sad. He had no friends so he told Coyote about his troubles.* Now Coyote was very wise and had learned many things. He could run very fast and had been all over the world.

He told Kathatkanave to build an oven and heat it with fire. Then he was to cut many tall rushes and place them in the hot oven in very straight rows. When he had done as Coyote directed, Kathatkanave sat back by the stream and began to doze in the warm sunshine.

Pretty soon he went over to the oven and removed some of the rushes. However, they were not baked so he called them White People and sent them away. Kathatkanave turned again to the oven and took out some more rushes. These were just right, a reddish-brown color and Kathatkanave said, "You are my people, the Indians. I will love and care for you forever."

* Many Indian stories tell of Coyote being present at the Creation, but few make any attempt to explain just how he got there.

Turning once again to the oven, he took out the remaining rushes, but they had burned too done. He called them the Black People and tossed them on an island in the Eastern Sea.——Walapai

WASHO

Living along the California-Nevada border, the Washo are not as well-known as many of their neighbors. Although they speak a dialect of the Hokan language, a rather alien language to the area and not related to the Shoshonean dialects spoken by their neighbors, they observed most of the same cultural traditions. They are a small tribe numbering only a few hundred. Actually, rather a "misfit" as far as linguistics and early history, they are erroneously considered by many as Paiutes and not recognized as a separate group. Many of the Washo activities centered around the large lakes in their homeland. These bodies of water, Pyramid and Tahoe Lakes, are critical elements to the desert dwelling Indians and are included in many of their stories. The tale of "How Spirit Lodge Came to Be" is typical

How Spirit Lodge Came to Be

Long ago, in the vicinity of Lake Tahoe, one tribe possessed the whole area and was strong, numerous, and rich. The time came, however, when another group rose up stronger than they and defeated and enslaved them. The Great Spirit sent an immense wave across the continent from the sea, and this wave engulfed the oppressor and the oppressed. All but a very small remnant perished in the great flood.

Then the taskmasters made the remaining slaves raise up a huge temple with a high tower so that they of the ruling class should have a refuge in case of another flood. In the tower atop the temple was kept a column of perpetual fire which was worshiped by the rulers.

Only a short time had elapsed, however, when the earth was again troubled. This time there were strong convulsions and thunderings, and the masters took refuge in their great tower, shutting the other people out. The poor slaves fled to the Humboldt River and, getting into canoes, paddled for life from the awful sight behind them.

The land was tossing like a troubled sea and casting up fire, smoke, and ashes. The flames went up to the very heavens and melted many stars so that they rained down in molten metal upon the earth, forming the ore that the white men seek. The Sierra was mounded up from the bosom of the earth, while the place where the great fort stood sank, leaving only the dome on top of the tower exposed above the waters of Lake Tahoe.

The inmates of the temple tower clung to this dome to save themselves from drowning. The Great Spirit walked on the water in his wrath and took the oppressors one by one like pebbles and threw them far into the recesses of a great cavern on the east side of the lake. There the waters shut them in and, to this day, the cave is called Spirit Lodge. There they must remain until a great volcanic burning, which is to overturn the whole earth, shall again set them free. In the depths of their cavern prison they may still be heard, wailing and moaning, when the snows melt and the waters swell in the lake.——Washo

YAQUI

The Yaqui homeland is in southern Sonora and northern Sinaloa in Mexico. These Uto-Aztecan speakers have a warlike reputation, earned in a series of uprisings and rebellions against the Spanish and the Mexican governments. Even after they were decisively defeated by Mexican troops in 1886, the Yaqui were not easily pacified. Small bands escaped and fled to mountain strongholds where they still exist almost totally independent and autonomous. The last serious Yaqui uprising was as recent as 1927.

During the turbulent years many Yaqui fled as refugees to Arizona where they live in six villages, including Pascua, near Tucson, and Guadalupe, near Phoenix. Present-day Yaqui culture represents a fusion of sixteenth century Spanish culture with the indigenous Yaqui ways. Their ceremonials are a blend of Spanish Catholicism with native Yaqui rites. They reach a climax during the forty days of Lent at which time the tribal ceremonial societies enact a colorful Easter Passion Play. Their tradition even declares that Jesus was born and lived in Yaqui country. One story provided in the following examples concerns such a belief.

Although many of the Yaqui oral traditions do indicate that Jesus was physically present, not all center around this concept. Stories such as "How the Toad Stole Fire" and "The Koo Bird" illustrate the undiluted Indian explanation of natural phenomena.

San Pedro and the One-Legged Chicken

One time San Pedro and Jesucristo* were walking along and Jesucristo said he was hungry. San Pedro said he would go to a nearby house and try to get some food. He knocked on the door and asked the housewife if she had anything cooked that he could present to Jesucristo.

The housewife had just finished roasting a chicken and was very happy to donate it to Jesucristo. She gave it to San Pedro and he started out to catch up with the Lord. As he hurried along, the odor of the chicken was more than he could endure. He pulled off a leg and ate it.

When Jesucristo saw what San Pedro brought, he asked, "Why has this chicken but one leg?" "It never had another leg," answered San Pedro. "All the chickens around here only have one leg."

They proceeded down the road and came to a big tree which had a number of sleeping chickens under it. They all had one leg tucked in under their feathers out of sight as chickens are prone to do.

San Pedro pointed to them and said, "You see! All of the chickens have only one leg."

Jesucristo picked up a rock and threw it at one of the chickens which immediately awoke and stood up on two legs.

"Oh," said San Pedro, "a miracle!" He then picked up some rocks and threw them at the rest of the flock. "You see," he said, "I can perform miracles, too."—Yaqui

How the Toad Stole Fire

Now, there is fire in the rocks and in all sticks, but a long time ago there was no fire in the world. All the people and the animals and all beings that had life came together in a great council to find why there was no fire.

They all knew that somewhere there was fire, but no one knew where it was. Perhaps it was in the sea, or maybe on some of the islands, or maybe clear on the other side of the sea. For this reason, Bobok, the Toad, offered to go find the fire and bring some of it back so everyone could use it. Crow and Roadrunner and Dog volunteered to help Toad in his task. Although the others were willing to do what they could, Bobok, the Toad, was the only one who could enter the sea without perishing.

* Yaqui for Jesus Christ and Saint Peter.

The God of Fire was very selfish and would not let anyone take any of his fire away. For this reason he still sends thunderbolts and lightning at anyone who carries light or fire. He is always killing them.

However, Bobok slipped into the house of the God of Fire and stole some fire. He carried it in his mouth and traveled through the waters toward home. Lightning and thunder made great noise and many flashes, but Bobok came on, safe beneath the water. Then there formed on the flooding water little whirlpools full of rubbish and driftwood.

Suddenly, not just one toad was to be seen, but many, many toads swam in the sea. They were all singing and carrying small portions of fire in their mouths. Bobok had met his sons and given some fire to each of them. These carried the fire to land where Dog, Crow, and Roadrunner waited. Bobok and his sons gave their fire to the three who could not enter the water.

The God of Fire saw what happened and he threw lightning at Crow and Roadrunner and Dog. Many toads kept coming through and passed fire on to all the other beings. The whole world now had fire and light, even the rocks and the sticks. Now men can make fire by using a wooden drill or by striking rocks together.——Yaqui

The Koo Bird

Once, long ago, in the desert country lived a very poor little bird. He was so poor that he didn't have one feather and ran around totally naked all the time. He suffered when the weather was cold and nearly froze to death every winter.

Many years passed like this until one day, the little Koo Bird worked up enough nerve to talk to Owl about his situation. Recognizing the wisdom of Owl, the Koo Bird asked to borrow just one owl feather to help protect him from the cold. Owl not only gave the little cold one a feather, but he went to each of the other birds and asked that they lend the Koo Bird one feather. All the birds agreed, and the next day they gathered and each bird contributed one feather until the Koo Bird's costume was complete.

A few days later the Koo Bird visited a spring filled with clear water. Here, many birds with beautiful plumage gathered to admire themselves and each other. The water served as a mirror and each could see the colors of their feathers.

When the Koo Bird arrived, all the other birds surrounded him and admired his gorgeous feathers. Not recognizing him, they thought him to be someone sent from the Great Spirit, and they paid homage to him. Some even called him the bird of a thousand colors.

As time passed and the popularity increased, the Koo Bird enjoyed the attention. One day, however, the beautifully colored bird simply disappeared. All the other birds looked for him but to no avail. Never again did he reappear.

To this day, Owl is still hunting for the Koo Bird. He searches and he calls his name: "Koo, Koo, Koo." He is not able to say more but he can sing "Koo, Koo, Koo."

Many centuries have passed and no one has seen the Koo Bird again. Some of the people claim he is enchanted and that he now lives near a waterhole to the west near the great sea. Some even say they have been there and heard him singing, but no one ever claims to have seen him.——Yaqui

YUMA

The Yuma are one of the chief tribes of the Yuman linguistic stock, to which they have given their name. The language is now considered to be a part of the larger Hokan linguistic family. They live on both sides of the Colorado River above the Cocopa, about fifty or sixty miles from the mouth of the river, just below the junction of the Gila River.

The first contact with whites was apparently in 1702 when Father Kino visited the area. Most of their territory became a part of the United States by the Treaty of Guadalupe Hidalgo in 1848 and the balance by the Gadsen Purchase of 1853. Most of the Yuma people were eventually concentrated on the Colorado River and the Yuma Reservations. Today there are approximately one thousand of these people left to perpetuate their tribal culture which has suffered severe erosion over the years. One of their tribal stories is provided here.

How the Great Flood Came to Earth

Long ago there was a time when Earth was a woman and Sky was a man. One day a drop of water fell from Sky and landed on Woman and she conceived twins. They came to being by emerging through a volcano.

At this time Earth and Sky were close together and the twins' first task was to raise the heavens and set the cardinal points. They next established the land and water and created all the inhabitants. One brother taught the newly created men all the good things, and the other brother taught the humans jealousy and war which brought about the division of mankind. This also brought on a feud between the two brothers, and the evil one in his rage caused a rain which lasted for many days. It eventually covered the earth with water and destroyed the world.

The good brother gathered up his people when the flood came and carried them in his arms until the water receded. They were then placed back on earth and became the grandparents of all humans.——Yuma

Three

The Central Plains Indians

The Central Plains Indians occupied a vast area extending from Hudson Bay on the north to Texas on the south and stretching from the Rocky Mountains to the Appalachians. Within this immense division of land were three basic regions: The Short Grass Prairies, the Tall Grass Prairies, and the Missouri, Ohio, and Mississippi River Basins.

To many non-Indians these Plains dwellers fill the stereotypic image made so popular by the media. When "Indian" is mentioned, most of America envisions a mounted warrior bedecked with feathers and wearing fringed buckskins as he chases the huge buffalo across the open prairie. After the chase covers many miles, the noble savage dispatches the fiery-eyed beast with one small arrow, dresses it, and carries the usable portions back to his tipi where his "squaw" timidly awaits to do the bidding of her lord and master.

The sad truth is that very little of this stereotype is exemplary of the lifestyle of any group of Indian people and the image was conjured up by thrill-seeking journalists intent only on selling newsprint; prevaricating military personnel and politicians attempting to establish a reason, or excuse, for their inept handling of relationships with the tribes; and psalm-singing missionaries evading the facts of life to perpetuate their influence over these "fallen sons of perdition." None of these depictions, inaccurate as they are, seems to have faded even as we became a more enlightened nation.

In reality, these Plains Indians led a highly organized life with extremely functional social, political, and spiritual perspectives and practices. They were a highly religious people whose way of life had evolved over thousands of years of living in ecological balance and harmony with nature. The family constituted the center of their culture, and everyone in the group was treated with respect, which allowed each to maintain dignity as a human being.

During the nineteenth century America was in the throes of Manifest Destiny and vitally concerned with removing the obstacles to westward expansion. The crimes of the Indians were protecting their families, their land, their religion, and their lives. For these "crimes" they were condemned, and sentenced to concentration camp styled reservations where they were robbed of their material as well as their spiritual possessions. The incarceration broke their spirits and their bodies and they died.

Occasionally there would be a resurgence, such as the Ghost Dance, which would strike a spark of revitalization. These were short-lived for the most part and, with the Wounded Knee Massacre of 1890, resistance totally ended. This was the low point for the Plains Indians and it took a great amount of intestinal fortitude for them to begin their climb back up the ladder of human dignity to the place they now occupy.*

During the years of depredation, while these people were at the very bottom of their existence, it was only their steadfast faith in their traditional spirituality which maintained them. When they began their uphill battle to regain their former status, it was this same faith which provided the impetus to accomplish their measure of success. The traditions did not die; they live on today. The stories provided in the following pages will indicate that much of the "old life" remains and gives succor which enables the people to survive.

ARIKARA

The Arikara, a Caddoan-speaking people closely related to the Pawnee, have a tradition that they were once a part of the Skidi Pawnee

* For a detailed explanation see William E. Coffer, *Phoenix: The Decline and Rebirth of the Indian People* (New York: Van Nostrand Reinhold Co., 1979.)

and lived in the Red River Valley in Minnesota and North Dakota. They comprised a confederacy of about ten small tribes each occupying their own village.

The tribe was drastically reduced by warfare with the Sioux and by smallpox which was introduced by white traders. They developed friendly relations with the Hidatsa and the Mandan, both of whom were similarly decimated by wars and disease. The United States government created the Fort Berthold Reservation for the three tribes in 1880 and they have been there ever since.

The Arikara, because of their loss of population and their integration with the Hidatsa (Gros Ventres) and Mandan and the assimilation pressure from the dominant society, have lost much of their culture. Some of the oral tradition remains and recently other facets of their lifeways have been revived. A sampling of Arikara stories are provided on the following pages.

How Things Came to Be

The great Sky Spirit, Nesaru, had charge over all of the creation. Below his world was a limitless body of water where two ducks swam forever at peace. Suddenly, they saw Wolf-Man and Lucky-Man. These two asked the ducks to dive and bring up mud with which to make earth. Wolf-Man made a great prairie for the animals to live in. Lucky-Man made ground with hills and valleys where, in the future, the Indians could hunt and find shelter. Between the two regions a great river began to run, as it still does.

Then Wolf-Man and Lucky-Man went under the earth to find the Two Spiders. These were male and female beings who were dirty and ugly. The two visitors were very surprised to find that the Spiders had no knowledge of how to reproduce. The visitors scrubbed the Two Spiders and explained to them the wonders of fertilization. Enlightened, the Two Spiders began to give birth to all kinds of animals and to a race of giants.

Nesaru was not pleased with these giants who lived under the earth and would not obey him as the Power Above. So Nesaru created maize and sent down its seeds for the animals to take under the earth. The seeds turned into a race of smaller people, who were human-sized. Nesaru then sent a flood which destroyed all the giants without harming the new people still under the earth. They developed in their dark underworld and, wondering if there was a better place, cried for help. Nesaru decided they should come out into the open world. He sent down a woman from his cornfields, Corn Mother. She walked far and wide, but found no one, until she heard Thunder in the east, who thrust her down into the underworld.

The people and animals clustered around her in the dark underworld. Calling upon the gods and the spirits, the animals were inspired to help her. Badger began the work of digging to the light, but could not bear the brightness as he came near the surface. Then Mole dug further, but the first rays of light blinded him, so he remained in his underground burrow. Lastly, Mouse made the breakthrough, but the light was so strong that it cut off his long snout and he became a short-nosed mouse. Then Corn Mother began to thrust her way into the light. Earth was still tight around her. Then, Thunder roared again in the east and shook the earth loose so Corn Mother and the whole creation of humans and animals could come up to the surface.

The people followed the trail westwards from the place of emergence. Many adventures followed. Kingfisher pointed the way. Owl led them through the dark forest. Loon led them across the lake.

They were given maize to plant and taught how to play games like shinny, a field hockey-like game, but with many, sometimes hundreds of people on each team. Corn Mother returned to the sky. Left to themselves, the people began to quarrel and fight over the games. Many were killed. Then one day they saw a beautiful man by the lake dressed like a chief. His hair was beautiful and hung to his waist. He carried a staff hung with captured scalps.* The man was Nesaru, and he told them how to live at peace together and work under the leadership of a chief. He showed them how to conduct wars and gave them rules of honor, including those that covered the taking of scalps. These scalps were to be the marks of bravery, and show which of the warriors was best suited to become a war chief. Then Corn Mother stood beside him to teach them how to grow maize. She told them of the stars,

---

* It is generally thought that the taking of scalps was introduced to the Indians by the Europeans, a means of collecting bounty. This story casts some doubt upon that theory. It also indicates how European concepts and values can creep into even these sacred oral traditions. As far as this author can ascertain, scalping was brought to America along with other gifts, such as smallpox, syphilis, materialism, greed, and other niceties of the Old World cultures.

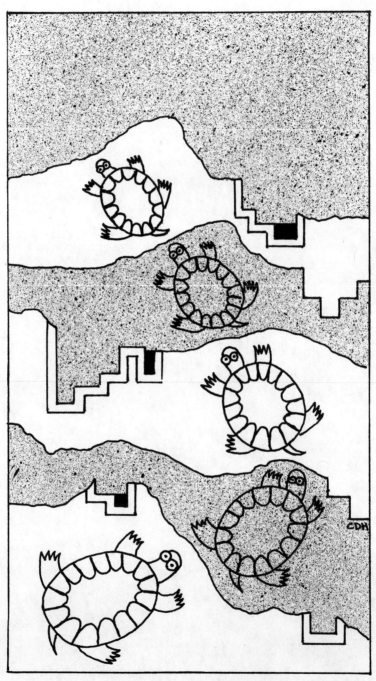

How the Turtle Beat the Coyote
Arikara

planets, sun, moon, and the gods in the sky. Finally, she told them that they must take the sacred symbols, which would be given to them and wrap them up to become the sacred medicine-bundles to help them through all dangers.

The people made offerings to the gods of the eight Directions of the Sky. Then there was a great roaring sound. It was the Wind of the Southeast, who had been forgotten. He was like a tornado and everyone he touched fell dead from disease. But a dog was sent from the sun with medicine to cure them. It told the people of the diseases of man and how to cure them, and explained the reason for the anger of the Wind of the Southeast. The people made offerings and appeased him. They learned to cure disease. Because of this, the people held a ceremony. They sacrificed a god so that its spirit would take messages to the gods.

Nesaru and Corn Mother, warning them that offerings of tobacco smoke must be given regularly to the Gods of the Eight Directions, then left. Nesaru left his medicine-bundle among them and Corn Mother gave them a cedar tree to represent her.——Arikara

How the Turtle Beat the Coyote

One time Turtle and Coyote were talking and Coyote began boasting about how fast he could run. Turtle challenged him to a race and they agreed to hold the contest the next day.

As soon as they parted, Turtle began to worry about the race and doubts started forming in his mind. He knew Coyote was a swift runner and he was not as confident as he had been earlier. But Turtle was wise and enlisted the help of a number of his brother Turtles to beat Coyote. He told each of them the place where they were to run and the distance they were to cover.

The next day all the Turtles went to their places and prepared to run. They placed one Turtle at the end of the course; then another a certain distance behind him; then another back of that one, and so on, and Turtle himself took his place at the starting line. Each Turtle then hid in the ground except the one who would start the race.

The Turtle gave the command to start, and as Coyote ran swiftly down the course, he merely crawled into his hole in the ground. When Coyote came to a knoll, there was the Turtle ahead of him. He caught up and passed the Turtle who crawled into the ground. The Coyote sped on, and upon reaching another hill, saw Turtle going on ahead of him. Coyote caught up and passed him, but at every hill he would see Turtle ahead again.

At the end of the course, there was Turtle waiting when Coyote arrived. Coyote gave up and conceded he had been beaten, but the strain of racing all those Turtles was too much, and he died.——Arikara

ASSINIBOIN

The Assiniboin belong to the Siouan linguistic family and were a branch of the Yanktonai Dakota. They live primarily in Canada on the Stony Reservation, at Moose Mountain, and at the Battleford, Edmonton, and Assiniboin agencies. Those living in the United States are generally located at the Fort Belknap and Fort Peck Reservations.

According to tribal tradition, the Assiniboin separated from the Yanktonai before the white man appeared on the Plains. They moved northward, settling around Lake Winnipeg and along the Assiniboin and Saskatchewan Rivers. They allied themselves with the Cree and became bitter enemies with their southern relatives, the Dakotas.

Estimated at having a population of ten thousand before white contact, the Assiniboin population has been drastically reduced because of warfare, disease, and acculturation. Much of their culture has remained relatively intact because of less assimilation pressure by the Canadian government and the comparatively lighter population explosion in Canada than in the United States.

As each year passes, however, a little more traditional Assiniboin life vanishes. The stories are fewer and the audiences grow smaller as the people become more "modern" in their lifestyle. One of the stories still told by Assiniboin elders is "The Beginning of the World."

The Beginning of the World

In the beginning there was nothing but water. Inktomi, the Creator, looked all around for some earth, but there was none with which He could make some land. He then sent Muskrat to the bottom of the water in search of some dirt. Muskrat dived and dived many times before he finally reached the bottom and brought up some mud. From this small ball of mud Inktomi made the fields and the woods, the rocks and the rivers, and everything. He and Muskrat and all the other animals lived together and enjoyed the new creation.

Frog complained about the pleasant weather and this angered Inktomi so He made it snow. After many days of snow, Frog begged Inktomi to make the sun shine. After much argument and discussion, it was decided there should be seven months of cold weather and five months of warm weather. And that is the way it is even today.

The animals were still not satisfied with the world. They wanted other creatures to share it with. Inktomi then made humans out of earth, and, so they would not eat all the other animals, created Buffalo to provide the humans with everything they needed. He taught men how to kill and dress the buffalo and how to make homes from the skins. He showed them how to use the bones and sinews for tools and to use even the droppings for fuel.

The humans had to work very hard to catch the buffalo on foot and to carry the meat and hides on their backs. They begged Inktomi to give them horses to bear their burdens, but Inktomi refused. He told them that if they wanted horses, they would have to steal them. So from that day, stealing horses, especially from an enemy, has been the way of life.——Assiniboin

CHIPPEWA (OJIBWA)

The Chippewa, according to tradition, were a part of a large group of Indians which came from the east. Their stories do not relate how far east from their current homes they originated but, after reaching a point north of the Great Lakes, the body of Indians separated into the Chippewa, Ottawa, and Potawatomi. These Algonquian speakers then spread around the Lakes with the Chippewa extending as far west as the Turtle Mountains in North Dakota. During the nineteenth century they were gradually compressed onto small reservations in their homeland and were never removed as a unit from that area.

Always a very large tribe, the Chippewa were estimated to have thirty-five thousand tribal members prior to white contact. By the 1920s the combined population in Canada and the United States was estimated at forty-five thousand and by 1970 this figure had about doubled. Living in their traditional homeland and not being subject to relocation as a tribe has helped the Chippewa. Set apart in small, iso-lated reservations and allowed to continue their lifestyle as they wanted, the tribe today retains an extremely traditional approach to many facets of life.

Chippewa culture is alive with stories passed orally from generation to generation. The corrosive forces of education and religion took their toll on the traditions of the group for a period of time, especially dur-ing the latter decades of the nineteenth century and the first half of the twentieth. Recently however, there has been a resurgence of Chippewa culture, and more and more people, especially the younger genera-tions, are aggressively turning back to the "old ways." Some of the stories which are once again popular with the youth are presented here.

How the Warrior Spirit Regained His Body

Once long ago, a warrior was killed on the field of battle and his friends left his body where it fell, facing the direction of his enemy's retreat. As they began their march homeward, the spirit of the slain one accompanied them and tried to assure them that he was not dead, but was with them. Of course, they did not know of his presence for his spirit was not able to be seen by mortal man. Even after the home vil-lage was reached and he heard the people talk of his heroism, he could not make them know of his presence. He could not console his father in his mourning nor could he get his mother to dress his wounds. When he shouted in the ear of his wife that he was hungry and thirsty, she heard only a faint rumbling.

Then the dead warrior remembered hearing how the spirit some-times forsakes its body, so he retraced the long journey to the field of battle. As he neared it, a fire appeared directly in his path. He changed his course, but the fire moved as he did. When he moved to the right, so did the fire. When he moved to the left, the fire followed and barred his way. He at last cried out, "I am a spirit and am trying to return to my body. You may purify me but you cannot keep me from my body. I have conquered my enemies and shall triumph over you, Spirit of Fire."

Giving a great shout, he darted through this mysterious flame and found his body. His soul and body were once more united and he awoke from his long trance on the field of battle. The young warrior once again returned to his people and was given a hero's welcome for he had not only conquered his enemies, but had reunited his soul and body in a triumph over the Spirit of Fire.——Chippewa

Why the Porcupine Has Quills

Long ago, when the world was very young, the porcupine had no quills. One day, when Porcupine was in the woods, a bear came along and tried to eat him. But Porcupine climbed to the top of a high tree and was safe.

The next day, when Porcupine was under a Hawthorn tree, one of the thorns pricked him and it hurt terribly. This gave him an idea. He broke off some of the branches of the Hawthorn and put them on his back. Then he went into the woods and waited for the bear. Pretty soon the bear came ambling along through the trees and spotted the porcupine. Being very hungry, the bear sprang on Porcupine and attempted to eat him. However, being stuck by the thorns from the Hawthorn tree was too much, so the bear had to go away.

Nanabozho saw what happened and called Porcupine to him and asked, "How did you know that trick?"

"I am always in danger when a bear comes along," replied Porcupine. "When I saw those thorns, I decided to use them to keep bears from eating me."

So Nanabozho took some branches from the Hawthorn tree and peeled off the bark until they were all white. Then he put some clay on the back of the porcupine, stuck some thorns in it, and made the whole thing part of his skin.

"Now go into the woods," said Nanabozho as he hid behind a tree to watch. Porcupine obeyed and slowly waddled off into the forest with his new armor.

Soon a wolf came along and sprang on Porcupine and ran away howling in pain. Next the bear came along, but, remembering his experience with the thorns, just went on by. For that reason, the porcupine has kept his quills until this day.——Chippewa

The Dancing Coyote

One moonlit night, Coyote was walking along the shore of a lake when he heard the sound of a great dance going on. Now Coyote loved to dance and thought he was a better dancer than anyone, so he decided to join the ceremony. He hurried on and came to a great crowd of dancers on the shore of the lake. He joined in their dance and was having a great time. He was so involved with his own dancing and in having such a good time, he hardly noticed the other dancers.

All night long they danced furiously, back and forth, waving their arms. They danced without stopping, bending and swaying and moaning. The more the other dancers swayed, the harder Coyote danced. When dawn came finally, Coyote was barely able to lift his feet, and they were so sore he secretly wished the dance would end.

As the sun rose and daylight broke over the lake, Coyote was very embarrassed. He looked around and discovered he had not been dancing with people at all. He was standing in the middle of a field of bulrushes.——Chippewa

The Story of the Two Sisters

Once long ago a young Indian had taken his long fast, received his vision and his song, and had been given his medicine. It was now time for him to look for a wife so he began looking in his village for a girl who suited him. He visited one home where there were two sisters, both beautiful and talented so there was very little difference between them. The young man went to see them many times but was unable to choose which he wanted for a wife. He finally decided to seek the advice of the chief Medicine Man of his tribe. So he went to the lodge of the Medicine Man and told him of his trouble.

After a while an old man came out of the Medicine Man's lodge, an old crippled man who walked slowly and leaned on a crooked stick for support. His eyes were dull and he could see very little, and he had no teeth and his chin quivered with age. His moccasins were worn out and his feet were sore from walking. He hobbled along until he came to the house of the two sisters.

He knocked on the door and the elder sister opened it. Seeing the old man, she slammed it shut and told him to go away.

The old man knocked again and this time the younger sister answered. She said, "Poor old man! You must be tired and hungry." She led him by the hand and had him sit on some soft skins to rest. She then bathed his tired feet in cool water and put on a new pair of moccasins she had just finished making. Gathering him some food the young girl cared for the old man until he had eaten and gone to sleep.

When he awoke he thanked the younger sister and prepared to leave. The older girl laughed at his quivering chin and his crippled walk as he left the house and made his way slowly back to the Medicine Man's lodge.

Not long afterward the young Indian appeared at the sisters' house again and brought a deer he had killed. He laid it at the feet of the younger girl, and as the older sister started to approach it, the young man stopped her.

"It is not for you," he said.

They looked down at his feet and there were the new moccasins the younger girl had given the old man just a short time before. He took the younger sister's hand and started to lead her out of the lodge, but the older girl insisted on going too.

When they were outside the young man spoke to the older sister. "I looked for a maiden to be the light of my life," he said, "And I found her. I was the old man who came to your house needing food and rest, and you turned me away. You laughed at the old man's quivering chin. So you will never again deceive anyone by making them think you are good, I will turn you into a tree. And as the old man's chin quivered, so shall your leaves always quiver."

And so it was; and an aspen tree stood by the door, its leaves always shaking. And so it is even today that when all the other leaves in the forest are still, the aspen leaves always quiver.——Chippewa

Why Dogs Do Not Like Cats

A long time ago, no one liked cats very much. They were sneaky and always doing things to cause trouble. Dogs worked for their masters and were well-liked and fed and petted.

One day all the cats got together and planned how to get even with the dogs. They devised a very devious plan to get their revenge. After many hours of howling and yowling and hissing and spitting, they elected one old tomcat as their leader.

He went into the town and approached the snarling dogs. They were wary of old Tom for no one trusted cats. Finally, after assuring the dogs he meant no evil, the old cat was allowed to speak. "We are having a great party tomorrow in the old empty barn at the edge of town and all you dogs are invited. There will be free food, all you can eat. Please come."

The dogs were suspicious but the thought of all that free food was just too much to pass up. "Of course, we'll come," they said. "We aren't afraid of you cats. We will be there."

The next day every dog in the country began to arrive at the old barn for the big party and the free food. At the door they were met by the old tomcat who greeted each one warmly and everything was quite friendly. As each dog entered he was directed to hang his tail and his anus on hooks which were placed on the wall. The dogs politely removed their tails and their anuses and hung them on the appropriate hooks and settled down to enjoy the festivities.

Before the party was hardly underway and before the free food was brought in, one cat leaped to the stage and shouted "Fire!" The small, lithe cats jumped out the windows but the larger and clumsier dogs began a stampede for the door. As they pushed and shoved each other in their panic, a problem arose.

It was fairly easy for each dog to recognize and grab his tail, but in the turmoil, the anuses got all mixed up. Not wanting to take time to sort them out for fear of being burned up, the dogs grabbed the nearest anus and made their escape.

To this day dogs hate cats for playing such a dastardly trick on them and chase them at every opportunity. This is also why when one dogs meets a new one, he immediately checks to see if the stranger has his anus. This inspection goes on even today and will continue until every dog has retrieved his own anus.——Chippewa

The Little Turkey Girl

There was a time, long before the white man came to this country, when ducks, geese, and turkeys were all tame and lived with the Indians the same as their ponies. They were shut up at night so the wolves and other wild animals would not get them, but all day they fed in the forest or by the stream.

Now in one village there was a girl they called the Turkey Girl. She took care of all the turkeys in the village. Every morning she took them out to feed and at night brought them back and shut them up. She did not belong to the people of the village and was not of their tribe. She had been taken prisoner during a war when she was very young. She was not allowed to come into the lodge with the other people of the village, but had to stay outside. In the winter she slept with the turkeys to keep from freezing.

It was in the spring time and there was to be a big celebration. The villagers would dance all day and all night, then the next day there would be a great feast. The little Turkey Girl overheard the other girls of the village talking about it and wished she could go. Of course they would not let he go and she knew better than to ask, but she was very sad just the same. That evening after the turkeys had been fastened up for the night, one old gobbler said to the other turkeys, "Do you not see that our little keeper is sad? I am sure she is unhappy because she cannot go to the big celebration."

All the turkeys felt badly because the little Turkey Girl was good to them, always providing what they needed and protecting them by shutting them up at night so the wolves wouldn't eat them. Finally, the old gobbler told the rest of the turkeys that he was a maker of magic and if they would help him, their little friend might go to the celebration after all. He instructed them to gather up all the feathers they could find and he explained his plan to them.

They gathered up so many feathers that they had a large pile in their pen. That evening when little Turkey Girl brought them all home, the old gobbler spoke to her. She was surprised for she did not know he could talk. The old gobbler asked her if she wanted to go to the festival. "Of course," said the girl, "but I have nothing but these rags to wear."

The old gobbler led her to the big pile of feathers and began sticking them all over her ragged dress. All at once the feathers turned into a beautiful deerskin dress all trimmed with fringe and beads. Then he put feathers on her feet and they turned into a lovely pair of moccasins, and he did a headband the same way. She looked so pretty no one would have ever thought she was the Turkey Girl.

So she went to the dance and all the young men looked at her for she was the most beautiful girl there. They danced with her until all the other girls were jealous but no one knew who she was.

Now the old gobbler had told her to leave their gate open and they would go out and feed themselves, but she must come for them before dark the next evening and bring them home—if she did not she would be found out.

All night she danced and had a wonderful time, and the next day she ate more at the feast than she had eaten in her entire life. She enjoyed herself so much with all the festivities that she forgot all about the turkeys and sunset. Suddenly as the sun went down, all her pretty clothes vanished and there she stood barefoot and in her old dirty rags. Then the people knew her and were very angry. They chased her out into the forest and no one ever saw her again.

And the turkeys, having no one to take them home, the wolves got in among them and ate some of them. The rest scattered all through the forests and ever since there have been wild turkeys in the woods.——— Chippewa

How Frogs Came to Be

Once, long ago, there was a strange, odd-looking group of people who lived on the top of a high mountain. At the bottom of the mountain lived a tribe of Indians who had everything they needed and were a happy group. There was always plenty of water for their corn and their families. The water came down the mountain in a big sparkling stream and everyone used it as it was needed.

One day the people noticed the stream seemed smaller than usual. They watched it for a few days and saw that each day the amount of water grew less and less. Soon there was not enough water left to take care of the village.

The corn dried up in the fields and the animals began to die from the lack of water. The people began to get sick and the Indians did not know what to do. Without water, they would all soon die.

One day the Great Rabbit, who was the maker of magic, came hopping into the village. "What is wrong?" he asked. "Why is everyone so sad? There is not water? Why, the top of the mountain has always been full of water. Where can it have gone?"

The people replied, "We are so glad to see you, Great Rabbit. Our corn had dried up and our animals lie dead in the feed lot, and now we are getting sick and will soon die too. Please go to the top of the mountain and set the water free for we are sure someone shut it up."

Seeing how badly the people needed water, the Great Rabbit started up the mountain. It only took three hops for him to get nearly to the top for he was so big. When he was almost at the top he heard voices and they sounded as if a quarrel was taking place. One big, deep voice was calling, "More! More!" Another tiny voice farther away kept repeating, "We've enough, we've enough."

So the Great Rabbit went on and peeked over the top of the mountain. He saw that someone had built a dam which shut all the water up in a big pool and kept any from going down the mountain. There were strange-looking people swimming around in the pool. "What do you mean by this, shutting up all the water on the top of the mountain so the people down at the bottom are dying of thirst," he said. "There is enough for all if you open this dam and let the water go."

"No," said the big fellow," there is not enough. We need MORE, MORE, MORE."

This made the Great Rabbit very angry so he kicked out the dam and let the water run down the mountain. He reached into the water and grabbed the big, selfish fellow by the neck. He held him so tight that his eyes bulged out, and the man was so scared that great chills came out on his back which was covered with green moss from the water. The Great Rabbit shook him and scolded him and threw the weird one to the ground. He fell in a heap, all bowlegged, his back humped, and his fingers spread apart. Great Rabbit then said to him in an angry voice, "You shall go all your life looking like this, and all your people, and your tribe forever."

And so the selfish man was turned into a frog. He still has green moss on his back, his eyes bulge; he is humped and still has big chills on his back. If you listen some warm summer night you can still hear him calling for more water.——Chippewa

CREE

The Cree are one of the two greatest divisions of the Algonquian linguistic family, the other being the Chippewa. Cree territory, before the whites came, extended along the entire area south of Hudson Bay from James Bay westward to Saskatchewan. The French made friends with these people early in the seventeenth century and utilized their services in promoting the fur trade. Later, the English followed the same pattern and established trading posts of the Hudson Bay Company. The two European powers developed a great rivalry for the friendship of the Cree.

Early estimates of Cree population are about ten thousand at the first white contact. Currently it is thought that about one-half this number still live, relatively undisturbed, in their original homeland. Because of their importance in the fur trade, the assimilation processes usually accorded Indians in America has not been forced on these natives.

Most Indian tribes retain and perpetuate their version of the Creation. The Cree are no exception and the following story is told over and over in many families.

How Wisagatcak Made the World

Wisagatcak* built a dam of stakes across a creek to trap the Giant Beaver when it swam from its lodge. He waited all day until evening came, and he saw the creature swimming toward him. He was ready to spear Giant Beaver when Muskrat suddenly bit him from behind and made him miss. Wisagatcak gave up for the day. The next morning, he decided to break down the dam, so he pulled out the stakes of the dam. Water flowed out and kept on flowing. But the level of the creek did not fall. The Giant Beaver had worked magic against Wisagatcak because he had broken the dam. All the land became covered. As the waters rose, Wisagatcak pulled up trees to make a raft and collected many different kinds of animals which were swimming in the water.

For two weeks the Beavers made the water rise until no land was left. At the end of two weeks, Muskrat left the raft and dove down but could not find any earth, and stayed below the surface so long that he died. Then Raven left the raft. He flew for a whole day and saw only water in all the four directions. Then Wisagatcak made his own magic and called for Wolf to help. Wolf ran around and around the raft with a ball of moss in his mouth. As he ran, the moss grew and the earth formed on it. Putting it down, they danced around it singing powerful spells. The earth grew. It spread over the raft and continued growing until it made the whole world.——Cree

DAKOTA (SIOUX)

One of the largest and best know groups of American Indians is the Sioux. They call themselves Dakota, meaning "allies" in the Santee or

* Wisagatcak was the trickster to the Eastern Cree much on the same order as Coyote or Raven to other tribes.

eastern dialect; in Yankton and in Assiniboin it is Nakota; and in Teton it is Lakota. The word Sioux which has become the common designation, was given them by the Chippewa, via the French, and means "enemies."

The Dakota have been a populous nation since the earliest white contact in 1640 when Jesuits met them in their homeland in Minnesota and Wisconsin. By 1780, it is estimated that there were over twenty-five thousand Sioux living in the Northern Plains area* and today's estimates about double that figure. Current ethnological classifications divide the people into seven distinct groups: (1) Mdewkanton, (2) Wahpeton, (3) Wahpekute, (4) Sisseton, (5) Yankton, (6) Yantonai, and (7) Teton. These are in turn divided into many subgroups which comprise the Dakota or Sioux Nation.

It was from these Plains Indians that America developed the stereotypic Indian that has been so popularized and romanticized by the media. After the Civil War when the United States was promulgating the concept of "Manifest Destiny," the Sioux became a household word, promoted by newspapermen who needed bizarre stories of blood and carnage to replace their wartime banners. America became quite aware of the buckskin-clad, buffalo-hunting, tipi-dwelling painted savage described by eastern newspapers. The sad rationale was developed and promoted which justified the extermination of these "obstacles to progress and freedom for Americans." Because of this biased reporting, thousands of Indians were murdered, starved, and herded as cattle into concentration camps designed for cultural and physical genocide.** One of the results of the Plains Indians' patriotic effort to defend their land, women, and children, and their very existence was this mental image which still permeates American society.

In spite of the maltreatment the Dakota received and despite the all-out efforts of the dominant society to perpetrate physical and cultural genocide, the Sioux survived. Although condemned to a high degree of acculturation and assimilation, they have tenaciously retained much of their cultural heritage and today are reviving even more of their "old ways." The Dakota still live, physically and spiritually.

* "We, The First Americans" published by the United States Department of Commerce, Bureau of the Census, June 1973.
** William E. Coffer. *Phoenix: The Decline and Rebirth of the Indian People* (New York: Van Nostrand Reinhold Co., 1979).

The following stories are offered as a tribute to these stalwart people and their indomitable will to survive.

Old Man Coyote and His Mother-In-Law

Old Man Coyote makes trouble wherever he goes. It doesn't make any difference to him if people like him or not. He will say and do whatever he pleases.

One day his wife went to visit her sister and left her mother behind to take care of Old Man and cook for him. Now, since it is forbidden that a man look at his mother-in-law, or speak to her, or even say her name, it made it quite difficult for the two of them to stay in the same lodge.

Old Man's mother-in-law sat by the tipi door in the cooking place and kept her back to her son-in-law. When she wanted to give him something to eat, she reached behind her and placed it on the floor. He would then pick it up and eat it. Except at mealtime, Old Many Coyote stayed outdoors and hunted or sat around talking to his friends.

One day a blizzard came up and Old Man couldn't go outside and had to stay in the tipi with his mother-in-law. By this time Old Man was pretty disgusted anyway because he had no one to speak to in his own tipi. Finally, he said, "I wish there was someone here to talk to." He looked directly at the tipi flaps and directed his comments to them.

"I feel the same way," the mother-in-law told the glowing embers of the cooking fire.

So they sat there all day, looking at the tipi flaps and the cooking fire, and talked about all sorts of things. Finally, it was time for bed and the woman spread the skins out for Old Man and then made her own bed. They both lay down, but before long Old Man began to complain about being cold.

"Put another log on the fire," his mother-in-law told him sleepily.

But even with the fire blazing, Old Man still complained of being too cold. "I'm used to my wife keeping me warm in bed. You are her mother and you ought to be even warmer."

The old lady was tired of hearing him complain so she slid over under his buffalo hide. In a few minutes Old Man was fast asleep and snoring and mother-in-law was able to get out of his bed. So he wouldn't know she was gone if he awoke during the night, she slipped

Why Crows Are Black
Dakota

the largest log from the woodpile and placed it beside him. When Old Man Coyote woke up in the morning and saw what had been keeping him warm all night, the only thing he said—and he said that to the tipi flaps—was, "I hope my wife gets home soon."

That's what happens to people who break the mother-in-law rules. ——Dakota

Why Crows Are Black

A long time ago crows were all white and lived in the northland in the summer and went south in the winter just like they do today. One summer, however, when all the crows were getting ready to head for the warm country, one decided to be different and stay in the north all winter.

Now, crows like to gossip and tattle, so this one crow had a time. He would fly from camp to camp and tipi to tipi and then he would go around tattling and telling what everyone was saying. One night the chiefs were talking about a herd of buffalo they had heard about and were laying plans on how to get their winter's supply of meat. The white crow heard them and flew over to the buffaloes and told them of the plans. Naturally, the herd moved on as fast as possible and when the hunters arrived, there was nothing but empty prairie before them.

When they returned to camp with no meat, everyone was extremely upset. A council was called and somehow it was decided that the white crow had warned the buffalo. The people caught the crow and built a large fire and hung the crow upside down over it. The black smoke billowed up and the crow began to beg the people to have pity on him. They split his tongue* and left him there hanging in the smoke all night. The next morning instead of his beautiful white feathers, the crow was covered with black ones.

And that is why crows are black today.——Dakota

The Story of Buffalo Maiden

Once, long ago, there was a large camp of Lakota (Sioux) at the foot of Paha Sapa, or as they are known today, the Black Hills. It had been a

* It is said by many people that crows have split tongues which enable them to mimic the human voice.

hard summer for the people and, now that autumn had come, things were even worse for there was no food. The men and women were hungry and the children cried constantly because of their empty stomachs.

The chief of this camp and the medicine man appointed two of the young men to pick out the best ponies and go out in search of game so the people could eat. The two set out in the direction of Paha Sapa and, after several days journey, stopped one evening on the top of a high hill. They heard a frightful howling sound and as they investigated the hill, they found the sound coming from a huge cave. It was a mournful sound and the young men were afraid but, to show their bravery, they camped at the entrance of the howling cave.

Soon, in spite of their fear, the two young men fell fast asleep. Sometime during the night, they were wakened by a noise and, as they opened their eyes, they saw a beautiful young maiden standing in the flickering light of their dying campfire. She was dressed in a white buckskin dress decorated with ornaments of bone and gems.

She spoke to the young men and instructed them to go to their people and bring back to her many tokens. The young men did as she bade them and returned to their encampment. They told the chief and the medicine man what the Buffalo Maiden had said. The two leaders went among the people, repeating the story, and collected all the best ornaments and tokens the people had. They put these items in a buckskin pouch along with some pemmican, jerky, and cherries and gave them to the medicine man to deliver. He, the two young men, and about twenty hunters began their journey back to the cave.

When they arrived at the cave, the howling sound was still to be heard and all the men were frightened. The hunters stayed behind a great rock and the medicine man and the two young men entered the cave.

The beautiful Buffalo Maiden appeared before them dressed in her finery and reached out to take the tokens sent by the people. She said, "Your people will hunger no more," and with that statement she disappeared. The three men were very frightened for the howling noise suddenly stopped. They ran back to where the hunters were hidden and were amazed as a herd of buffalo came out of the cave.

The hunters killed enough of the buffalo to feed their families, taking care not to slay more than they could use. From that time on, Buffalo Maiden always sent enough of the animals that the Lakota were never hungry.——Lakota

The Lakota and the Cottonwood

Indians, living close to nature, perceive things differently from whites. Every object of the Creation was placed on earth for a specific purpose. It is the Indian's responsibility to ascertain that purpose and utilize the object toward its true meaning. The Lakota (Sioux) of the high plains learned the secrets of much of Creation and used them in their everyday life. This is especially true of the trees and, more explicitly, the cottonwood.

The chokecherry tree furnished the straight shafts necessary for arrows; the dogwood was best for tepee stakes; the elm with its tough core was used for mortars; the post oak made the best pestles; and the ash branches with their straight grain, made the best material for pipe stems.

The cottonwood, however, was a special tree, blessed by the Great Spirit with multitudinous uses. The Mandans used its large timbers in the construction of their permanent lodges, and the Hopi and Zuni use the soft roots to carve their kachina dolls from. The Pawnee used the soft inner bark to feed their horses during hard winters and also used this same substance for a sweet "ice cream" type food.

Since the slightest breeze set the leaves of the cottonwood in motion, many tribes hold them in reverence for they feel this tree is more sensitive to the presence of the Great Spirit. Because of this, some tribes think it inappropriate to burn cottonwood in cooking fires. Since it has such sacred qualities, cottonwood is appropriate for use in ceremonial fires and is widely used as the center pole in the Sun Dance Lodge by many tribal groups.

The Lakota held the cottonwood tree sacred for at least two other reasons. According to their oral tradition, it was from the shape of its leaf, folded edge to edge, that the Lakota learned the design of their tepee. If you cut an upper limb of the great cottonwood crosswise, you find a five-pointed star, a sign of the Great Spirit.——Lakota

The Pipe and the White Buffalo Calf Woman

A long, long time ago two young men were out looking for buffalo. They climbed to the top of a high hill and looked all around the horizon. They saw something moving toward them from the north and, as it drew nearer, they saw that it was a woman. One of the men had some bad thoughts and made some comments, but the other rebuked him severely for he recognized that she was a sacred woman.

When she came closer, the men saw that she wore a fine white buckskin dress, that her hair was long, and that she was very beautiful. The foolish one again had bad thoughts and started toward the young woman. But as he neared her he was covered by a white cloud, and when it blew away the foolish man was a skeleton covered with worms.

The woman then spoke to the man who was left, "Go home and tell your people that I am coming and that a large tipi shall be built for me in the center of the nation." The man, who was very much afraid, went quickly and explained what had happened. The people did as they were told and constructed a large tipi in the center of the nation and waited for the sacred woman.

After a while she came among them and they marveled at her great beauty. She sang them a beautiful song as she entered the great tipi.

> With visible breath I am walking.
> A voice I am sending as I walk.
> In a sacred manner I am walking.
> With visible tracks I am walking.
> In a sacred manner I walk.

As she sang, there came from her mouth a white cloud with a very pleasant smell. Then she gave something to the chief. It was a pipe with a buffalo calf carved on one side to represent the earth that bears and feeds us. There were twelve eagle feathers hanging down from the stem to illustrate the sky and the twelve moons, and these were tied with a grass that never breaks.

"Behold!" she said. "With this you shall multiply and become a great nation. Nothing but good shall come from it and only the hands of the good will take care of it and the bad shall not even see it." Then she sang her song again and went into the tipi, and as the people watched, she turned into a great white buffalo who snorted and galloped away, and soon it was gone.——Dakota

How the Dakotas Learned to Pray

Many years ago, long before they moved to the Northern Plains where they live today, the Dakotas, or Sioux as they are now called, lived around the Great Lakes and in Canada. They had a happy life and everything they needed was at hand. One day, however, some of the people began to become sick with some new kind of disease. Each day more would become ill and soon the sick ones began to die. The medicine men used all their herbs and all their rituals but nothing seemed to help. They had no power over the awful sickness.

One day, a young man of the tribe was hunting for food for his people. He came upon a mud turtle crossing between water holes who had been overcome by the heat. Turtle had underestimated the distance he must cross to reach the next water and was about to die.

The young man was about to pass the dying turtle when he heard the creature speak to him. "Please help me! If you leave me here, I will surely die but, if you help get to the next water hole, I will give you great power which you can use to cure your people."

The young hunter was kind-hearted and would have saved the turtle regardless of the promise of power, so he gently picked up brother turtle and carried him to the next water hole. There he placed the turtle in the water and watched him sink slowly in the cool water. Soon, however, the turtle rose to the surface and thanked the young hunter. Then, suddenly, in the place of the turtle, was a young Indian man, dressed in buckskin and feathers as if he were a Dakota.

The turtle who had turned to a young Indian said, "Return to your home and fast for three days. Speak to the Great Spirit and you will be shown the way to cure your people."

The young man followed the turtle's orders and returned to his home. He went to the top of the highest hill and fasted for three days. Finally, fainting from the heat and hunger, he heard the Great Spirit speaking to him. Suddenly, there was a beautiful Indian maiden standing before him. She wore the finest of clothing and ornaments and held a bundle in her arms. This bundle was wrapped in beaver fur and tied with the skin of a rattlesnake.

The girl told the young man to take the bundle to his village and to gather all the members for a ceremony. She explained that in the bundle was the sacred pipe which, if the people smoked it in the proper manner, would drive away the killing disease.

The young man did as the girl bade him and a great ceremony was held by the Dakota people. They danced and prayed to the Great Spirit for health and they smoked tobacco in the sacred pipe. A small amount of special tobacco was placed in the bowl and puffs of the sacred tobacco smoke were sent to the four directions by the elders.

Soon the illness left the people and they were cured. From that day to this, the Dakota people dance and fast and offer the smoke from the sacred pipe to the Great Spirit.——Dakota

How the Badlands Were Made

Long ago, where the Badlands of South Dakota now are located, stood a high plain covered with grass and trees. Deer, buffalo, and elk were plentiful there and each autumn many tribes gathered there to get their winter's supply of meat. These groups of people, some deadly enemies, laid aside all their differences and there was no quarreling or fighting while they camped and hunted.

This peaceful hunting time existed for many years, until one autumn a fierce tribe from the western mountains appeared on the scene. They took over the hunting grounds and would not let any other tribe use it. The original tribes, the Sioux and their friends, banded together and tried to drive the newcomers away, but to no avail. These fierce intruders were too strong and awesome in battle for the plains people to defeat.

Again and again attempts were made to regain their hunting grounds and many brave plains warriors were killed, but the mountain people were always victorious. The plains people called a great council to discuss the situation. They prayed and fasted and presented the spirits all their ceremonies in an attempt to gain their favor. They received no answer even though the medicine men performed all the dances and rituals they knew. Things looked hopeless and the people were very sad and discouraged.

One day, however, the spirits sent their answer. In the middle of the day the sky grew dark as night. The lightning flashed and the thunder rolled and the whole earth shook. Strange fires lighted up the entire country with their flames and peculiar things began to happen.

The land began to roll as if it were great ocean waves. The mountain tribes were caught in these huge earthen waves and swallowed up. The whole tribe with its horses and their tipis were engulfed, and with them went the game and the grass and the trees. Everything that made this area a paradise was lost.

Just as suddenly as it had begun, the noise and commotion stopped. When the dawn came, the peaceloving tribes saw that the rolling waves of earth had become stark bare rocks and there was now a wasteland where nothing would ever grow.

The spirits in their wrath had taken away the cause of the fighting. They changed the special hunting area to a place of barren desolation over which no one would ever quarrel. To those who lived, the Badlands remain to this day as a reminder of the anger and the power of the spirits.——Dakota

The Separation of Man and Animals

In the beginning there was Father Sun and Mother Earth and nothing else. The warmth of the Sun entered into the bosom of the Earth, and she immediately conceived and brought forth life, animal and vegetable. Then came First Born, a being in the likeness of man and yet he was much more than that. He roamed solitary among the animal people and understood their ways and conversed with them. They held him in great awe for they could do nothing without him knowing. He pitched his tent in the center of the land and he could see every spot in the country.

After a time, First Born became lonely for someone of his own kind so he made himself a companion, a brother, from a splinter in his big toe. He was called Little Boy Man for he was not made full-grown but as a child, innocent and helpless. First Born was his teacher through every stage of human progress and it is the rules he laid down and his advice to Little Boy Man which formed most of the traditions and beliefs of life and customs which guide the people yet today.

There dwelt among the animals at that time a powerful trickster, a troublemaker, who watched the growth and development of Little Boy Man. Spider, that was the name of the evil one, tried to convince the other animals to kill the boy, and told them if they didn't do away with him, the boy would soon be master of them all. But tney loved Little Boy Man because he was friendly and played with them and none would do him any harm. The monsters of the deep sea heeded the counsel of Spider and killed the boy, hiding his body at the bottom of the sea.

First Born, finding his brother's bones, used his magic to restore him to life by making a vapor bath. On the shore of the Great Water he dug two round holes. Over one of them he built a low enclosure of fragrant cedar boughs, and here he placed the bones of his brother. In the other pit he built a fire and heated four round stones which he rolled into the lodge of cedar limbs. He then closed all the openings except one and, as he sang his mystic song, thrust his arm in the opening and sprinkled water on the hot stones with a bunch of sage. Immediately, steam arose and restored life to the bones of Little Boy Man. The process was repeated four times and the boy was completely back to his former self.

Once more the boy roamed the land with his animal friends who were in those days a powerful people. He learned their ways and their language—for at that time all the animals spoke in one tongue. He learned to sing like the birds and swim like the fish. He even learned to climb over the rocky cliffs like the mountain sheep and goats.

Once more Spider began to sow dissention among the animals and this time the evil power worked. Messages were sent to all the animal tribes to unite and declare war on this solitary man.

Elder Brother, learning of the plot, armed the boy with a bow and flint-tipped arrows, a war-club, and a spear. He tossed four pebbles into the air and, as they landed on the earth, they formed barricades on all four sides of Little Boy Man. He was instructed then to exert his supremacy over the animal people since they had started the trouble.

The animals attacked and, for the first time on earth, the bow was strung. Hundreds of flint-headed arrows found their mark in the bodies of the animals and each time Little Boy Man swung his war-club, the animals fell in countless numbers.

Finally the insects, the little people of the air, attacked him. They filled his eyes and ears and tormented him with their sharp spears until he was frantic. He called to First Born for help, who ordered him to strike the rocks with his stone war-club. He did so and sparks flew out setting fire to the prairie grass. A mighty smoke ascended, driving away all the tormenting swarms of insects, and frightening away all the other animals.

This was the separation of man and animals, and the animals were subdued. In the peace agreement it was provided that the animals must forever furnish man with meat for his food and skins for clothing. The insect people refused to make any concessions, and have ever since been the tormentors of man. However, the birds, who were not persuaded by Spider to attack Little Boy Man, declared that they would punish the insects for their stubbornness, and this they continue to this day.——Dakota

IOWA

The Iowa Nation were a Siouan-speaking people who moved about a great deal but generally within the state which bears their name. Never a very large group, the maximum population estimated by Swanton was only twelve hundred; the Iowa fill very few pages in even the most detailed accounts of the history of the area. Swanton claims that Iowa tradition links their origin to the Winnebago, Otoe, and Missouri tribes.* In a publication, *The Davenport Conspiracy,* marketed by the office of the State Archaeologist of Iowa in 1970, excavations of mounds in the state prove conclusively that humans inhabited the area during the time of mastedons in America. However, the archeologists investigating these sites disclaim any relationship between these Mound Builders and the local Indians.

Whatever the case, the Iowa Nation has nearly disappeared as an identifiable entity in the Indian community. Today, as a result of the many forces brought to bear on the Indian people, there are only about one hundred Iowa Indians living in Oklahoma, their last homeland. Most of their culture has disappeared and they live generally as an integral part of American society. A few facets of their cultural heritage is still in evidence, however, in oral tradition. Their rather comical, yet very pragmatic explanation of "Why Buzzard Stinks" is an example of the stories which survive.

Why Buzzard Stinks

One day Coyote or Old Man saw Buzzard flying high above him. He thought it would be glorious to soar about so high above the world where there was no danger so he began to beg Buzzard for a ride.

"No," replied Buzzard. "You belong on earth and I belong up in the sky. You wouldn't like it up here, anyway."

But Coyote persisted with his begging until Buzzard finally gave in.

* Swanton, op. cit.

He took Coyote up a little way and then returned him. This did not
satisfy him so Coyote pleaded to be taken up again and higher. This
went on for four times and each time Coyote wanted to go higher. Finally Buzzard flew very high and dipped and soared until Coyote became very frightened and cried to be returned.

By this time Buzzard was tired of Coyote and his pestering so he
dipped low over the forest and dropped Coyote. When he hit the trees
Coyote became stuck in a hollow stump. His cries attracted the other
animals who pulled and tugged and eventually managed to free Coyote. His fur was so ragged and tousled from the experience that he
looks this way even today.

After such a bad time, Coyote was very angry with Buzzard and
swore to get revenge. He thought and thought of some way he could
ruin Buzzard's beautiful coat of glistening feathers and make him look
ugly too. Finally he hit upon a scheme and set out to trick Buzzard.

Since Coyote was a powerful magician, he changed himself into a
dead horse and lay down to attract Buzzard. He fooled most of the
birds, even the crows who pecked at his buttocks, but Buzzard was not
fooled. Coyote next turneed himself into a dead bear but Buzzard still
did not accept the bait. Finally, Coyote pretended to be a dead elk and
this did the trick. The birds came and ate most of his rear-end, and the
crows even went in and out of his body. This was too much and Buzzard came down from the sky to join in the feast. He came and pecked
at the edge of the opening and then stretched his neck out and put his
head far inside to eat more.

All at once Coyote closed the opening and Buzzard was caught. He
pulled and tugged, trying to get his head out, but Coyote held fast.
He then began walking away, dragging Buzzard along behind him. He
kept Buzzard there a long time until he felt he had been revenged.
Then he released the poor bird and stood back to look at the awful
sight.

And that is why Buzzard's head is bald even today, and stinks.——
Iowa

MENOMINEE

The Menominee, "Wild Rice Men," so called because wild rice was the
primary commodity in their diet, belong to the Algonquian language

family. They lived along the Menominee River in Wisconsin and claimed a large territory on either side of it. Their tradition speaks of a migration to this land, but they were already in the Wisconsin area when first contacted by whites.

Of all tribes of Indians in the United States the Menominee were as assimilated as any when the Federal government terminated them through the Eighty-third Congress. The date established for the final severance of the governmental relationship was 1957, but as complications developed the deadline was extended several times. Finally, in 1961 Menominee County was formed comprising the former reservation, and a corporation with a tribally elected board of directors was formed to manage the assets of the tribe. It was only a short time until the Menominee Nation, the second wealthiest in America, became the poorest of Wisconsin's seventy-two counties.

In 1973, after twenty years as Indians without a country (they lost reservation status in 1953), the Menominees were restored to the status of Indian by the Nixon administration. This stands as one of the few bright spots for Indians in American history.

Never having more than about three thousand people, the Menominee have had a very difficult time trying to retain any portion of their culture. With assimilation procedures being applied first by the French, then the English, and later the United States, and all the while educational and Christianizing pressures being extremely strong, it is a wonder the Menominee have any cultural perspective left intact.

They have, however, been able to maintain and perpetuate some of their oral tradition. The following stories illustrate a minute portion of Menominee culture.

How the Dandelion Came to Be

Once, many years ago when the world was new, there lived a very lazy Indian. His home was in the warm, sunny southland and he was the keeper of the South Wind. One day as he was sitting in the doorway of his lodge enjoying the warm sunshine, he looked across the meadow and saw a beautiful maiden, standing there. She was slender and beautiful and had golden yellow hair and was wrapped in a bright green shawl. As this lazy fellow looked at her beauty he breathed a warm, soft sigh, and a gentle South Wind went across the land to where she stood. Her green shawl waved in the warm wind and she swayed gently back and forth, looking very beautiful.

The boy watched her and greatly admired her. He wondered where she came from and how long she would be in his village. He thought he would like to win her for his wife but he was too lazy just then; maybe tomorrow.

The next day when he came to sit in the sunshine by his door, he saw the little maiden with the golden yellow hair was still standing in the meadow. He wished she would come closer for she was too far away to woo. She seemed to be calling to him as she swayed in the soft summer breeze. The young man again felt he would like this beautiful maiden for his wife but he was just too tired right now. He thought to himself, "Perhaps tomorrow I will go meet her."

But tomorrow was just the same as today. She was still there beckoning to him, but she was still so far away. He made up his mind that if she was still there the next day, he would go to her and ask her to come live with him and be his wife.

The next day, however, when he went to look at her, the golden yellow hair had turned white over night and it was like a great white halo around her head. The young, lazy Indian had waited too long and the young maiden was no longer of this earth but had become a spirit. He heaved a great sigh, for he was very sad. As he did this the gentle South Wind blew to the spirit maiden and her white halo went all to pieces and scattered about over the land.

The next year wherever one of the pieces of the halo had dropped, a yellow flower grew, the dandelion, to remind the young man that he had lost a beautiful bride by being too lazy to go after her.

That is how the dandelion came to be.——Menominee

Why the Hell-Diver's Eyes Are Red

Manabozho was a great trickster who sometimes did things for the good of the people and sometimes did evil things. One day as he was walking along the lake he came on a large group of water-fowl and decided he would have a feast. A swan saw him and asked fearfully, "Where are you going, Manabozho?" Whereupon he replied, "I am going to have a song."

Pulling out his rhythm sticks, he invited the birds to dance around him and sing as loudly as they could while he beat the two sticks together.

"Keep your eyes closed and dance around me," he said. "The first one who opens his eyes will have them turn sore and red."

As the birds circled him singing at the top of their voices, Manabozho reached out and grabbed one of the swans by the neck. It screamed loudly but Manabozho wrung its neck and told the other birds to keep singing as loud as they could. He grabbed another and another and killed them. Finally, the Hell-diver, peeking to see why the singing had nearly stopped, shouted, "Manabozho is killing us!"

All the birds who were left took off for the lake to escape. Manabozho chased after the Hell-diver and caught him by the tail just as they reached the edge of the water. Hell-diver struggled and flapped his wings so hard that all his tail feathers came out and he escaped. However, to this day, Hell-divers are tailless and red-eyed because of Manabozho's trick.——Menominee

MESQUAKIE

The Mesquakie people, generally called Fox, are speakers of a dialect of the Algonquian language similar to that of the Sauk and Kickapoo. They call themselves "Meshquakihug" meaning "red earth people" from the kind of earth from which they were created. The name "Fox" is derived from the Fox clan and was applied to the entire tribe through ignorance.

In 1842, after the Black Hawk War, the Mesquakies and the Sauk, who had taken refuge with them, sold their lands in Iowa where they had migrated earlier. They moved across the Missouri River into Kansas where they lived together for a time. The Mesquakie became angry with the Sauk about 1858 for disposing of land without consulting with them and returned to Iowa where a few of their people had remained. They purchased some land near Tama and increased it by buying adjacent plots until they now own more than three thousand acres. Today about six hundred Mesquakies live on their small reservation.

Throughout their history, the Mesquakie have been a very independent people and, although quite isolated from most of "Indian America," have maintained a very traditional perspective. Their stories are not just folktales but are a distinct part of a vital culture. The explanation provided in the following tale is typical of Mesquakie stories.

The Great Bear in the Sky

One day, many years ago when the world was young, three young Indian hunters went out in search of game. One of them took his dog along to help find the animals. It had snowed the night before and the hunters hoped to find a trail.

They hunted in vain for several hours and were getting discouraged. Finally they came to a place beside a river where the bushes grew very thick, and discovered fresh tracks in the snow. They followed the trail as it wound in and out of the trees and up over a large hill. It eventually led them to a cave in the side of the mountain, and the boys knew they had found the den of a bear.

Now that they had found the bear's cave, the young hunters were faced with the problem of what to do next. After much discussion, it was decided that the oldest boy would go into the cave and chase out the bear. The others could then shoot him with arrows and they would have enough meat for their people.

The oldest hunter crawled into the cave and began to poke the bear with his bow. This woke the bear who was so startled he ran out of the cave so fast the hunters could not shoot him. Away he went over the hill with the three hunters and the dog chasing him.

They ran to the east to the place where the sun comes from, and then they ran to the north where the cold winter winds and the snow is born. They could not catch the bear but the boys were able to change the direction of the chase. The bear turned and headed in the direction of the place where the sun falls down, the west, and the boys and the dog followed.

They ran and ran until one of the boys looked down and saw Grandmother Earth far below. The bear had led them up into the sky, and they could not get down. They had run so far that they were now in the Sky World.

Finally, the hunters caught up with the bear and killed him. They piled up maple and sumac branches and butchered the bear on them. Even to this day the leaves of those two trees turn blood-red in the fall.

The hunters then cut off the bear's head and threw it to the east.

Even now, early in the winter's morning, a group of stars shaped like a bear's head appears low in the sky just before daybreak.

Next, the boys cut up the bear and threw his backbone to the north. Today, if you look to the north during a cold winter's night, you can see a group of stars outlining the bear's backbone.

If you look in the right place in the sky anytime at night, you can see four bright stars forming a square and, behind them, three bright stars and a tiny, dim one in a row. The square of stars is the bear, the three bright ones trailing are the three hunters, and the little, dim one is the little dog.

Those eight stars go around and around in the sky all year long. They do not rest like the other stars do. Until they catch up with the bear, the hunters and the little dog can never rest.——Mesquakie

OSAGE

The Osage Nation was a Siouan-speaking group of Indians indigenous to the area which is now the State of Missouri. Their tradition indicates they once lived in the Ohio River Valley, but, at the time of the first European contact, they were located in Missouri and Arkansas. On November 10, 1808, the Osage signed a treaty with the United States, ceding their lands in these two states and following treaties signed in 1825, 1839, and 1865, they were assigned a reservation in Oklahoma Territory on July 15, 1870. They remained on this reservation until Oklahoma became a state in 1907 when they were allotted land in severalty and became citizens of the State. Today there are a little over three thousand Osage left in Oklahoma, about one-half the population of the Nation before white contact.

The Osage Nation became highly integrated when oil was discovered in their territory. Tribal rolls grew tremendously in a very short time as politicians, bureaucrats, their in-laws and out-laws, and every carpetbagger who could became Osage. The true Osage people were exploited and many lost their legal rights to the plentiful "oil money." Many of the "oil rich Indians" are actually not related by blood to any Osage who ever lived, but are Osage by decree.

With this kind of "integration" it became extremely difficult for the traditional Osage people to maintain their culture. Through perseverance and cultural integrity, some facets do remain and are kept alive today. The story of "The Beginning of the Osage Nation" is one of the stories reverently retained by the people.

The Beginning of the Osage Nation

A long time ago, a snail lived very happily on the banks of the Missouri River for there he found plenty of food and everything he needed was close at hand. One day a great flood came and he was caught by the water. He climbed on a log and clung on with all his strength. Floating helplessly for many days, he found himself in a strange land, covered with river slime and mud. The sun shone brightly and the heat was terrible. The mud and the slime dried and hardened and the snail, even today, is covered with this substance.

Covered with mud, hot and hungry, the snail resigned himself to die. Suddenly, though, a new feeling surged through him and he gained back his strength. His shell split and his head gradually rose above the ground. His lower extremities gradually became legs and feet, arms grew from his sides and at their ends they divided and became fingers. Rising to an upright position, he became a noble-looking man given his being by the effects of the warm sunlight.

For a while his brain did not function, but after a bit he began to think. Memory became strong in him and he slowly returned up the river to where he formerly lived. He was naked and ignorant and very hungry. As he walked along he saw much game which was edible but, since he did not know how to kill it, he nearly starved.

At last he became so weak he lay down and prepared to die. He had not been on the ground very long when he heard a voice calling him by name, "Wasbashas, Wasbashas!" He looked up and saw the Great Spirit and was frightened. The Great Spirit sat on a beautiful white animal and He had eyes which sparkled as stars and the hair of His head shone like the sun. Trembling, Wasbashas could not bear to look upon him and lowered his eyes. The voice said very softly and kindly, "Wasbashas, why are you afraid?" Wasbashas replied, "I tremble because I stand before Him who raised me from the ground. I am weak and hungry for I have eaten nothing since I was left a little shell on the shore of a strange land."

The Great Spirit then showed Wasbashas a bow and some arrows and, telling Wasbashas to observe, placed the arrow on the string of the bow and sent it into the air. He fired the arrow into the air, striking a beautiful bird which fell dead to the ground. A deer appeared and the Great Spirit shot it through the heart. "There," He said to Wasbashas, "is your food, and these are your weapons," and gave him the bow and arrows. Wasbashas was then instructed how to dress the game and how to use all the parts. "You are naked," He said, "and must be clothed. Although it is warm now, the skies will soon change and you will need the skins to cover your body." He then gave Wasbashas some fire to keep him warm and to cook his food. He gave him authority over all the animals and made him custodian of the earth. Having done this, the Great Spirit rose in the air and vanished.

Wasbashas refreshed himself with food and continued his journey to his native land. After walking a long way, he seated himself on the bank of the river to rest and to meditate on what had transpired. Suddenly a great beaver surfaced in the river and called to him, "Who are you that comes to disturb me and my home?"

"I am a man," Wasbashas answered. "I once was a creeping shell but now am a man. Who are you?"

"I am the king of the nation of beavers and lead my people up and down this stream. We are a busy people and this river is my kingdom," replied the beaver.

"We will share the river and the land," said Wasbashas, "for the Great Spirit has made me the custodian to care for all the animals and birds and the fishes and plants."

"We are then brothers," said the beaver. "Come with me to my lodge and refresh yourself after your journey." So saying, he led Wasbashas, who gladly accepted the invitation, to a beautiful village. There he was entertained in the chief's lodge which was built in the shape of a cone and had the floor covered with pine mats. Wasbashas was very pleased and happy.

After they had seated themselves, the chief ordered his wife and his beautiful daughter to prepare their choicest foods for their guest. While they waited the chief told how the beavers built their lodges and described how they cut the trees with their teeth, felling them across the streams so as to dam up the water. He also explained how they finished the dams with leaves and clay and made their underwater homes dry and comfortable.

Beaver mother and daughter then brought in their finest peeled poplar and cedar and sassafras bark. This was their choicest food and Wasbashas politely attempted to eat. He was not able to devour much of the bark but the beavers ate it with great relish. The beautiful young daughter of the chief, however, did attract the eyes of Wasbashas.

Her modesty and clean attire, her response to her father's requests, and her attention to him increased Wasbashas' interest and he fell in love with this lovely young beaver. Finally, he asked the father beaver for his daughter's hand in marriage to which the chief gladly agreed. Since the daughter was as enamoured as Wasbashas, they were married. A great feast and party was held and all the beavers and friendly animals were invited. From this union of the snail and beaver the Osage nation had its origin.——Osage

OTO

The Oto are a Siouan-speaking group and are closely related with the Winnebago. They lived in the Missouri-Iowa section of the United States, west of the Mississippi River. After a series of treaties with the government, the Oto and the Missouri surrendered all their lands and accepted reservation life in Oklahoma.

The Oto-Missouri were never a very populous group, usually numbering about one thousand people. Currently, there are about that number living in Oklahoma much in the same manner as other citizens of the state. Most of the traditional way of life has been eroded by the close association with the dominant society. Recently, however, as with many groups of Indians in America, there has been a resurgence of native culture. Remnants of traditional lifestyles have been pieced together and revitalized culture is emerging.

One facet of traditional life which has surfaced is the telling of tribal stories. The following are examples of Oto stories now being told in their communities.

How the Bobcat Lost His Tail

One cold winter day Bobcat came out of his den at the base of a big oak tree. He had not eaten in several days and was very hungry, so he went in search of some food. He had gone only a short way when he came upon a mink who was carrying a fine mess of fish to his den.

"Where did you get such a fine mess of fish," asked Bobcat as his mouth watered, "and how did you manage to catch them?"

Mink replied, "I got them in the river. The ice has thawed now, so if you will sit by the edge of the water and hang your tail in the water, the fish will come up and nibble it. When you have had a great number of nibbles you will know you have a lot of fish on your tail. If you will pull it out very quickly, you will have a nice mess of fish for supper."

The bobcat hurried down to the river and sat on the edge with his tail in the water just as Mink had told him to do. All day long he sat there with his stomach hurting from hunger. He felt a number of nibbles but did not pull his tail out for he wanted a large mess of fish.

Along toward evening his tail began to hurt and he began to feel very cold. He patiently waited though, for he wanted a lot of fish. He felt more and more nibbles, but he still waited. Finally, about sundown he could stand the pain no longer and decided to jerk his tail out of the water very quickly as Mink had instructed.

He tried to yank his tail out but found it was held fast in the water. He pulled and pulled but his tail was frozen fast. Finally, he gave a vicious jerk and pulled his tail right off. He ran toward his den feeling hungry and very angry, and he had a terrible hurt where his tail had been. He pounced on every bird and small animal he could find. Even to this day, Bobcat has a very short temper and is hard to get along with. And he is still looking for Mink to make him pay for his trick.
——Oto

How the Cranes Got Their Long Legs

In the far-back times, soon after the Creation had taken place, all the birds of the earth looked alike. They all belonged to the same tribe, all talked the same language, had their homes all built alike and even ate the same kind of food. There were no differences in colors or size and they all lived in a huge tree near a shallow river. They gathered each day along the banks of this stream to eat the berries and seeds that grew there.

One day Wokonda, the Great Spirit, told the birds He was going to send a great flood to widen the river. He told them they must stay away from the edge of the river so they wouldn't get drowned when the heavy water came. He even provided a pond for them in a nearby meadow and made foods grow there for them. Most of the birds heeded Wokonda's advice and went to the pond, but some didn't want to stay away from the river. They thought they were wise enough to take care of themselves and they continued going to the river every day to look for food.

Suddenly one day, without any warning, the flood came with a great roaring and rushing of water. The birds who had disobeyed Wokonda were caught in the rushing water and tossed about as if they were twigs. Their wings were water-soaked and they could not fly to safety and the water was too deep for their short legs to allow them to stand. They were all about to drown when one of the birds who had obeyed called out, "O Wokonda, please save those foolish ones who disobeyed you. Put some stilts on my legs and I can wade into the water and rescue them."

Wokonda smiled on the water and it became calm. He sent a gentle breeze to blow the foolish birds to the shallow water near the river bank. Then He said to the bird who had asked for mercy, "Now you have the stilts you wanted. Wade into the water and rescue the foolish ones."

The bird looked down and his legs had grown very long and he was able to wade into much deeper water than ever before. He looked at the others who had obeyed Wokonda and saw they, too, had long legs and they had all grown larger bodies. He called his brothers and they waded into the water and carried the other birds to safety.

Ever since that time there have been many different clans of birds. Some have long legs and some have short ones and some have long beaks and others short ones. All the clans have different songs and different colored feathers.

The sandhill crane is called the Bird-On-Stilts and has great wisdom and courage for he was blessed by Wokonda that day.——Oto

SAUK

The Sauk, the "people of the yellow earth," are an Algonquian speaking people very closely related to the Mesquakie and Kickapoo. Originally from the Wisconsin-Michigan area, they were forced to remove west of the Mississippi River following the Black Hawk War in 1832. As a result of the loss of that conflict, the Sauk sought refuge with the Mesquakie who were established at Tama, Iowa.

The two tribes accepted land in Kansas and, as related earlier, in 1858 they split and the Mesquakie returned to Iowa. The Sauk moved to Indian Territory in 1867, and in 1889 they took land in severalty and sold the surplus to the government.

Although separated from the Mesquakie for many years, they are still generally identified as Sauk and Fox Indians. Today there are about one thousand living in Oklahoma, almost completely acculturated. A few of their stories remain intact and, like others in their assimilated condition, they remember and retell their version of "How the World was Created."

How the World Was Created

In the beginning the gods created every living being which was intended to have life upon the face of the whole earth, and then were formed every species of living animal. After this the gods also formed man, whom they perceived to be both cruel and foolish. They then put into man the heart of the best beast they had created, but they beheld that man still continued cruel and foolish.

After this it came to pass that the Great Spirit took a piece of Himself, of which He made a heart for the man, and when he received it, he immediately became wise above every other animal on the earth.

And it came to pass in the process of much time, that the earth, its first fruit in abundance, and all the living beasts, were greatly multiplied. The earth about this time was also inhabited by an inumerable host of giants and gods. And the gods whose habitation was under the seas, made war upon Wesukkah, the chief god upon the earth, and joined with the giants against him. Nevertheless, they were still afraid of Wesukkah and his immense host of gods, therefore they called a council upon the earth. When they were all assembled upon the earth, at the council, both the giants and the gods from under the seas, after much debate and long consultation, made a resolution. They resolved to make a great feast upon the earth, and to invite Wesukkah, that they might thus beguile him, and at the feast lay hands upon him and slay him.

And when the council had appointed a delegate to visit Wesukkah and commanded him to invite Wesukkah to the great feast which they were preparing for him, behold, the younger brother of Wesukkah was discovered in the midst of the council. Being confused in the whole assembly, they asked, "Where is your brother, Wesukkah?" And he replied that he was not his brother's keeper and did not know where Wesukkah was. The council, realizing all their plans were known to the younger brother, were extremely angry and with one accord the whole assembly rushed violently upon him, and slew him.

Now when Wesukkah heard of the death of his younger brother, he was extremely sorrowful and wept aloud. The gods whose habitations were above the clouds heard the voice of his lamentations, and they allied with him to avenge the blood of his brother. At this time the lower gods had fled from the face of the earth to their own habitations under the seas, and the giants were thus forsaken and left alone to defend themselves against Wesukkah and his allies.

Now the scene of battle where Wesukkah and his allies fought the giants was in a flame of fire. The whole race of giants was destroyed with a great slaughter, so that there was not one left upon the face of the whole earth. And when the gods under the seas knew the dreadful fate of their allies, the giants whom they had deserted, they were sore afraid. They cried aloud to Nanamakeh, the god of thunder, to come to their assistance.

Nanamakeh heard their cries and accepted their request and sent his sub god Notahtesseah, god of the wind, to Papoanetesseah, god of the cold, to invite him to come with all his dreadful host of frost, snow, hail, ice, and northwind, to their relief. When this destroying army came from the north, they smote the whole earth with frost, converting the waters of every river, lake, and sea into solid masses of ice, and covering the whole earth with an immense sheet of snow and hail. Thus perished all the first inhabitants of the earth, both men and beasts, except a few choice ones of each kind which Wesukkah preserved with himself upon the earth.

And again it came to pass in the process of a long time, that the gods under the seas came forth again upon the earth. When they saw Wesukkah and that he was almost alone on the earth, they rejoiced in assurance of being able to destroy him. But when they had exhausted every scheme, attempted every plan, and executed every effort to no avail, perceiving that all their councils and designs were well known to Wesukkah, they became mad with despair. They resolved to destroy Wesukkah by spoiling forever the whole face of the earth, which they desired so much to inhabit. To this end, therefore, they returned to their homes under the seas and entreated Nanamakeh, the god of thunder, to drown the whole earth with a flood.

And Nanamakeh again hearkened to their cries and calling all the clouds to gather themselves together, they obeyed his voice and came. When all the clouds were assembled, he commanded them, and they poured down water upon the earth, a tremendous torrent, until the whole surface of the earth, even the tops of the highest mountains, were covered with water. But, it came to pass that when Wesukkah saw the water coming upon the earth, he took some air and made a large boat. Getting into it himself, he took with him all sorts of living beasts, and man. When the waters rose upon the earth the boat was lifted up and floated upon the surface until the tops of the highest mountains were covered with the flood.

When the boat had remained for a long time upon the surface of the flood, Wesukkah commanded one of the animals which was with him in the boat to go down through the water to the earth and to bring some of it back to him. After many repeated efforts and with great difficulty, the animal at length returned bringing in its mouth some earth. When Wesukkah received it, he formed this earth and spread it forth upon the surface of the water. He then went forth himself and all that were with him in the boat, and occupied the dry land, as they still do today.——Sauk*

SHAWNEE

The Shawnee belong to the Algonquian linguistic stock and are close relatives of the Mesquakie, Sauk, and Kickapoo. They were one of the most nomadic of all Indian nations and lived throughout the eastern part of the United States at one time or another. They were noted as warriors, and from the beginning of the French and Indian War in 1690 to the signing of the Treaty of Greenville in 1795, the main body of Shawnee were almost constantly fighting the English or the Americans. During these years they were driven from place to place according to the fortunes of war. In 1793, a large group of Shawnee settled in Spanish territory west of the Mississippi River near Cape Girardeau,

* Most of the information in this story came from *The Great Indian Chief of the West or Life and Adventures of Black Hawk*. The publication does not identify the author, but it was published in Cincinnati in 1854 by Applegate & Company.

Missouri. In 1798 the main body of the tribe moved to the White River in Indiana by invitation of the Delaware.

The great Shawnee leader, Tecumseh, began an earnest campaign to unite the various Indian nations east of the Mississippi in an effort to ally them with the British and expel the Americans. In 1812, war broke out between the Americans and the British, and Tecumseh, along with all the Indians he could enlist, joined in the fight. The cause, however, was hopeless and the Indians, along with their English allies, suffered a decisive defeat. Tecumseh died in the Battle of the Thames in 1814.

Gradually, all the various components of the Shawnee Nation were moved to Oklahoma Territory where they settled on a small reservation and, after Oklahoma statehood came about in 1907, became citizens. Of the estimated three thousand Shawnee in prewhite times, some twelve hundred of their descendants now are residents of the State of Oklahoma.

The Shawnees were exposed to many tribes during their transiency, and to the strong influence of white society after final location in Indian Territory. Each of these exposures eroded a little of the Shawnee cultural perspective and added a small alien segment. Very little of the traditional Shawnee lifestyle remains intact. However, a few of their traditional stories do survive and are being perpetuated in Shawnee communities. One of these, the prophesy concerning the end of the world, is provided here.

The End of the World

At one time the Shawnee was a great and powerful nation with many, many people. One time, long, long ago, they were all called together for a conference to decide on the important issues which would affect the course of the nation. They assembled on a pleasant, smooth, and level prairie to prepare for the meeting, arranging their camp according to bands and clans within the nation.

After having been in camp for a number of hours, about half of the people fell asleep and slept through the night. The other half remained awake until dawn and, as the sun arose, began a march to the east. When the sleeping group awoke, seeing the others had left, they broke camp and moved to the west towards the land where the sun sets. This was the origin of the two nations of the Shawnee people. The first group who moved to the east were called Shawnee and the second who followed the sun to the west was called Kickapoo.

Now, prior to this separation, these two nations were united and on extremely friendly terms. They worked together and cooperated in gathering foods, farming, and hunting. They shared and were blessed by the Great Spirit as much or more than any other nation of people. Since they became disunited and became two tribes, He withdrew these blessings from them. One of the gifts He withdrew from them was their ability to walk upon the surface of the water.

It was because of this special power that the Shawnee were able to cross the great sea without the aid of canoes or rafts, moving from the east to these shores. The Great Spirit also withdrew the power of restoring the dead through the use of the understanding of natural medicine. Other powers lost were prophecy and comprehension of great mysteries and the ability to perform miracles.

One prophecy which is very alive with the Shawnee and Kickapoo is the prediction that when the Shawnees have wandered as far west as possible and returned to their homeland where the separation occurred, the world will cease to be.——Shawnee*

WINNEBAGO

The Winnebago speak the Siouan language but, in their homeland south of the Great Lakes, they were surrounded by Algonquians. It is thought by many that they were probably left behind when the other Siouan groups moved westward out of the area.

The tribe was usually on friendly terms with its neighbors and did not suffer heavily from warfare. It was disease brought into the area by whites which depleted the population in the 1830s. It was about this time that the Winnebago people started a series of moves which eventually located them with the Omaha Nation in Nebraska. They now have an assigned area of trust land where about one thousand Winnebago make their home, north of Omaha, Nebraska, along the Missouri River.

Much of their culture has been diluted, but Winnebago oral tradi-

---

* It is noteworthy that these people reached the extreme western point; the Pacific Ocean, and are now moving back toward their eastern homeland.

tion still exists much as it has for centuries. Their prophesy of the destruction of the Evil Spirit and his disciples is related to the people as an aid in enduring the hardships found in everyday life.

The Story of the Evil Spirit

The Great Spirit created the world and all the good things in it. He made the deer, the buffalo, the rabbit, the ducks and geese, and all the other animals which provide food and clothing. He made the pine, oak, and juniper trees and placed the helpful herbs to grow on the earth. All was peaceful and happy. The Great Spirit then made the Indian and put him on earth to care for the Creation.

Now while the Great Spirit had been at work making the world a pleasant place, the Evil Spirit had been asleep. When he awoke and saw all the good things which the Great Spirit had created, he became very jealous and started to work himself, quite sure he could do as well. His first work was to try to make a duplicate of the Indian. He got some of the ingredients mixed up though and the black man was produced. Next the Evil Spirit tried to make a black bear, but it turned out to be the mean-tempered grizzly. He then made several snakes and they were filled with poison. The next creations were insects which plague man to this day: gnats, flies, mosquitoes, and fleas. All of his animal creations were failures.

Next, the Evil Spirit commenced work on the vegetable line, but had the same results. He produced poison ivy, thorn trees, thistles, and some twisted and gnarled trees but none of the beautiful trees such as the Great Spirit had made. All his creations looked very bad when compared to the beauty the Great Spirit had placed on earth.

Since he could not compete with the Great Spirit in creating things, the Evil Spirit began to change the good things. He placed briars on the berry bushes, put thick hulls on the walnut, gave the wasps and bees stingers and the skunk he provided with a bad smell. Even some of the Indians were taught to murder, lie, and steal and some were taught to forget that they were the caretakers of the earth and its inhabitants. He tried his best to outdo the Great Spirit and to make everything evil.

Some day the Great Spirit and the Evil Spirit will have a great battle to decide who will have his way in the world. At that time there will be no light for four days and nights and earth will be in darkness. There will be great storms and the thunder will roll and the lightning will flash across the sky. The earth itself will shudder and tremble with fear and great destruction will be everywhere. Great floods will cover the lands and earth will be destroyed. The wicked ones will go to the Evil Spirit and be seen no more.

It is at that time that the Great Spirit, who will always exist, will restore the earth for His children who have followed His way, and all will be happiness forever.——Winnebago

The Northeast Indians

For the presentation of the Northeastern section of this book, boundaries will be restricted to the area from the Atlantic Ocean to the eastern Great Lakes, and from northeastern Canada south to lower New York. The Iroquois nations are inhabitants of this area along with a large number of Algonquian groups.

The northeastern tribes have been exposed to European contact for a very long time and, although not so affected by esthetic change, were changed tremendously in their commercial association. The French were the first to move into the area and perhaps their unique attitude toward acculturation influenced this situation.

Rather than attempting stringent acculturation activity, the French trappers and traders reversed the general European approach. The French, not the Indians, usually assimilated. They accepted Indian customs, married Indian women, and became a part of the Indian community. This willingness to allow credence to Indians and their value system made them much more acceptable than their counterparts. It required a great amount of sophisticated and subtle political maneuvering and a considerable military effort by the English to wrest control from the Frenchmen. Even today in many areas, the French influence is strongly visible in Indian communities, especially in Canada.

Until the fall of "New France" in 1760, for example, the Iroquois were able to maintain a large degree of autonomy. They balanced white powers against each other and were able to control much of their own lives. After 1760, the Iroquois were quickly overrun by white settlement and they became pawns of the American and British forces.

This section of the book represents people who live or have lived in the Northeast during the period of time which has been the most well-documented period of American history. Most historians however, restrict or distort the history of native people in their presentations. During the many years of forced study of United States history in our educational institutions, we find students quite able to communicate facts and concepts concerning George Washington, Concord and Lexington, New Amsterdam, Cabot, Cartier, and other white oriented portions. We likewise find though that, aside from scalping expeditions, torture, and other negative connotations about the "barbarous savages," they have very little knowledge, especially valid knowledge, concerning the native people.

What bits of "Indian" history of this area that are presented are generally held to the Iroquois. Nothing is found which relates to the genocide of the Pequot Nation. There are no depictions of the disappearance of the Narragansets, the Rappahanocks, the Massachusets, the great Powhatan Confederacy, or the many other nations of people who are no more.

Nevertheless, the lessons that these nations learned in their dealings with the Europeans enabled many of them to retain their traditions and a sense of identity. The exploitation of a group sometimes strengthens these facets of culture, for the oppressed will "grasp at straws" and turn to spiritual support in order to survive the ordeals forced on them. The following pages illustrate some of these "straws" the northeastern Indians perpetuate today.

ABNAKI

The Abnaki are an Algonquian-speaking people who lived in what is now the State of Maine. They are closely related to the Malecite, Penobscot, and Pennacook tribes and a little more distantly related to the Passamaquoddy. They were never a large nation, numbering only about three thousand before the coming of the whites.

Because of their geographic location they were probably one of the tribes contacted by the Norsemen nearly one thousand years ago. Since then they have seen a succession of European people as they were visited by fishermen and explorers from many countries. They developed a strong relationship with the French, and when England began to encroach into the area, they resisted. After several military defeats at the hands of the British army, they moved to Canada to be under the protection of their French friends. After Canada was lost to England the Abnaki remained along the St. Lawrence waterway east of the City of Quebec where they are today.

Although acculturated to a great degree, the Abnaki still retain some of their native traditions and rely on the stories of their elders to provide spiritual strength to the people. One of their favorite tales is related here.

How the Indians Got Corn

Many years ago when the Indians were first made, there was one man who lived by himself, far from any other Indian people. He knew nothing of fire or of cooking, so he lived on roots, nuts, berries, and bark. After a time, he became tired of digging and scratching and felt very lonesome. He needed someone to talk with so he decided to fast and obtain a vision which would tell him how to keep from being so lonely.

For several days the Indian ate no food and lay in the sunshine daydreaming. One day he awoke sharply and saw a lovely young woman standing nearby. She had long, golden hair, quite unlike other Indian hair, and was extremely beautiful. He called to the maiden and asked her to come to him, but she would not. As he tried to approach her, she kept a certain distance between them. The young man sang to her of his loneliness and begged her to stay with him and never leave. Finally, she told him if he would carefully follow her instructions, he would have her with him forever. Of course, the young man promised to do exactly as she instructed him.

The beautiful maiden led the young man to a place where there was some very dry grass. She then gave him two sticks and told him to rub them together very fast while holding them in the dry grass. Soon the heat became so intense the grass caught fire and the entire areas was burned over.

Then the young woman said, "When the sun sets, take me by the hair and drag me over the burned ground."

Of course, the young man did not want to do this, but he had promised to obey. The girl told him that wherever he dragged her, a new and wonderful plant would grow. She said that he would see her hair coming out between the leaves and the seeds of the plant would be for him to use for food.

The young man did as he was instructed, and to this day, when Indians see the golden silk on the cornstalk, they know the young maiden has not forgotten them.——Abnaki

DELAWARE

The Delaware Indians, or as they call themselves, "Lenape," are an Algonquin-speaking people closely related to the Chippewa and Shawnee Indians. Before the appearance of the Europeans, the Lenape territory was the Delaware River Valley and much of what is now the State of New Jersey. As more whites arrived, pressure on the Indians became greater and they began moving westward. The Lenape relocated in the Pennsylvania area where they were contacted by William Penn and the Quakers. The dealings between this religious organization and the Lenape were harmonious and very fair. This pattern of honesty and respect has carried through the years and is still quite evident in contemporary operation.*

As the newly formed United States began to recognize the need for legal methods of negotiation with the native people, acceptance of the Indian groups as sovereign nations was extended and transactions were implemented in the form of treaties. The first treaty between the United States and an Indian nation was signed at Fort Pitt with the powerful Delaware Nation on September 17, 1778. From that time the Lenape were forced to make many moves as the Federal government, hostile Indians, and white settlers harassed and coerced them. Eventually settled principally in Kansas and Oklahoma, the remnants of this important nation of people are now but a small number with little of their cultural heritage evident.

* The Quaker (Friends) Church is the only Christian organization known to this author which has never exploited the native people and has an unblemished record of true advocacy for their rights. They have always totally upheld the principles of their religious doctrines without extracting spiritual payment in the form of proselytism of the Indian.

The Walum Olum, "painted record," is one of the few remaining traditions. The work was originally in the form of pictographs inscribed on wood or bark and passed from one generation to the next. Translations from the pictographs to the Lenape language and then to English has diluted somewhat the authenticity of the historic story but much of the beauty of the epic survives.

The following pages present the first three sections of the Walum Olum which tell of the Creation and the establishment of the earth.

Walum Olum

I

At first, in that place, at all times, above the earth,

On the earth, [was] an extended fog, and there the great Manito was.

At first, forever, lost in space, everywhere, the great Manito was.

He made the extended land and the sky.

He made the sun, the moon, the stars.

He made them all to move evenly.

Then the wind blew violently, and it cleared, and the water flowed off far and strong.

And groups of islands grew newly, and there remained.

Anew spoke the great Manito, a manito to manitos,

To beings, mortals, souls and all,

And ever after he was a manito to men, and their grandfather.

He gave the first mother, the mother of beings.

He gave the fish, he gave the turtles, he gave the beasts, he gave the birds.

But an evil Manito made evil beings only, monsters,

He made the flies, he made the gnats.

All beings were then friendly.

Truly the manitos were active and kindly

To those very first men, and to those first mothers; fetched them wives,

And fetched them food, when first they desired it.

All had cheerful knowledge, all had leisure, all thought in gladness.

But very secretly an evil being, a mighty magician, came on earth,

And with him brought baldness, quarreling, unhappiness,

Brought bad weather, brought sickness, brought death.

All this took place of old on the earth, beyond the great tidewater, at the first.

II
Long ago there was a mighty snake and beings evil to men.

This mighty snake hated those who were there [and] greatly disquieted those whom he hated.

They both did harm, they both injured each other, both were not in peace.

Driven from their homes they fought with this murderer.

The mighty snake firmly resolved to harm the men.

He brought three persons, he brought a monster, he brought a rushing water.

Between the hills the water rushed and rushed, dashing through and through, destroying much.

Nanabush, the Strong White One, grandfather of beings, grandfather of men, was on the Turtle Island.

There he was walking and creating, as he passed by and created the turtle.

Beings and men all go forth, they walk in the floods and shallow waters, downstream thither to the Turtle Island.

There were many monster fishes, which ate some of them.

The Manito daughter, coming, helped with her canoe, helped all as they came and came.

(And also) Nanabush, Nanabush, the grandfather of all, the grandfather of beings, the grandfather of men, the grandfather of the turtle.

The men then were together on the turtle, like to turtles.

Frightened on the turtle, they prayed on the turtle that what was spoiled should be restored.

The water ran off, the earth dried, the lakes were at rest, all was silent, and the mighty snake departed.

III
After the rushing waters (had subsided) the Lenape of the turtle were close together, in hollow houses, living together there.

It freezes where they abode, it snows where they abode, it storms where they abode, it is cold where they abode.

At this northern place they speak favorably of mild, cool [lands], with many deer and buffaloes.

As they journeyed, some being strong, some rich, they separated into house-builders and hunters;

The strongest, the most united, the purest, were the hunters.

The hunters showed themselves at the north, at the east, at the south, at the west.

In that ancient country, in that northern country, in that turtle country, the best of the Lenape were the Turtle men.

All the cabin fires of that land were disquieted, and all said to their priest, "Let us go."

To the Snake land to the east they went forth, going away, earnestly grieving.

Split asunder, weak, trembling, their land burned, they went, torn and broken, to the Snake Island.

Those from the North being free, without care, went forth from the land of snow, in different directions.

The fathers of the Bald Eagle and the White Wolf remain along the sea, rich in fish and mussels.

Floating up the streams in their canoes, our fathers were rich, they were in the light, when they were at those islands.

Head Beaver and Big Bird said,
"Let us go to Snake Island," they said.

All say they will go along to destroy all the land.

Those of the north agreed,
Those of the east agreed.
Over the water, the frozen sea,
They went to enjoy it.

On the wonderful slippery water,
On the stone-hard water all went,
On the great Tidal Sea, the mussel-bearing sea.

Ten thousand at night,
All in one night,
To the Snake Island, to the east, at night,
They walk and walk, all of them.

The men from the north, the east, the south,
The Eagle clan, the Beaver clan, the Wolf clan,
The best men, the rich men, the head men,
Those with wives, those with daughters, those with dogs,

They all come, they tarry at the land of the spruce pines;
Those from the west come with hesitation,
Esteeming highly their old home at the Turtle land.——Delaware
(Lenape)

HURON

The Huron people were great traders since their territory lay on both sides of the St. Lawrence River and bordered on Lake Ontario and Lake Huron. Indians from all over the area utilized these waterways to transport their wares to exchange for Huron products. As the Europeans entered the area, this trade was stimulated by their insatiable desire for furs, especially by the French.

Decimated by wars with the Mohawk and the Seneca tribes, the Hurons retreated to an island which was unfit for anything except that it was easy to defend. Most of these refugees starved during the winter of 1649–50. Only about five hundred survived and they moved to Quebec where their descendants still live.

Thus the Huron Nation was reduced from eighteen villages with a combined population of thirty to forty thousand to five hundred miserable refugees. This loss can be attributed directly to the influence of the European invaders who, using tactics which are successful even today, pitted one group of natives against another with disastrous results to the Indians.

The Wyandots were a Southern branch of the Hurons, not involved in the inter-tribal warfare, who allied with the British in the War of 1812. They were rewarded with a large tract of land in Ohio and Michigan. After selling most of it, the tribe settled on small reservations until 1842 when they were removed to Kansas. In 1867 they were once again moved, this time to a small reservation in northeastern Oklahoma. When the territory became a state in 1907, the Wyandots, like their peers, became citizens. The people assimilated for the most part and became a part of the dominant society.

Along with the loss of the people and their homeland, the culture and traditions of the Huron and Wyandot also suffered tremendous losses. Very little of these remain today and little hope is apparent that any revival will occur.

A few stories remain and are told by the elders of the tribe. Two versions of the Creation Story are related here.

How the World Was Made

Far above us in the sky is another world. The people who live there are just like us, only taller and more beautiful and with no trouble to mar their happiness. They live in the same type lodges and wear the same type clothing as worn in our world. If you look up on a clear night you can see the lights from their world peeping through the holes in the floor of the sky.

One time, many years ago, there was no world here below, only water stretching over everything. The only dwellers were the animals that lived in the sea, toad, frog, fish, turtle, beaver, and the sea birds.

One day a pregnant woman fell from a hole in the sky. Two loons, seeing her fall and fearing she would drown in the sea, spread their wings together and caught her just before she hit the water. The loons called to the other animals for help, but none heard them. They called and called and their sad wailing forms their song even today.

Finally, Turtle heard the loons' call and gathered the other water animals to give assistance.

Turtle, who now carried the world on his back, had many strange and wonderful powers. He placed the woman on his shell and, knowing she and her baby would need earth to live on, sent beaver to the bottom of the ocean for some mud. Beaver dove under the water but was unable to go deep enough to bring back any mud. Muskrat next tried, but he too failed to find the bottom.

Toad then asked Turtle if he could try, but he was so small that Turtle refused to give him permission. But Toad persisted and was finally allowed to try. He dived into the water and disappeared.

As the time passed and Toad did not come back, the animals became discouraged for they thought the little toad had drowned. Finally Toad reappeared, nearly dead, but with a small amount of mud in his mouth. Turtle handed the mud to the Sky Woman who spread it over his shell. Gradually it began to grow, larger and larger, until it formed the world as we know it now. It began to take shape, making hills and valleys, until it was ready for the trees and other plants.

Then the woman gave birth to twins who were the exact opposites in personality. One, who was kind and gentle, made all the good things on earth, such as the dog, deer, bear, turkey, and the helpful plants. The other made the fierce animals, snakes, mosquitoes and the noxious plants.

Thus, the earth, man, animals, plants, good and bad were made.
——Huron

The Creation of the World

The first people lived in the sky because there was no earth. Below the sky was nothing but an endless sea of water. In the sky home one day, a young maiden became ill. The medicine man instucted the people to dig up a tree and lay the ill girl beside the hole. The people began to dig but as they did so, the tree fell right through the hole they had made and the girl slipped through also.

Below, on the endless sheet of water, were two swans. They heard the commotion from above and looked up just in time to see the tree break through the sky and fall into the water. Then they saw the girl falling after it so they swam to her and supported her on their backs. She was far too beautiful to let drown.

The swans then swam to the Great Turtle who was the leader of all the animals, and he called a council. When the council was assembled, Turtle explained what had happened and that the appearance of the young girl was a sign that they would have good fortune. Since the tree had dirt on its roots, Turtle commanded the other animals to find

The Creation of the World
Huron

where it had sunk. He told them to bring some of the dirt and put it on his back to make an island for the maiden to live on.

The swans led the animals to where the tree had sunk. First, Otter, then Muskrat, and then Beaver dived under the water. As each one came back from the great depths, they rolled over exhausted, and died. Many other animals tried to follow Great Turtle's command, but they all met the same fate. Finally, old lady Toad volunteered to try her luck. She dived and was gone so long everyone knew she was lost too. At last she surfaced and, just before she died, she managed to spit a little dirt on the Great Turtle's back.

This dirt was magical and had the power to grow. When it was large enough, the swans placed the woman on the island on Great Turtle's back. The swans continued to swim about and watch the earth grow. It spread and spread until at last it became the world island as it is today, supported in the great waters on the back of the Great Turtle.

There was no light on earth and all was darkness so Great Turtle called another council of the animals. After lengthy consideration and discussion, it was decided to place a great light in the sky to illuminate the world. The biggest question was how to get the light up to the sky for the way was dangerous and full of obstacles. Finally, it was decided that Little Turtle would attempt the journey.

All the animals used their magic powers to help and a large, black cloud was formed. It was full of crashing rocks and their moving and bumping against one another caused great flashing of lightning and much noise. Little Turtle climbed on this cloud and was carried high into the sky. First she made a great bright ball of light and put it into place. She then decided there should be more light so she made a smaller ball and set it in its proper position. The first ball became the sun and the second ball became the moon. She then returned to earth to report what she had done.

Great Turtle was pleased with Little Turtle's work but thought there should be more variety than constant daylight so he again called the animals to council. He explained that there should be a rest period for the great lights and while one worked the other should sleep. He commanded the burrowing animals to make holes in the corners of the sky so the sun and moon could go down through one to rest and come up through the other to work. This is why we have day and night.——— Wyandot (Huron)

MICMAC

The history of the Micmac Indians closely parallels that of their relatives, the Abnaki. They were missionized by the French early in the seventeenth century and became middlemen in trading between the Europeans and Indians further west and south. After the French gave up their Canadian interests, some trouble developed between the Mimacs and the English. When this warfare stopped in 1779, the Mimacs became peaceful and assimilated pretty thoroughly into the dominant society.

Today it is quite difficult to identify very many of these people and no estimates of their population can be found. There do remain however, a number of pockets of traditional Mimacs who diligently perpetuate portions of their culture. One facet which can still be found are the stories told by the people. One of these, "How the World was Made," is provided here.

How the World Was Made

At first, there was only the great expanse of water which had been made by the chief Creator. There was a secondary creator, under the Great Spirit, and his name was Glooskap. He possessed a dual personality, one good and one bad, and was full of virtue and also all kinds of trickery.*

One day Glooskap and a woman were sitting on a log which floated on the great ocean which was the world. They were surrounded by all kinds of animals, and a discussion was held as to what it was that existed at the bottom of the water. Four animals were sent down to find what was there. Three failed, but the last, Muskrat, returned with some mud in his forepaw. The woman scraped it off and began to work it around in her hands.

The mud began to grow rapidly and, when the woman placed it in the water, it expanded to be the earth we know today. As the mud grew, the animals scattered throughout the world. The Wolf began to be troublesome and the woman got angry with him. She scolded him

---

* This dual personality, good and evil, helpful and mischievous, was not uncommon in the oral traditions of many tribes. "Characters" such as coyote, raven, and some of the spirits are imbued with this trait.

and finally threw him on an island. He ran around the outside, making indentations with his paws, making the shores of rivers and lakes to be harder than any other soil.

Herbs and trees began to grow on the earth and one small shrub the woman planted grew so tall it reached the sky. Overhead there was a strange object which was so beautiful it fascinated all creatures below. The woman sent the man up the tree to find out what it was. It looked like an old woman and the man caught it in a snare. The woman was angry with the man and sent several animals up to release the object.

The racoon climbed the tree but the heat from the captive object was so great that he was scorched and fell out of the tree. Even today his fur appears as if the tips of the hair has been burned.

Next, the mole climbed up and he, too, was nearly overcome by the heat. He did manage to reach the snare and gnaw through it. This allowed the beautiful object, the Sun, to continue on its journey across the sky. Poor Mole, though, had gotten so close that his nose was burned and to this day, no hair grows on it.——Micmac

MOHAWK

Home for most Mohawks today refers to the St. Regis Reservation near Hogansburg, New York. These thirty-nine thousand acres stretch along the St. Lawrence River with part under the jurisdiction of the United States and part under Canadian control. These people who are called Mohawk are known to nearly every literate inhabitant of our country. Every United States history textbook describes in a very biased and one-sided manner the way the dreadful Iroquois tortured and killed early settlers in the New World.

We think of the early colonists as brave and honorable pioneers carving a civilization out of the wilderness and being treat miserably by the uncivilized heathens who were totally wrong. True, the colonists were brave, but we should not forget that America was not a wilderness and it was not inhabited by uncivilized people. The "cruelty" of the Indian was in defense of their homes, their land, their women and children, and their very existence.

The Mohawks are a member of the great Iroquois League, sometimes called The Six Nations, or The Iroquois Confederacy. This association of Iroquois-speaking natives was a well-organized group of

Indians who designed and implemented a highly sophisticated democracy operated under their constitution, "The Great Law of Peace." This political instrument formed the basis for the establishment of the governing documents of the United States. Drawn up and presented to the people by Tekanawita, the law giver, it assigns specific political functions for each of the nations. The Mohawks were mandated as follows:

> I, Tekanawita, appoint the Mohawk statesmen the head and the Leaders of the Five Nations League.* The Mohawk Statesmen are the foundation of the Great Peace, and it shall therefore be against the Great Binding Law to pass measures in the Council of the League after the Mohawk statesmen have protested against them.
> No Council of the League shall be legal unless all of the statesmen of the Mohawks are present.**

These people resisted the European invaders and tried valiantly to maintain their traditional way of life. Even today, the resistance to outside influence is very evident. In 1973, a group of Mohawks occupied a six hundred acre portion of land, drove out the non-Indians, and have withstood all forcible removable since then.

Many traditional leaders have assisted in keeping the culture of "The People of the Longhouse" alive. The following stories are offered as a tribute to Tom Porter, Tom Sullivan, and the other traditional Mohawks this writer has known.

Saratoga Lake

The Mohawks deeply revered the stillness of Saratoga Lake for they thought the quiet was sacred and honored the Great Spirit. They firmly believed that if a sound were to be made while crossing its waters, the canoe would sink.

One day, the wife of an early settler was to be transported to the dis-

---

* Originally there were five nations in the confederacy, Mohawk, Seneca, Cayuga, Onondaga, and Oneida. After colonial pressures became too great, the Tuscarora requested and gained permission to become the sixth nation.
** The Great Law of Peace of the People of the Longhouse published by the Mohawk Nation at Akwesasne via Rooseveltown, New York from the teachings of Tekanawita.

tant shore of the lake by several Mohawks. Before the journey was begun, she was warned of the need for absolute silence, and the importance of the silence was stressed as a sacred tradition. As they neared the center of the lake the woman, in an attempt to illustrate that the Indians' belief was only superstition, uttered a loud shriek.

The Indians were startled and frightened and a gloomy feeling settled over them as they redoubled their efforts and hurriedly reached the shore. As they stepped ashore the woman began to berate the men for their superstitious fears, when one of the Mohawks scornfully put her in her place by answering, "The Great Spirit is merciful, He knows that a white woman cannot hold her tongue!"——Mohawk

Why Mosquitoes Bite

Long ago in the land of the Real People, two giant mosquitoes appeared. The huge creatures were as tall as the pine trees and they frightened the people greatly. They stood on either side of a stream and, as the Indians paddled their canoes down the river, the giant creatures would bend their heads and attack them with their gigantic beaks.

The mosquitoes killed many people and the rest were forced to use other rivers for they knew they would be attacked if they paddled their canoes on the mosquitoes' stream. It was at this time that the giant creatures moved to other waterways to seek their prey.

For a long time the Indians lived in terror, for they never knew when or where they might be attacked and eaten by the monsters. Finally, they formed a war party and after proper ceremonies and dances they began to seek out the giant mosquitoes so they could destroy them.

Twenty brave warriors in two great canoes floated down a river where they thought the creatures might be. They were all armed with bows and arrows, and each man had his knife and war-club. Suddenly two shadows loomed over them and a huge beak pierced one of the canoes. Instantly the warriors gave their war cry and filled the air with arrows. The battle was on!

The giant mosquitoes fought savagely and seemed to be everywhere at the same time. It was not long before they had killed half the warriors. The remainder determined to die with courage and began to sing their death songs as they attacked the huge creatures on land.

They hid in the bushes and behind trees and surround the mosquitoes who could not get at them because of the branches. The fighters fired arrow after arrow into the giant insects and, just as they were about to run out of arrows, the two mosquitoes fell to earth.

Immediately the warriors fell on them with their knives and clubs and tore the bodies apart. From the blood of the two giant mosquitoes there appeared many little ones, and soon the air was filled with them. These little mosquitoes, like their grandfathers, were very fond of the taste of blood. They hate man for killing their grandfathers and are constantly trying to get revenge. This is how mosquitoes came to be and why they are always biting people.——Mohawk

The Big Dipper

Many years ago there was a village of bark houses along the Oswego River. One day a group of hunters from the settlement discovered some huge bear tracks. The prints were so large that the men knew they had to come from a bear much larger than any they had seen before.

After that, they saw the tracks many times, and sometimes the tracks would circle the village very close but no one ever saw the giant beast. Soon the animals began to disappear from the forest and the Indians knew the great Bear was killing them and carrying them away. Because of the vanishing of the game animals, it was not long before the people became very hungry. The meat racks were empty and famine spread through the community.

It was decided that, even though the giant Bear was a dangerous foe, he must be killed to preserve the people. At once a group of hunters set out in search of the Bear. They came upon his tracks and followed them for many days. Finally they located their prey and set about destroying him. The air was filled with arrows, but to the surprise of the hunters they failed to pierce the hide of the Bear and many broken arrows fell from his tough skin.

The huge animal then let out an awful roar and charged the hunters. Many were killed by the first attack and those who attempted to flee were soon overtaken and killed also. Only two men escaped and they returned to the village to tell what had happened. The Indians were even more sure that the great Bear must be slain. Group after group were sent on the mission but they always failed. There were many battles fought and many Indians were slain.

As time passed, more and more game vanished from the forest and the people became very thin because of the lack of food. They were filled with fear and huddled around their fires at night to seek protection from the great beast who circled the town every night. They were afraid to leave their village because as soon as they did they could hear the great Bear roar his warning.

One night three brothers had the same dream, that they had tracked the giant Bear and killed him. For three successive nights they had the same vision. The council interpreted this as a sign from the spirits so they decided to send one more war party against the Bear. The group gathered all the weapons they could and, with what little food they had, started out on the trail.

For many months the hunters tracked the great Bear. Finally, they came to the end of the world and, looking ahead, they saw the great beast leap from earth into the heavens. When the group came to the jumping-off place, it was decided only the three brothers who had dreamed of killing the Bear should continue. Without hesitation, the three followed the Bear into the sky. They have never quite caught up to the Bear, but in the winter sky you can see them still on the chase.

In the fall of the year, when the Bear gets ready for his long sleep, the three hunters get near enough to shoot their arrows into his body. His dripping blood caused by the wounds turns the autumn leaves red. However, the Bear always manages to escape from the hunters and for a time he is invisible while he recovers from his wounds. Then he reappears and, when the Indians see the Big Dipper in the sky, they know the three hunters are still chasing the great Bear.——Mohawk

OTTAWA

The Ottawa Nation belongs to the Algonquian linguistic family and they are most closely related with the Chippewa and Potawatomi people. Living on the rivers and lakes, they were heavily involved in trading with the other native units as well as the Europeans after their arrival. Theirs is a long history of move after move in an attempt to escape harassment from the warlike Iroquois and, later, the colonists.

The Ottawa warriors joined Tecumseh in his stand against the Americans in the early 1800s. They were led by their famous war-chief, Pontiac, who distinguished himself in fights against the British and the Americans. Finally signing a treaty with the British, he was murdered by a Kaskaskia Indian after a night of drinking.

After the passage of the Removal Act of 1830, the Ottawas were again removed to new lands, this time beyond the Mississippi River. They were provided with a small reservation in the northeastern corner of Oklahoma. When that territory became a state in 1907, the Ottawa Reservation was absorbed. Today there is some government controlled land in the area held in trust for the tribe, but for the most part the Ottawas became Oklahomans.

Although suffering extreme assimilation pressures and being nearly wiped out as an Indian entity, some Ottawa tradition was kept alive by the spiritual leaders of the tribe. One of their stories, "The Flood" is provided here to honor the Ottawa Nation.

The Flood

Long ago, Nanaboozho, who possessed miraculous powers, lived for a time among the humans. During that time he made his winter quarters near a large lake in which lived some evil monsters. Nanaboozho told his favorite son, Wolf, not to go out on the ice when he was hunting but to always go around the lake so the monsters would not attack him. For a time, Wolf followed his father's orders, but one evening as he was returning home, he disobeyed. He was tired and hungry and the lake was frozen so deep that he decided to take a short-cut across the ice.

He was about half way across when strange rumbling noises started coming from under the ice. The smooth frozen surface began to rise and buckle as if some great force was pushing from beneath. Wolf became terribly afraid and began to run as fast as he could toward shore, but the ice broke and he was thrown into the water where he soon perished.

Nanaboozho was deeply enraged at the loss of his favorite son, and vowed revenge on the monsters. He decided to wait until summer to do anything for he knew when the weather was warm, the monsters would leave the water to sun themselves on the shore.

When the snow and ice had gone, he took his best bow and arrows and went to the lake to slay the monsters. He changed himself to a pine tree so he wouldn't be detected and stood in a convenient place on the shore. Sure enough, about noon, when the sun was quite warm, the monsters began coming ashore and stretching out in the warm sunshine. Since they were not accustomed to this fresh air and warm sun, they soon went soundly to sleep.

When all was quite, Nanaboozho changed from the pine tree to a man's form. He took deliberate aim and began to shoot arrows into the great beasts. Aroused from their sleep, they were enraged and some were sorely wounded. They hastily plunged into the water, which they agitated until it rose and overflowed the banks. Such was the force of the water that it destroyed everything in its path.

Nanaboozho was forced to the top of the highest mountain peak, but soon the water rose even that high. He climbed on a pine log as it floated past and remained there until the water quieted. After the monsters quit stirring up the flood, Nanaboozho had a lot of time to think as he floated around. He began to devise schemes in his mind as to how he could restore the world.

While meditating one day, he saw Muskrat sitting on a log and commanded him to dive down and bring him a piece of mud from the bottom. Muskrat did as he was commanded and dove to the bottom of the water. He was gone a long time and nearly drowned. Finally he surfaced and Nanaboozho found a piece of clay under one of Muskrat's shoulders. He pressed it between his hands until it became thin and flat and then laid it gently on the surface of the water. In a few days it had grown and was the Earth as we now know it.

Nanaboozho then placed large numbers of people and animals on it and provided all the vegetation and all things that were necessary to sustain man and animals.

At first the ground was flat but there soon came a large animal that began to paw the plastic soil. This produced deep indentations and made the mountains, valleys, and the river courses.

For some time after the flood, Nanaboozho lived with his people and instructed them in all things relating to their welfare. One day he told them he was going to leave them and make his new home far to the north. He said he loved his people and would watch over them even though he was far off. He told them that periodically he would build large fires in the north country, and they would see them and know he still watched over them.

The northern lights are the reflection of the great fires built by Nanaboozho according to the promise he gave to his people.——Ottawa

PENOBSCOT

The Penobscot are members of the Algonquian linquistic family and are closely related to the Abnaki, Passamaquoddy, Malecite, and Pennacook tribes. They lived on the shores of Penobscot Bay and along the Penobscot River in what is now the State of Maine.

The tribe, like most of their neighbors, were contacted by European fishermen and explorers early in the sixteenth century and have been exposed to their acculturation strategies almost constantly since that time. Never a very large group, estimated at about one thousand in colonial times, they have never been a political factor in America. Making peace with the English in 1749, they have remained in their homeland ever since.

Although the Penobscot have a tradition of migrating to their homeland from the Southwest, none of their stories reflect any characteristics of that area and are much like those of their Algonquian peers. A few of their stories are included in the next few pages.

The Hunter and the Eagle

Once there was a hunter who was known for his skill in hunting deer. He knew how to call them to eat in the open fields where they were easy targets for his arrows. As his fame grew, he was not content to be known as just a great deer hunter. He began to call to the eagles to come feast on the deer-meat and, when they would alight to eat, he would shoot them and take their feathers. Since eagles are sacred birds and are not to be killed, the people warned the hunter that what he was doing was extremely dangerous.

One day as the hunter called the eagles, the Mother of all Eagles soared over the field. The hunter was very frightened for he knew of the power of the great bird so he crawled into a hollow log to hide. The Eagle Mother picked up the log, with the man inside, and carried it away to her nest so her chicks could enjoy a meal by eating the hunter.

Glooscap and the Frog
Penobscot

Luckily the man had his leather carrying-thongs and some dried meat with him. When Eagle Mother left the nest again, the hunter tossed small portions of dried meat out to the young birds. When they lowered their heads to eat, the hunter bound their beaks shut with the thongs.

For two days Eagle Mother tried to untie the thongs which held her babies' mouths closed, but she could not release them. Finally she was forced to make an agreement with the man. She would return him to earth if he promised to shoot only deer and never again kill an eagle, provided he would first untie the beaks of her children. The hunter agreed and was returned to his people.

Until this time, his descendants keep the promise the hunter made to the Eagle Mother. Whenever a deer is killed, the shaman calls the eagles to come and eat in safety.——Penobscot

Glooscap Leaves the World

After dwelling on the land with his people for a long time, Glooscap finally rid the world of monsters. The giants no longer wandered about the wilderness; the giant flying monster, Cullo, terrified man no more as it spread its great wings and blocked out the sun; the Chenoo of the North no longer preyed on man; and no evil beasts, devils, or serpents were to be found near the home of man. Great Glooscap had, moreover, taught men the arts which made them happier. They were not, however, grateful to the Master, and although they worshipped him, they were still wicked.

When his children performed their evil deeds, lied and stole, killed and robbed, it made Glooscap very unhappy. Finally, he could stand no more and he made a rich feast by the shore of the Great Lake. All the animals came to it, and when the feast was over he got into a great canoe and paddled away. The beasts watched him until he disappeared from sight and still they could hear him singing. They listened to his song as it grew fainter and fainter until they could hear it no more. A deep silence fell on all the land as the animals realized their Great Father was gone.

Until now, the animals had all spoken one language but they realized that they could no longer understand each other. They became frightened and fled and to this day they have never again met in council. Until the day when Glooscap returns and makes men and animals live together once more in peace and contentment, all nature mourns.

Meanwhile, Glooscap still lives far away beyond the horizon. If a person travels far and long and is not afraid, and if his heart is pure, he may still find the home of the Great Glooscap. He may find the great wigwam where he is busy making arrows. The wigwam is half full of arrows now and when it is full Glooscap will come forth and make war on the monsters again.

And on whom will he make war? He will make war on the white people. He will expel them from his land. He will kill them all.——
Penobscot

Glooscap and the Frog

Glooscap had been sitting around with nothing to do for days, and he had become bored with home life. He bade Grandmother farewell and went out to inspect the rivers. He paddled his great stone canoe up and down all the streams of the land. In some he reduced the size of water-falls and in others cleared the rapids to make them more navigable. At one place he left his canoe (it remains to this day near the present-day town of Castine) and proceeded on foot. It was not long until he came to a village full of distressed people.

The people told him that Oglebamu, the giant frog, had taken over the stream and the people had no water and were dying of thirst. Glooscap went to the Spring which formed the river and, sure enough, there sat a huge frog, Oglebamu. All around the trees and grasses were dead and the frog drank the water as fast as it came out of the ground.

Give the people some water," said Glooscap.

They-can't-have-any," replied the frog.

Glooscap became furious at the frog's ignoring his command. He stamped his feet and roared with rage but the frog just kept on drink-ing the water. Glooscap grasped his great ax and swung it as if it were a feather, bringing it down upon the back of Oglebamu. So great was the blow that it broke the frog's back and caused him to vomit up all the water.

Still very angry, Glooscap grabbed the frog in his hands and squeezed him small. At first Glooscap was so upset that he denied the frog any water ever, but Oglebamu pleaded so hard that Glooscap's heart was softened. He gave the frog permission to live around the edge of ponds and streams but he could never have all the water. To this day you can see the marks on the back of the frog caused by Glooscap's ax which was swung with such fury long ago.

When the water gushed out of Oglebamu, it formed the Penobscot River. Many people, so happy to have the water back, plunged into the stream and were transformed into the many fishes and water-creatures we know today.——Penobscot

How the Negro Came to Be

Once there was a boy who laughed constantly at his parents and his friends. No matter how serious the situation or how sad other people were, this boy just laughed at them. Every time anyone said anything, he would laugh until he was black in the face.

This angered the Spirits so they turned him black and he became the father of the negro race. To this day, they are always laughing and showing their teeth.——Penobscot

SENECA

The westernmost of the Five (later Six) Nations, of the Iroquois Confederacy was the Seneca. Their territory extended from their neighboring Iroquoian neighbors the Cayuga on the east to the shores of Lake Erie on the west. The Confederacy compared their geographic locations to a longhouse compartmented by tribes, and under this arrangement the Seneca were "the keepers of the western door." It was through this door that all Iroquois nations passed to war or trade with other Indians to the south or west. All other Indians whether at peace or war must knock at this "western door" before entering the home country of the Confederacy.

The Seneca were the most powerful and most populous of the nations of the Confederacy. In the early days before white contact, they numbered about four thousand. Today there are still about that same number living in New York and another small group in the northeastern corner of Oklahoma. Like most Indians in America, the exposure to and pressure from the dominant society has taken its toll on the traditional Seneca way of life. Cultural attributes have been eroded and the people have seemingly assimilated to a great degree. Many facets of Seneca culture remain however, and are tenaciously held by the majority of the tribe.

Tribal structure, religion, the clan system, matriarchal dominance, and oral tradition are still very much alive in the Seneca people. Some of their stories are provided here as an indication that they do survive.

The Good Hunter or the Story of Little Water

There was once a young hunter who was loved by all the animals because of the kindness he showed them even though he had to kill them to survive.* He never shot a deer while it was swimming or took a doe that had a fawn. He never killed any animal from ambush or one he had taken by surprise or that was tired from long pursuit. The quarry was always given a chance to make his escape.

When the young man made a kill, some of the remains were always left behind for the "meat eaters" and he never completely harvested the wild honey he found but would always leave some for the bears. The entrails and other organic portions would be thrown into the lakes and streams to share with the fish and other water animals.

One day, while he was hunting, he was captured and scalped by some enemy tribesmen. When they had departed, Wolf smelled the blood and came to the young man and licked the bloody head. He howled a message to the rest of the animals, who gathered around and mourned for their friend. Bear felt the body and found a warm spot which let him know there was still a little life left in his friend. While the bear held the body to keep it warm, the birds met in a council to decide how to revive the young man. Only Turkey Buzzard did not agree and wanted to let him die so he could eat him.

Each of the birds and animals contributed a bit of themselves to a compound which would restore life—some a bit of brain, others a portion of heart or other vital part. The mixture of all these parts was so concentrated by the animals that it could all be contained in one small acorn shell.**

---

* Many tribal stories relate that the deer and other edible animals were placed on earth to provide food for man and are happy when they can fulfill the mission for which they were created.
** Because the mixture was so concentrated, the story and the ceremony are called Little Water.

It was clear to everyone that in order for the young man to live, he must have his scalp, but who was going to get it from the enemy tribe? One after another each animal volunteered but were found incapable of carrying out the task. Finally it was decided that the legged animals could not do it and it must be performed by some very clever bird. The choice eventually was made that Crow, who is the messenger for all birds, should be the one to retrieve the scalp.

Crow flew to the Cherokee village, for it was a Cherokee war party which had scalped the young man, and there he saw the scalp. It had been stretched on a hoop and hung up to dry over the smoke hole. He swooped down and grabbed it and flew away as fast as he could. The Cherokees saw him and started shooting arrows at him, but Crow flew too high for them to do any harm.

When the scalp was brought to the council, they found it had dried out too much to be worn by a living man. The Great Crow had to vomit on it and the Dew Eagle, who carried a pool of dew on his back, sprinkled some dew-drops on it. This made it supple and moist enough to grow back on the hunter's head. Since the birds had given the young man the medicine and had put his scalp back, he began to revive.

As he lay, still with his eyes closed, he realized he could understand the languages of the birds and the animals as they sang a wonderful song to him. He listened to it and was amazed that later he remembered every word. They told him to form a group and sing the song when their help was needed. The young man then asked for the formula for the magic medicine but the birds could not tell him, for he was not a virgin. They told him the secret would be revealed at a ceremony to someone when it was needed and would be told by singing their song.

The bear helped the young man to his feet, but when he opened his eyes, there was no one there. He saw only a circle of tracks around him, but the animals were all gone. Since it was now dawn, he went back to his village and related his experiences to his people. To this day the Little Water ceremony is observed by his tribe to honor the animals and thank them for saving the young man's life.——Seneca

The Little People

Many years ago an Iroquois boy was hunting for food for his family. He came to a deep ravine in which grew a tall tree. The top of this tree was about even with the boy as he stood on the edge of the ravine. As he looked across, he saw a black squirrel sitting on one of the top limbs. Just as the boy was about to loose his arrow at the squirrel, he heard strange voices which seemed to be coming from the base of the cliff below him.

He crawled to the edge and peered down. There he saw two little men who were shooting at the squirrel with their tiny bows and arrows but they could not shoot more than halfway up the tall tree. The boy shot the squirrel and it fell at the feet of the little men who were very excited at seeing such an enormous arrow. They tugged on it but could not get it out of the squirrel. They looked up and saw the boy and asked him to come down and remove the arrow. He did so and the little men asked if they could have the squirrel. They explained that black squirrel meat to them was like buffalo meat for the Indians. The boy not only agreed that they should have the game, but also gave them two gray squirrels he had shot earlier. The little men invited the boy to their camp to share a meal and to become their friend.

They went off through the woods until they came to a cave in the side of a hill which was the home of the little men. Inside was a little old man and a little old woman, the parents of the two hunters. The woman was pounding corn with a tiny mortar and pestle and gave the boy some corn soup in a tiny wooden bowl. He thought this would not be enough soup for someone his size, but no matter how much he ate, the bowl was always full. They then told him about themselves.

There were three tribes of the Great Little People. One lived along the Genesee River and under its falls, and this group was called the Stone Throwers. They were terribly strong and could hurl huge boulders and pull trees out of the ground, roots and all.

They told of another tribe who took care of the plants which grew in the area. It was their responsibility to awaken them when it was springtime, to see that the flowers bloomed, and turn the fruit so that it got the sun.

The third tribe lived in the caverns and it was their special task to guard all the entrances to the underworld. They were to prevent the white buffalo that lived there from breaking out and wreaking havoc on earth. When these buffalo did manage to escape, it was the job of this tribe to herd them back to the underground. In this sense the Little

People worked for the Indians and had always wanted to make their acquaintance.

The mother then prepared a feast: corn soup, using the meat of the black squirrel, and a drink of berry juice. The rest of the tribe joined the party: little men, women, and tiny children. They ate and then burned the sacred tobacco and sang the sacred songs to the beat of the tiny drum. They told the boy to learn them so he stayed for several days and they repeated the same rituals every night until the boy could go through the entire ceremony.

The Little People told him to perform this ritual three days after his return home and they and their kind would come and feast with the Indians. If the Indians heard the Little People drumming they were to go to the ravines and gulches from which the sound came and throw some tobacco down for the drummers. They also requested that the young people of the boy's tribe collect cut fingernails and throw them down, for when the animals which the Little People fear smelled the fingernails, they would think there were humans around and leave them alone. They then gave the young man a round white stone which would be a charm to help him when he was hunting.

They then took him to the cliff where their meeting took place and the boy returned to his own tribe. Upon arrival, however, he found everything changed. The village was overgrown with trees and there were no people there. He searched for his tribe and finally found them, but they did not recognize him. He had grown much older, for every day he had spent with the Little People was a year to the humans. He related his experiences with them and from that time, the Indians have never failed to give feasts for the Little People.——Seneca

How the Chipmunk Got Its Stripes

Many years ago, a grandmother and a granddaughter lived together. They had a skin blanket which they used to cover themselves at night to keep off the cold. Grandmother had had the blanket for many years and it was old and much of the hair was worn off.

The two women went into the forest to cut wood and took the blanket with them. After a few days in the forest they discovered their blanket had come to life and was very angry. They threw it down and started running for their home as fast as they could. The blanket had turned into a bear and was following them, growling and snarling. When they reached home, the bear was so near that as they pushed open the door to enter the cabin, the bear clawed at them and scratched their backs.

The old woman and her granddaughter were chipmunks, and, although they escaped the bear, since that time all chipmunks have stripes on their backs because of the bear scratches.——Seneca

How the Seneca Got Beans

When the Creator made the Seneca people he gave them corn and taught them how to plant and grow it. However, Corn grew alone in the fields and was very lonely.

One day the people heard some very beautiful singing and as it grew louder they realized it was coming from a lovely young lady as she walked down the banks of a stream. Her song was very sad, and, as she came closer, the Senecas could hear the words she sang:

> Who shall marry me?
> Who shall marry me?
> Let him ask for my hand.
> Oh, who shall marry me?

A great black bear appeared suddenly out of the woods and stood with his forepaws waving in the air. "I will marry you and care for you all your life."

The beautiful woman seemed frightened at the loud voice from this huge creature and asked timidly, "If I marry you, what kind of food will you bring me to eat?"

The bear bellowed his answer, "I'll bring you berries and nuts, and since I am the strongest animal in the woods, I'll give you all you want to eat, lots of blackberries, lots of blueberries, many walnuts and pecans. This is what I will give you to eat."

The beautiful lady sadly shook her head, "I would surely starve to death on that food. I cannot live with you." And she began to sing her song again:

> Who shall marry me?
> Who shall marry me?
> Let him ask for my hand!
> Oh, who shall marry me?

Suddenly a great buck deer came crashing out of the woods. He stood on the riverbank and held his huge rack of horns up proudly and said, "I will marry you."

The woman looked at the deer and asked the same question, "If I marry you, what will you bring me to eat?"

The buck deer replied, "I know where the tender leaves and buds and shoots grow and I will bring the best of these for you to eat."

The woman shook her head and sadly said, "I could never eat that food. I would surely starve to death if I should marry you. I am sorry, Buck Deer." She then began her sad song again.

> Who shall marry me?
> Who shall marry me?
> Let him ask for my hand!
> Oh, who shall marry me?

All at once, a great roar shook the forest and a huge mountain lion sprang onto a log beside the river. "I will marry you," he said.

"And what would you bring me to eat?" replied the beautiful woman.

The mountain lion answered, "I am the greatest hunter in the whole world, and our lodge would always have plenty of fresh meat. That is what I would bring you to eat."

The beautiful woman shook her head and replied, "I would never be able to live with you for I would surely starve with only fresh meat to eat. I cannot marry you," and sadly she began her song again:

> Who shall marry me?
> Who shall marry me?
> Let him ask for my hand!
> Oh, who will marry me?

Suddenly a great gray wolf leaped out of the woods, lifted his head high, and gave a mighty howl. Every creature in the forest trembled with fear when they heard his loud voice, "I will marry you, beautiful lady," he said.

She looked at him and asked the same question she had asked of the other animals, "If I marry you, what kind of food will you bring me to eat?"

The huge wolf lifted his head and howled, "I am the most cunning hunter in these woods, and I will always bring you plenty of venison and rabbits to eat. You will never go hungry if you marry me."

The beautiful lady shook her head. "I never eat such food and if I lived with you, I would surely starve." She shook her head even more sadly than before and once again began to sing her song:

> Who shall marry me?
> Who shall marry me?
> Let him ask for my hand!
> Oh, who will marry me?

A handsome young man appeared and walked over to the river bank. He sat down on a log and looked at the beautiful woman. He looked at her a very long time and listened to her sad song. At last he said to her, "I will marry you." The woman stopped singing and looked at the handsome young man. Finally, she asked him the same question she had asked all the animals, "If I marry you, what kind of food will you bring me?"

The young man answered, "If you marry me I will give you corn to eat. Corn is the gift of the Creator, and this is what I will give to you."

The beautiful young woman smiled happily and replied, "Of all the foods in the world, I love corn best of all. If that is the food you will bring to me, I will be glad to marry you." The woman ran to him and threw her arms around his neck and hugged him tightly. They walked off into the woods together and disappeared.

The Senecas who were hiding in the woods watching what had happened were very frightened for this was truly an unusual thing they had seen. They told all the villages what they had seen and heard and everyone wondered what it meant.

The next morning as the Senecas went out to work in their corn fields they were greeted by a strange sight. In each hill of corn there was a strange plant growing. Its vines grew up the corn and its arms hugged the corn plant as tightly as the beautiful woman had hugged the handsome young man. It was only then that the people realized what they had seen the day before. The beautiful woman was the spirit of the bean plant who had come to live among the Seneca and the young man was the spirit of corn.

Ever since that day, which was a very long time ago, the Seneca people have planted beans in each hill of corn. The beautiful bean woman and the handsome corn man have lived happily together to this very day.——Seneca

How the People Received the Plants

Once, long ago, Sky Woman had a beautiful daughter. The girl had a lover who appeared in the image of a vine. Soon the young girl became pregnant and eventually gave birth to twin boys. These sons were not at all alike and Elder One made his mother happy while Warty One caused her great pain and eventually killed her. Elder One, called Good Mind, helped Sky Woman prepare his mother's burial place.

When her daughter was ready to be placed in the grave, Sky Woman spoke to her: "Soon you will receive many beings from below and you must be ready for them, for the path will be trodden by many."

After the burial, Good Mind stayed and carefully watered the earth above his mother's grave. Soon buds began to appear and plants began to grow all over the grave. From the area of his mother's head sprouted the tobacco plant which was used in ceremonials to assure wisdom. From her breasts grew corn which nourished all the people. From her abdomen came the squash plant whose fruit is shaped like her stomach. The bean plant sprang from her hands, the pods resembling the long fingers of the woman, and from her feet grew the potato plant with its tubers looking like her toes.

Thus from the body of the daughter of Sky Woman came the vegetable foods which sustain the people to this day.——Seneca

Five

The Northwest Indians

This section deals with groups of people indigenous to the northwestern portion of the North American Continent, such as the Eskimo and Athapaskan, the Pacific coastal tribes, those who inhabit the Columbia Plateau, and some elements who are native to the Rocky Mountains. This huge geographic area is the homeland of a multitude of diverse peoples who speak numerous dialects belonging to several linguistic stocks.

The Eskimo is not Indian but is one of the native groups under the jurisdiction of the Bureau of Indian Affairs, is of Asiatic ethnological and physiological orientation and speaks the non-Indian Eskimunian language.

In general the coastal tribes shared vigorous, dramatic cultures. Normally, more advanced cultures in America were always agriculturally based. The northwestern coastal Indians, however, have developed stable, complex societies marked by wealth-consciousness, technical specialization, class distinction, and highly developed artistic traditions.

Some of the facets of the Northwest Coast cultures are most interesting. The carving and utilization of totem poles in their esthetic life and the celebration of potlatch ceremonies are, to a degree, unique. Physiologically these people are somewhat different from their peers in that fairly heavy growths of face and body hair are not unusual and a fair complexion is quite common.

The Plateau area is defined by the drainages of the Fraser, Columbia, and Snake Rivers. This area formed a center for cultures on the periphery and cultural perspectives of these marginal units are evidenced with those living on the Plateau. The eastern segments show portions of Rocky Mountain aspects, southern units have definite Basin characteristics, and western tribes show a close relationship with the coastal groups.

Rocky Mountain Indians display a combination of gathering, hunting, and semiagricultural cultural activities. Integration and acculturation has had definite effects on these people with acceptance varying from isolation and rejection, as with the Blackfeet, to very early invitations and overt efforts at integration displayed by the Nez Percé and Cayuse people.

Each tribal unit in this very large area has been subjected to varying degrees of assimilation pressures. Some have acculturated markedly and others have maintained cultural integrity and have kept the perspectives which have sustained their needs for countless centuries.

It would be an impossible task to present the oral traditions of any one of the groups represented in its entirety. The author offers the few stories in the following section as a mere sampling in order to illustrate that the stories do exist and are being perpetuated.

ATHAPASCAN

The Athapascan language family is made up of dialects of myriad tribes generally located in the Alaskan interior, the Yukon, and along the northwest Pacific coastal region. The most notable exceptions are the Navajo and the various Apache groups in the southwestern United States.

The Nahane form a major division of the Athapascan linguistic stock. They live in small nomadic bands in northern British Columbia and the Yukon Territory between the coast range and the Rocky Mountains and extending north to the Mackenzie River. Although scattered over a wide expanse, the population of the Nahane was never more than one thousand to fifteen hundred.

The Navajo, with today's population of around one hundred and fifty thousand, constitutes the largest tribe in America. They and the various Apache bands made their exodus from the North in the comparatively recent past, arriving in the Southwest only a short time before the Spaniards. These groups' stories were dealt with in another section of this book, so the following story is representative of the Nahane Athapascans of the Northwest.

Why Animals Are Lean in Winter

There is a certain being who lives in the moon which decides whether a hunt shall be successful or not. It is necessary to request his assistance before an expedition is started or it is doomed to failure.

This personage once lived with the people long ago when the world was young. He appeared among them as a poor ragged boy that an old woman had found and taken into her home and was bringing up as her own son.

The young man made himself look ridiculous to the other members of the group by constructing a pair of gigantic snowshoes. His friends could not comprehend why such a scrawny person would make such large snowshoes. Each day, however, he would leave camp by himself on the huge snowshoes and always return in the evening with no game. The other men, even though they could scarcely ever make a kill, seemed to regularly come on trails that would lead them to one or two freshly killed animals. They were extremely glad to get the game, for without it the people might have starved. They were very curious as to where and how the game always was there waiting for them when they had such poor hunting experiences.

Suspicion at last pointed to the boy and his great shoes as being implicated some way in the matter, and he was watched closely by the other members of his tribe. It soon became evident that it was he who had kept the group alive by leaving the carcasses for the hunters to find. Surprisingly, the people were not grateful, even though he had saved their lives, and continued to treat him with disrespect.

On one occasion the people, eating the meat which he had supplied, refused him a certain piece of fat he had requested. That night the boy disappeared, leaving his clothes hanging on a tree. He returned to them in a month, however, appearing as a full-grown man and dressed as

"Scarface," the Star Boy
Blackfeet

such. He told them he had made his home in the moon and that he would always look down with a kindly eye to their success in hunting. He added, though, that as a punishment for their greed and ingratitude in refusing the piece of fat, all animals should be lean the long winter through and fat only during the short summer months. And it has been that way ever since.——Athapascan

BLACKFEET

The Siksika, or Blackfeet, are made up of three major subtribes: the Siksika or Blackfeet proper, the Kainah or Bloods, and the Piegan. They belong to the Algonquian linguistic stock and are located in the territory stretching from North Saskatchewan River, Canada, to the southern headstreams of the Missouri River in Montana.

The Blackfeet were one of the largest and more warlike of the northern Plains tribes. They fought at one time or another with most of their neighbors and had a distinct dislike for explorers and traders. They were the only group of Indians to provide trouble for the Lewis and Clark Expedition.

The population of the Blackfeet has not varied as drastically as that of many tribes, and today there are about twelve thousand recognized Blackfeet, compared to fifteen thousand estimated by Mooney in 1780.

Because of their rather isolated location, they have been able to maintain many of their traditional ways. Aside from a couple of epidemics of smallpox, little interference has been noted from white society. Acculturation has taken place but more in the material aspects of life than the spiritual. Coersive pressures have been less evident with the Blackfeet than with most Indian groups.

The story of "Scarface" is one of the many stories kept alive by these resolute people.

"Scarface," the Star Boy

Long ago a maiden named Feather Woman was sleeping in the grass beside her tipi. The Morning Star loved her and she became with child. From then on she suffered the disdain and ridicule of her tribesfolk. One day, as she went to the river for water, she met a young man who said he was her husband, Morning Star. She saw in his hair a yellow feather, and in his hand a juniper branch with a spider web hanging from it. He was tall and straight and his hair was long and shining. His beautiful clothes were of soft-tanned skins and from them came a fragrance of sweetgrass and sage.

Morning Star placed the feather in the hair of Feather Woman and, giving her the juniper branch, directed her to shut her eyes. She was then told to hold the upper strand of the spider web in her hand and to place her foot in the lower one. In a moment she was transported to the sky. Morning Star then led her to the lodge of his parents, the Sun and the Moon. There she gave birth to a son, Star Boy (Jupiter).

The Moon, her mother-in-law, gave her a root-digger and told her she could dig up whatever roots she wanted except the large turnip which grew near the home of Spider Man. Curiousity finally overcame her fear and Feather Woman, with the aid of two cranes, uprooted the forbidden turnip and found that it covered a window in the sky which looked down to the earth she had left. Peering through the window, she saw the camp of her people and became very homesick. The Sun, her husband's father, decreed that she must be banished from the sky and returned to earth. Morning Star took her to the home of Spider Man, whose web had drawn her to the sky, and with her baby, Star Boy, in her arms, she was lowered back to the earth. Here, pining for her husband and the lost sky-land, she died having first told her people her story.

Her son grew up in poverty and, because of a scar on his face, was named "Scarface." When he grew up, he fell in love with a beautiful maiden, but she refused him because of the scar. A medicine woman told him the scar could only be removed by the Sun God himself. The boy set out for the lodge of the solar deity, traveling westward toward where the sun set every day. He eventually came to the shore of a great sea where he fasted for three days. On the fourth day, he saw a bright trail leading across the water, and following it, he came to the lodge of the Sun God.

In the sky world, Star Boy killed seven huge birds who were threatening the life of Morning Star and, as a reward, the Sun not only removed the scar from his face, but also taught him the ritual of the Sun Dance. He then gave Star Boy raven feathers to wear as a sign that he came from the Sun, and gave him a lover's flute and a song which would win the heart of the maiden he loved.

The Sun sent him back to earth by way of the short path, Milky Way, telling him to instruct his people in the ritual of the dance. He did as he was instructed, teaching his people all about the Sun Dance, and then Star Boy and his love returned to the sky world. This is how the Blackfeet learned the ritual of the Sun Dance.——Blackfeet

CAYUSE

Prior to the coming of the white man, the Cayuse Indians controlled an area of land around the headwaters of the Wallawalla, Umatilla, and Grande Ronde Rivers. Their first contact with the invading European society was in 1804 when the Lewis and Clark Expedition entered their country. Later they became well known to explorers and hunters, and, while they were fierce warriors, they generally were friendly to whites.

In 1838 a mission was established among them by the noted Reverend Marcus Whitman. In 1847, however, smallpox killed a number of the tribe, and the Cayuse, believing the missionaries had caused the epidemic, murdered Whitman and many other whites and destroyed the mission. Warfare followed, and the tribe was drastically reduced in number, and by 1851 they had partially merged with the Nez Perce. Two years later they signed the treaty which created the Umatilla Reservation in Oregon where the few remaining tribespeople now live.

Warfare, integration, and suppression have nearly obliterated the Cayuse and their cultural institutions. The following story is one of the last fragments of Cayuse culture remaining.

How the Falls of the Palouse Were Made

At one time there was a family of giants living along the Palouse River. It consisted of four brothers and a sister. One day the girl begged the boys to get her some beaver fat. This was no easy task for there was only one beaver in the entire country, and he was an animal of extraordinary size and activity. The four boys, in spite of this fact, set out to find the monster. Soon they caught sight of him near the mouth of the Palouse, then a quiet peaceful river gliding through an even, winding channel.

They at once gave chase, heading the giant beaver up the river. They had not chased him far when they succeeded in making the first strike with their spears. The beaver shook and thrashed around in the river, forming the first rapids of the Palouse, and then ran further upstream. Again the brothers overtook him, pinning him to the river bed with their weapons, and again the vigorous beast writhed away, making in the process the second falls of the Palouse.

Another chase, and in a third and fatal attack, the four spears were thrust through the broad wounded back. There was a last stubborn struggle at the spot and the great falls called Aputaput were made. There was a tearing of earth and a lashing of water in the fierce death-flurry and then the great beaver was dead.

The brothers, having secured the skin and fat, cut up the body and threw it in all the various directions. From these pieces originated the many nations of Indian people who now live in the country.——Cayuse

ESKIMO

The Eskimo constitute a separate linguistic stock of the aboriginal inhabitants of this hemisphere. Although they are not technically Indians, but distinctly Asiatic by race, they are included in the responsibility of the Bureau of Indian Affairs. On physical and linguistic grounds they are usually set apart from the other natives of America.

The Eskimo are known to have ocupied a large area of North America at one time. They extended from the Gulf of St. Lawrence, around the entire northeastern and northern coast of Canada to the Alaskan boundary, and around the Alaskan peninsula to the Aleutian Islands. They also lived in Baffin Land and many other islands in the Arctic as well as the entire west coast and most of the east coast of Greenland. Eskimo settlements are also found today along the north coast of Siberia.

The Norse settlers of Greenland were probably the first whites to see these unique people, about A.D. 1000. Other explorers contacted them in the eighteenth and nineteenth centuries but it was well into the twentieth century before the inland Eskimos were known.

The population of these people in the prewhite era has been estimated at about seventy-five thousand. Current Eskimo population, scattered throughout northern Alaska and Canada is considered to be only about one-half that number, about thirty-five thousand. The en-

croachment into their hunting grounds by outsiders, the unbalancing
of natural ecology, introduction of diseases for which there was no natural immunity, and other forces brought on by contact with whites has
caused the drastic reduction in the number of Eskimo people.

Along with the depletion of population, the acculturation by association and the influence of missionary activity has seriously eroded the
cultural integrity of traditional Eskimo beliefs. Some facets of the traditional culture remain intact, however, especially in the rural areas.
As with many other native groups, there has been a revival of the "old
ways" and a return to the age-old traditions. Stories which have been
passed down from generation to generation for centuries are becoming
popular and are being recorded for the first time in books and manu-
scripts.

Two such stories are offered here as a tribute to the Eskimo people
and their struggle for cultural survival.

The Giant Child

Once, long ago, lived two giants. No one knows how they were created
or by whom or even who they were. They lived by hunting as the Eskimos do today. Somehow they had a girl child who grew very rapidly
and had an enormous appetite, even for a giant child. Even worse than
her great appetite was her desire to eat flesh whenever she could find it.

One night she even began to eat the limbs of her sleeping parents.
Waking in horror, they grabbed the terrible girl and took her far out to
the deepest parts of the sea in an umiak (a large skin-covered boat used
for whale hunting and transportation). Once they were at the deepest
water, the parents cut off the girl's fingers. As they fell in the water, the
severed fingers became schools of fish and whales and seals. The giant
parents became even more frightened at this and, throwing the child in
the water, paddled home as fast as they could. They lived to be very
old and finally fell asleep and were frozen in the same manner as some
Eskimos did and still do.

The evil child, living beneath the sea, became Sedna, mother of all
sea creatures. She was responsible for storms at sea, and she directed
migration of her many children—the whales, seals, and fish of all
kinds.

The Eskimo believe that Sedna is always there and could always be approached by the angakok (shaman) while he was in a trance. Great spiritual power was given to the angakok and when there was a crisis, such as a shortage of food, he would go into a trance to speak with Sedna. His soul would leave his body and go beneath the sea. There he would visit with Sedna in her beautiful tent. She would listen to the requests of her people, sung as a hymn by the soul of the shaman.

Finally, Sedna would give the angakok a message. It would either be a threat of death unless the people moved to another location or a promise of food from her inexhaustible supply. The soul of the angakok would then return to his body and he would become conscious and recount, in a magic song, what Sedna had told him. The people would then act on her wishes and survive——Eskimo

Eskimo Traditional Beliefs

Newborn female babies are wiped off with the skin of a ground squirrel to insure beauty. If the baby is a male child, the skin from the forehead of a bull caribou is used so he will be a good hunter.

The beak of a yellow-bellied loon is touched to the lips of a newborn male to make the child a good singer.

Male babies have special charms sewn to their clothing: two little bones from the foot of a wolf to give staying power on the hunt, a ptarmigan feather to give camouflage ability, fox hair to ensure agility, or the hair of the weasel or ermine to make him a great killer of game.

When a death occurs, the body remains in the house four days and for five days the women in the family remain on the sleeping platform. Neither men nor women can take part in sewing or sawing for four days and they cannot hammer anything or break any bones.

After killing his first seal, an Eskimo boy wipes the blood off the head and pours some fresh water in its mouth.

The Queen of the Underworld

Long ago on the shores of the Arctic Ocean lived a beautiful maiden with her father. Her beauty had attracted many young men but she had never given her heart to any of them. One Spring day, however, she was wooed and won by the lyric song of the great fulmar bird, who promised her all his love and the luxuries of the world. The young girl ran off with the great bird, only to find she had been deceived. She lived in misery until her father came to rescue her.

He killed the fulmar and fled with his daughter in his boat. Many other fulmars flew after the pair and beat up a violent storm with their great wings. The cowardly father offered the girl to the birds. He pushed her overboard and, as she clung to the edge of the boat, cut off the ends of her fingers, which fell into the sea and became whales. She would still not let go, so the father next cut off the rest of her fingers, which became seals. The fulmars did not want the girl so they flew away. The father then pulled his daughter back into the boat and they returned home.

When they arrived, the girl was so angry with her father for what he did to her that she set the dogs on him. Suddenly, during the turmoil, father and daughter slipped into a hole in the earth and dropped to the underworld where ever since the girl has reigned as queen.——Eskimo

FLATHEADS

There is no Flathead Nation or tribe per se, the name is derived from the practice of some groups of Indians in the Plateau area of Idaho, Washington and Montana of binding the foreheads of infants to flatten them. Today, Flatheads are generally the descendants of Salish and Kutenai people who intermarried and who live on the Flathead Reservation in western Montana.

These Plateau Indians have always lived peacefully with their neighbors and in the early nineteenth century welcomed the Lewis and Clark Expedition as it made its way through their country. In 1825, Sir George Simpson, administrator for the Hudson's Bay Company, held council with the Flathead and other tribes in the area to establish fur trade with them. The Flatheads requested that missionaries be sent to teach them the white man's religion and ways. When no one came to fulfill their request, delegates from the Indians in 1831 were dispatched on a two thousand mile trip to St. Louis to seek assistance. It was not until 1835, however, that religious teachers began to arrive in the Plateau country.

Since they were peaceful and welcomed the whites, the Flatheads integrated easily, and native customs and traditions were hard to maintain. Although much of the oral tradition disappeared, a few of their stories still remain. The following are examples of these:

The Giant Beaver

In the mountains, in what is now northwestern Montana, a long timne ago lived a giant beaver. Beaver was so large that a dozen of the bravest warriors were no match for him. He lived in a large lake and ruled the entire country, doing just as he pleased.

Beaver was so large that his lake was too shallow for him. He decided to build a large dam across one end and make the water much deeper. As his dam got higher and higher, the lake got deeper and deeper, and the river below the dam got drier and drier. Soon there was no water at all in the river and Beaver was very happy.

One winter, however, there was more snow than usual and it piled up very high on the frozen lake and on the nearby mountains. Toward the end of winter a warm Chinook wind began blowing in the valley where the Beaver's lake was located. In one night, as the temperature climbed much higher than usual, all the snow on the lake melted and much of it on the mountains also thawed. This made more water than the dam could hold and before long the pressure was so great the whole thing washed out. The water poured out of the broken dam and flooded the valley below, carving a new course for the river.

Beaver was killed in the flood but you can still see the remnants of his dam at the south end of Flathead Lake.——Flathead

How the Sun and Moon Came to Be

Long ago when the earth was young, there was no light, and the animals, who were made first, lived in darkness. Even after the creation of man, everything was done without light for there was no sun or moon.

The leader of all the creatures on earth decided that there should be light and called all the people and animals together for a great council. He called on everyone for suggestions, and finally the skunk suggested that one of the animals should go up into the sky and become the Sun. Beaver added that there should also be a Moon to give lesser light by night. Now the question was posed as to who would be the Sun, for there could be only one, and who would be the Moon.

After much deliberation, Raven was selected to go to the sky and become the Sun. He was very happy and flew off into the sky. In the morning, Raven started across the sky from the east and in the evening he went down behind the west edge of the world. Then he came back to the village. The animals were not happy with the Raven Sun for he was so black, it had stayed dark all day.

They discussed the situation at great length and decided Chicken Hawk might make a good Sun since he was a large bird and his feathers were not black like Raven's.

Everyone agreed to let Chicken Hawk play the sun the next day. So, early in the morning Chicken Hawk rose in the eastern sky and started his journey across the sky. He went down in the west that evening and made his way back home. The animals, however, were not satisfied with his performance for all day, everything was yellow. It looked as if a great storm was going to come on them and they knew they could not be comfortable with a yellow sky.

Coyote was the next to try to be the Sun. He rose in the east and made his way across the sky until he went down in the west. However, the entire day was so hot the animals had to jump in the river to keep from burning up. Even the river got so hot it nearly cooked the animals. It was quite evident that Coyote could not be the Sun.

Some of the children heard the animals were playing Sun, and they wanted to be included. Elder Brother and Younger Brother both wanted to play the Sun but, since there could only be one Sun, Elder Brother was allowed to try first. The next morning Elder Brother rose in the eastern sky and made his way toward the west. The animals were very pleased for Elder Brother was neither too hot nor too bright.

Now Younger Brother wanted to be the Sun, too, and raised quite a commotion. Since the animals were quite content with Elder Brother for the Sun, it was decided that Younger Brother could be the Sun at night while Elder Brother was sleeping. So Younger Brother went up into the sky, and when Elder Brother went into his house in the west to sleep, Younger Brother played the Sun. He was a very good Night Sun, neither too warm nor too bright. It was decided that Younger Brother would be called Moon and there would never be anyone else to play Sun or Moon.

And that is the way it is, even today.——Kutenai (Flathead)

HAIDA

The Haida are rather typical of the general public's concept of Northwest Coast Indians. They are fishermen and traders, live along the water on Queen Charlotte Islands, carve totem poles and have potlatch ceremonies. These facets of Haida culture seem quite like that of their neighbors but aside from these apparent similarities the groups are quite diverse.

Each Haida village maintained its independence and had its own tribal government. Since the clan and moiety system of the Haida and the operation of their internal affairs is so complicated that the missionaries could not comprehend it, pressures to change have been lighter than on other indigenous people. The potlatch ceremony, which constitutes an important portion of Haida religious life, has been retained in its original form. The following stories illustrate the oral tradition still very much alive in the Haida communities.

How Raven Brought Light

A long time ago, darkness was everywhere beneath the clouds and the people were miserable. This was because a powerful chief far up the Nass River had a great carved box in which he kept the ball of light.

One day Raven was in the Queen Charlotte Islands helping the Haida people when he heard about the plight of the people on the mainland. When his tasks were completed, Raven decided to fly to the headwaters of the Nass River. Gathering all of the small pebbles he could carry with him, Raven took off on his eastward flight across Hecate Strait. Whenever he became tired, Raven dropped a pebble which splashed into the sea below and became an island on which he could alight and rest. He dropped his small stones all the way to the mouth of the Nass River on the mainland. The islands are still there today if one knows where to look.

Now Raven knew that the powerful chief who owned the box containing the light also had a daughter, and when he arrived at the headwaters of the Nass River, he observed that the chief's daughter went every day to a certain spring for water. Consequently, after much cunning thought, Raven decided upon a clever plan by which he would trick the chief. So he flew down to the spring and changed himself into a spruce needle floating on the water.

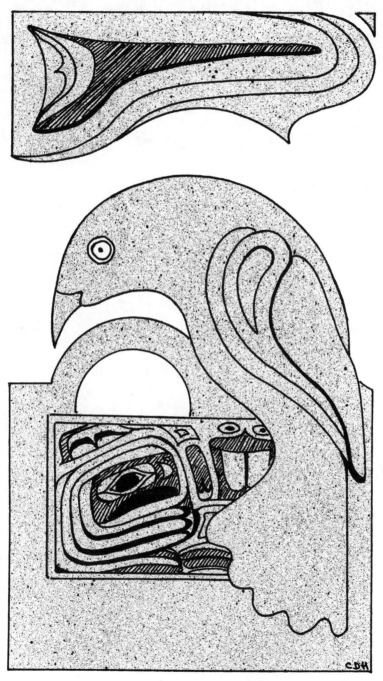

How Raven Brought Light
Haida

Presently along came the daughter of the selfish chief. As was her daily custom, the daughter drank several sips of the clear, cool spring water before filling the water containers for her father's house. As she sipped the water, the spruce needle washed down her throat. After a time it became obvious that the chief's daughter was pregnant. When the baby—who was really Raven—was born, the chief was delighted to be the grandfather of a healthy baby boy. The baby grew very rapidly because his grandfather stretched him every day, as was the custom of fathers who wanted strong, tall boys. Soon the baby was crawling all over the chief's great house and exploring every corner. He seemed to be searching for something among the many carved storage boxes which contained food, clothing, blankets, weapons, and ceremonial masks.

One day the baby boy began to wail and cry. Whenever his mother or his grandfather tried to comfort him the baby cried more loudly. So the chief called the elders and wise men of his clan to council. He asked each of them what should be done to comfort the baby and make him happy. This was exactly what the baby wanted the chief to do. One after the other, the wise men tried to discover what the baby wanted. Finally Raven caused one of the elders to suggest giving the baby the ball of light to play with.

The chief ordered his servants to bring him the great carved cedar box from its place near the wall. After lifting the lid of the box, the chief took out the precious ball of light and placed it on the floor beside the baby. Immediately the baby stopped crying and played happily with the ball, rolling around the floor and talking baby talk. After playing for a while, the baby rolled the ball to one side pretending to be tired. Happy to see his grandson contented, the chief put the ball of light safely in its box. The baby did not cry again.

Now for the first time since the baby began to crawl about, the household could sleep. Every day the baby was given the ball of light to play with, and every day his grandfather stretched him to help him grow stronger and taller. All the time the baby was secretly scheming. As he played with the light ball, he planned how he could escape and fly away with the magic daylight. Because the smoke hole in the roof was never open when he played with the ball of light, the baby decided to watch for the door to be opened.

One day during the season of fishing when people were going to and coming from the chief's house, the baby was playing with the ball. For a short time the door stood open, and while rolling the ball around, the baby managed to approach it without being noticed.

Suddenly the supernatural baby transformed itself to his true Raven form, clutched the ball of light in his talons, and before his mother or grandfather could interfere, flew through the open doorway toward the river. Downstream flew the mischievous Raven until he became hungry.

Alighting in the top branches of a tall cedar tree, Raven watched the people fishing in the darkness. The only light to pierce the gloom was from their fish-oil torches. Finally, when his hunger got the best of him, Raven called out loudly for the people to give him some fish to eat. But the people, busy with their nets in the Nass River, told him to come and get his own fish, as they were having trouble catching enough for themselves.

The Raven threatened to let the light out of the daylight ball if they refused to give him some fish. The very bright light would blind them if it was let out of the daylight ball. The people thought about the matter. Then they asked the Raven how he could get the ball of light because it was a holy thing kept in a great carved box by a chief at the head of the river.

This remark made Raven very angry. The people evidently did not realize that he was the creator and that he was therefore supernatural. Holding the light ball so the people could see it, he commanded that they give him fish or he would break the ball and they would all die. The people dared the Raven to break the ball, saying they would be able to see better to fish with bright light. And they shouted with much laughter and mocked Raven.

With this disrespectful reply from the fishermen below, Raven clutched the ball tightly with his talons and with his strong beak pecked a hole in it.

All of a sudden light flashed throughout the entire Nass River valley. With cries of alarm the people fishing on the river below perished. To the last person the fishermen vanished, never to be seen again because they were all ghost people.

Now that light had come to the world of the Nass River, other people, real human beings, came from all around to fish for the eulachon, which are called candlefish today. The new people had plenty of oil for their night lamps and for seasoning their food. These new people were the first Indians in that region. They built cedar-plank houses, made dug-out canoes, totem poles, and masks and formed the Tsimshian tribes of the Nass, where many of them still live.——Haida

How Mosquitoes Started

Once many years ago, five brothers were out hunting when a strange man came into their camp. After he had been there for a while, the eldest brother began to complain of a headache. The pain became so great that he cried and moaned and nothing his brothers could do seemed to bring any relief.

Finally, the stranger asked if he could try, and, upon receiving permission, secretly sucked the brains from the sick brother's head. The man was really an evil ogre who was dressed to look like a man.

Then the evil one killed all the brothers except the youngest who escaped by running away. He ran around the forest and through the meadows and the ogre was always close behind. The brother ran to the mountains where he saw a large lake. He came to a large log floating in the water made of two trees growing together so as to make a fork. He ran out on the log and threw himself in the crotch and the ogre followed.

However, when the evil one got to the fork in the log, he saw the brother's shadow in the water and sprang on it, falling into the lake.

The brother commenced singing a magic song, and the lake began to freeze. As the ogre struggled to escape the ice, the brother sang louder and the lake froze so fast, it captured the ogre. Only his head was above the ice. The brother then cut a lot of dry wood and piled it on the head of the ogre and lit a great fire. As the head burned, the ashes which arose from it turned into mosquitoes. And that is how they started.——Haida

How the Cedar Trees Grew

In the long ago when the Great Tetl, the Maker of the World, was seeking a land where His people might live, His friend Butterfly hovered around His head wherever He went. They finally came to a place where there was plenty of greenery, a land where islands dotted the coast, and where there were many bears. Butterfly alighted on Tetl's shoulder and pointed to this beautiful place. He said, "Wherever you find bears, you find salmon and honey, herbs and berries. This is a good place for our people to live."

No sooner had the Haida come to this land of peace and plenty though, than they immediately began to quarrel. The Great Tetl warned them that if they did not stop their bickering and live in peace, they would be destroyed. They begged for another chance and Tetl granted their wishes.

It was not long, however, until evil deeds and greed returned and the fighting started all over again. It was then the Great Tetl told them they would suffer the punishment they deserved.

A great darkness descended on the land and no sunshine was seen for many days. Everything was covered with fog and mist. After a time, the light came again and all the people had turned into huge cedar trees.

A great voice thundered across the land saying, "When men who can live in peace among themselves come again to occupy this fair land, it is from these red cedars they will get the boards with which to build their homes. The trunks of these great trees will be used to make canoes. From the fibers they will weave their clothing and from the roots they will make their baskets and mats. They will even use the inner bark for food in the early part of Spring.

Thus, from evil came great good, for the cedar trees can furnish all the needs for man's daily life.——Haida

NEZ PERCÉ

The Nez Percé, a French term meaning "pierced noses," once occupied a large part of central Idaho and sections of southeastern Washington and northeastern Oregon. Their first extensive exposure to the white man was when the Lewis and Clark Expedition passed through their territory in 1805. Friendly relations developed and the Nez Percé supplied the whites and provided them with guides who directed their journey all the way to the Pacific Ocean. The first friction followed the discovery of gold in the West which caused a constant influx of white miners and settlers.

By treaties concluded in 1855 and 1863, the Nez Percé, in an effort to keep peace, ceded all their lands to the United States except one large reservation. The band which lived in the Wallowa Valley refused to agree to the final treaty which called for them to give up their homeland, and the Nez Percé War began in 1877. It was during this conflict that Chief Joseph made his daring retreat in an attempt to remove his people to Canada.

After his ultimate defeat, marked by his eloquent surrender speech, Joseph and about four hundred of his followers were sent to Oklahoma. Because of the heavy loss of life brought on by living in this alien country, in 1885 this small group of Nez Percé were allowed to move to the Colville Reservation in eastern Washington.

Today there are about one thousand Nez Percé living on the Lapwai Reservation in Idaho and a few descendants of Joseph's band living at the Colville Reservation. This is all that remains of the six thousand people who welcomed Lewis and Clark in 1805.

Although their only crimes were being friendly to the Americans, accepting and even seeking Christianity, and wanting to escape the pressure of white society when it became unbearable, these noble people suffered tremendously. A few of their stories are still told by the elders in spite of the extreme acculturation the tribe has experienced. Samples of this oral tradition are related here.

How the Blind Man Got Even

Once there was a man who was blind. His wife was very cruel to him and fed him only snow while she ate dried salmon and berries. She thought that if she fed the blind man only snow, he would soon die.

One day a large grizzly bear who had been hunting along the river wandered into the camp. The woman was extremely frightened and called to her husband to shoot the bear. She helped him place the arrow in the bow and aimed it for him. The arrow flew straight to its mark, hitting the grizzly in the heart. The woman, seeing a way to further punish her blind husband, told him he had missed the bear and only frightened it away. After ridiculing the blind man, she secretly skinned the bear and cooked the meat. While she greedily ate the bear meat, her blind husband was fed only snow.

Now the blind man thought his wife was deceiving him for he had heard his arrow hit the bear. He asked the woman to bring him the arrow he had shot. When she threw it down beside the old man, he could still smell the scent of the bear blood on it, so he knew his wife was not being truthful with him.

He was confused and could not think straight so that night he left the cabin and made his way through the snow to Bitter Lake. As he sat on the bank feeling sorry for himself, Loon popped his head out of the water and asked why he was so sad.

Blind Man replied, "I am old and blind and no good for anything. I wish I could die."

The loon answered the man, "Lie down and weep and your troubles will be over."

The blind man lay down in the snow and wept and out of his eyes came blood and smoke, ashes and dust and hair. And when he opened his eyes, he saw the lake, the trees, the snow, and the moonlight. He was not blind anymore!

He heard his wife calling his name and he ran and hid in the underbrush. When the woman found his blood and hair and the ashes, she was overjoyed. She thought some animal had killed and eaten her husband so she laughed and sang and ran back home.

The man was heartbroken but he realized he was not old and useless and decided to punish his wife for her wickedness. He made his way back to their camp where he saw the woman cooking meat behind the cabin. The smell of the food was tantalizing, but he slipped inside the house and barred the door and then sat down and waited.

As evening came, the wife having eaten all the meat she could, came to the cabin door and tried to get in. When she found the door barred she called out, "Blind Man, you are dead. Wild animals ate you. You cannot be inside the house."

The man answered, "I am alive and can see. You are the one who is dead."

"Let me in, I am cold," she cried.

"I cannot let you in now," he said, "I am eating snow."

The man sat up all night just feasting his eyes on the things he had not seen for so long. The cries of the woman got softer and softer and finally stopped.

The next morning the man opened the door and looked at the sunrise. There on the ground lay his wife, frozen to death, with her mouth filled with white, glistening snow.——Nez Percé

Coyote Makes Man

One day, a long time ago, when there were only animals living in the world, a huge monster came down from the North. He was a mean monster and began to eat all the animals. Soon there were no more deer, no more bear, no more rabbits, no more squirrels. The monster ate everything in sight.

Coyote could not find any of his friends, and, after learning what had happened, decided to get rid of the monster. He went to the top of the highest peak in the Wallowa Mountains and called a challenge to the monster.

The monster let out a roar and charged after Coyote. Now the Wallowa Mountains were steep and high with many peaks and valleys. Try as hard as he could, the monster could not catch up with Coyote who dodged through narrow canyons and scampered up the steep sides of the cliffs where Monster couldn't go. Finally, Monster gave up and tried to make friends with the cunning Coyote. He invited Coyote to come and live with him.

One day Coyote told the monster he was lonely and wanted to visit his friends who had been eaten. Monster agreed and opened his huge mouth so Coyote could go inside and see his friends.

Upon arrival in the monster's belly, Coyote found his friends were safe. He decided to help them escape and decided on a plan of action. He built a large fire in Monster's stomach. Then he took out his knife and cut out Monster's heart. The monster died and all the animals escaped.

Coyote then said he would create a new animal which he would call "Man." He then began to cut up the monster's body and cast the pieces to the four winds. Wherever a piece of Monster landed, a group of people was born. Some formed in the North, some in the South, some in the East and some in the West. Many pieces fell in the canyons and along the rivers where new tribes sprang up.

When he was finished he washed the blood from his hands and where the drops fell to the ground, a new people were formed. Coyote said, "This tribe will be few in number, but they will be pure and strong."

And this how the Nez Percé were made.——Nez Percé

The Origin of Fire

Long ago when the world was young, the Nimipoo had no fire. On occasion they could see fire in the sky, so they knew there was fire someplace. The "sky-fire" was kept by the Great Power in great black bags which floated about. When these bags bumped into each other there was a crashing, tearing sound, and through the hole which the collision caused, the people could see the fire sparkle.

The people wanted fire, for without it they had to eat meat and fish and roots and berries raw, as the animals had to do. They needed it to warm the little children when the weather was cold. They would sit around looking blue and shivering. Nothing the medicine men could do seemed to bring any fire. They beat their drums and sang their songs but still no fire came from the sky.

Finally a young man, just old enough to try to prove his manhood, said that he would get the fire. All the people laughed at him and the medicine men became angry at his audacity.

The boy went on and made his plans though, and the first time he saw the black bags in the sky, he got everything ready. The first thing he did was to cleanse himself in the stream and brush himself with fir branches until he was clean and fragrant with the scent of fir.

He wrapped his best arrowhead with inner bark from a cedar tree and laid it on the ground next to his best bow. Next to them he placed a large white shell he used in his ceremonies. Then he prayed to the Great Power to help his special arrow reach one of the black bags. This frightened his friends for they feared the Great Power would be angry.

However, the boy waited until the largest bag was directly above him. He then raised his bow and shot the special arrow straight at the bag. Suddenly there was a tremendous crash, and the people saw a large flash of fire in the sky. Then the burning arrow came streaking out of the sky and struck the white shell, leaving a small fire of cedar bark.

The people were overjoyed and rushed to light sticks and bark and carry the fire to their lodges. Everyone celebrated with much singing and dancing.

When they had quieted and began to settle down, they looked for the young man to thank him for bringing them fire. He had disappeared, leaving his bow and the white shell. All the men examined the strange bow, but even the strongest was unable to bend it.

They then looked at the shell and saw that where the arrow had burned it, it still showed the color of the fire. The boy was never seen again, but his abalone shell is still beautiful and still shows the colors of the flame. The fire he brought from the black bag is still in the center of each lodge, the blessing of every home.——Nez Percé

NOOTKA

The Nootka people live along the western coast of Vancouver Island, the large body of land lying northwest of the State of Washington. The name is also sometimes applied to the Makah tribe in Washington but more often the Makah are treated independently. One possible reason for this is that Vancouver Island is totally owned by Canada and this brings the two related groups under the jurisdiction of different countries.

Heavily influenced by the Roman Catholic Church and their native ceremonies regulated by the Canadian government, the Nootka culture has suffered severe erosion. The whaling rituals, for these were great whale hunters, and the Wolf Dance, the main ceremony of the Nootkas, are things of the past for the most part. Very little, if any, of these rituals is observed today. Some of the oral tradition survives as the grandfathers pass the stories down to the children. One of these is the tale of "The Cry of the Loon."

The Cry of the Loon

Many years ago, the first person who ever lived was called Quawteaht. He was a thickset, hairy person and He made the land and the water and the animals who lived in the one or the other. In each of these animals when they were first created resided the embryo or the essence of man.

One day a canoe came down the coast paddled by two personages in the form of man, although such form was unknown to the animals of that time. The animals were all frightened out of their wits by these strange forms and fled, each from his own house, in such haste that he left behind him that human essence that he usually carried in his body. These abandoned embryos rapidly developed into men and they multiplied. They made use of the huts deserted by the animals and gradually became as men are today.

When Quawteaht made the world and created animals, He, for some unknown reason withheld fire from them. The one exception was the cuttlefish who always had fire in his home. The other animals tried various tricks to steal this fire but always failed. Finally, one day the deer succeeded in hiding a little of it in the joint of his hind leg and escaped to introduce this element to general use.

Not all the animals we know today were created by Quawteaht, for the loon and the crow were actually metamorphosed men. This came about when one day two fishermen were out to sea in their canoes and they got into a quarrel. One had caught many more fish than the other and began ridiculing the other for his small success. Finally, the unsuccessful man became so infuriated by the taunts of his companion that he knocked him on the head and stole his fish. He then cut out his tongue in case he managed to recover and reach the shore.

This precaution was well taken for the mutilated man did recover and reach land. When he tried to denounce his companion, he could not since he had no tongue. The only sound he could utter was the sound of the loon we hear today. Quawteaht became so indiscriminately angry at the whole affair that He changed the poor mute into a loon and his assailant into a crow.

So when the mournful voice of the loon is heard from the silent lake or river it is still the poor fisherman we hear trying to make himself understood and to tell the hard story of his wrongs.———Nootka

SALISH

The Salish people today live generally in the Flathead country described earlier. They and other tribes of the Northwest which utilized the practice of head-deformation on infants are usually lumped together under the rubric of Flathead. Some of the Salish people lived along the Pacific coastal area and others inhabited inland locations. The two geographically separated groups maintained close ties and were in harmony with their cultural relationship.

Like their neighbors the Nootkas, the Salish were heavily influenced by Roman Catholic missionaries who not only looked after the ecclesiastic needs of the Indians but also ran the legal affairs of the villages. The custom of the Canadian government issuing Magistrates' Commissions to missionaries gave these proselytizers absolute control over their congregations. This allowed the missionary zeal to reach into the private and tribal traditional activities and caused rapid assimilation.

Naturally the Salish people resisted such intrusion and control and a sense of spiritual rebellion was created. Even after over one hundred years of close scrutiny and attempted spiritual genocide, much of the Salish oral tradition remains very much alive today. A few examples are given on the following pages.

How the Animals Were Made

Long, long ago when the world was very young, the Creator found Himself to be alone. He was the only living being, surrounded by water and air, and He became very lonely. To overcome His loneliness, He created muskrat, beaver, otter, mink, and the other water animals.

One day the Creator realized He wanted other company but there was too much water. The water was not solid and He thought if He could have something solid on which to stand, things would be better. He even imagined if water was solid He might even be able to walk around. However, since water was not solid, He must try something else.

After much consideration, He decided on a plan. He tied a long cord onto Muskrat and told him to dive to the bottom of the water and bring up something solid. Muskrat did as he was told and dived into the water. He went down, down, deeper and deeper. When he had been gone a long time, everyone was afraid he would not be back. Finally he did come up but he was so tired that he died. Muskrat had not failed though, for in his paws the Creator found a tiny bit of mud.

The Creator took the little piece of mud and began to roll it. He rolled it and rolled it and shaped it and molded it and the mud began to grow. It got larger and larger until it was big enough for the Creator to walk on it. There was room for all the animals and all the new ones which were created. Plants and birds were made and so were rocks and forests. Lakes and rivers were left so the animals could drink the cool water. Now the Creator could have lots of company in His new world. He was very proud and happy with his beautiful creation.

It makes the Creator sad and unhappy when He sees His creatures abusing and misusing His handiwork, and someday He may become

very angry and destroy this world and make a new one.——Songhes
Band of Coastal Salish

The Healing Sticks

Once, a long time ago, there was a small boy who was being raised by
his grandfather who was a very old man. One day the grandfather said
to the boy, "Go to the mountains and climb to the very highest peak.
There you will find a stream of pure, cold water. Drink this water and
you will have great power to heal."

The boy did as his grandfather had said and started climbing the
mountains. Every time he got to the top of what he thought was the
highest peak, he would look across the ridges and see one which was a
little higher. After many years of toil and disappointment, he finally
found the mountain which stood above all the rest.

When he reached the peak, he found a cold, pure stream of water
coming out of the rocks. He drank from this spring and immediately
felt the power surging through his body. He knew grandfather was
right.

Upon returning to his village, he found a sick child there. The medicine man was unable to cure the sickness in the little one. The boy
asked if he could use his power to heal the child and the medicine man
told him to go ahead. The boy asked that food be brought and ordered a large fire built. He then began to dance around the fire and
sing. He then threw some of the food on the fire. Then he went to
the ill baby and rubbed him with his hands and drew the evil spirits
from the infant and threw them into the fire. The baby then became
well.

This healing went on for many years until the boy became an old
man and was ready to die. He called the people around him and instructed them how to use his healing power. He told them to make two
pieces of wood exactly the same. When this was done, he blessed the
sticks and said, "My power is now in these sticks. Protect and care for
them and throw some food on the fire before trying to use them to
cure." He then showed them how to use the sticks for healing and then
the old man died.

The people remembered the healer's words, and to this day these magic sticks are used to remove evil spirits and to heal in the Cowichan Valley.——Cowichan Band of Coastal Salish

The First Mosquitoes

Once, a long time ago, a young Indian was out in the forest hunting for food. He crept silently through the trees looking for Brother Deer. Suddenly, he heard twigs breaking and some animal breathing heavily. He stopped and waited to see what it was. Secretly he hoped it was the vicious mountain lion which had killed a number of his tribesmen. He would earn an honored place if he could kill such a beast.

Suddenly he saw what was making the noise and is blood froze. It was a huge mountain lion and it was coming straight toward him. He quietly notched an arrow in his bow and took careful aim. Away flew the arrow and it hit the great creature but it did not kill him. Roaring and angered by the stinging arrow, the mountain lion charged and pounced on the hunter.

The young man fought bravely and tried to plunge his knife into the heart of the giant cat. Finally he got the beast down and drove his blade deep into his body. The animal's blood gushed out and, at last, the killer was dead.

The young hunter quickly built a fire and burned the body of the mountain lion as he had been instructed by the older hunters of his tribe. As the last burning embers of the fire died out, the wind arose and scattered the ashes. As they rose into the air the ashes became mosquitoes. And that is why mosquitoes suck blood to this very day.——Salish

NISQUALLY

Before the coming of the white man, the Indians of the northwestern coast of what is now the United States were some of the wealthiest people in America. They were one of the few groups who produced much more than was needed for bare subsistence. The basis for this economic phenomenon was fishing and more particularly, salmon fishing. The salmon however, was not just a part of the Indians' diet, it was the very heart of their existence. Such a tribe was the Nisqually.

Nisqually tradition necessarily incorporates many water animals for these creatures provided everything for the Indian. Even in today's society, the Nisqually are constantly involved with the fight for their special relationship with fish.*

Although never a very large tribe, perhaps two thousand members in prewhite times, the Nisqually have tenaciously held on to their cere-monies, rituals, and stories. One of the tales heard in the evening, told by the elders, is "Why Porpoise and Seals Are Enemies."

Why Porpoise and Seals Are Enemies

A long time ago a family of Indians lived on the shore of the Pacific Ocean in what is now the State of Washington. The mother was twice widowed and had four sons, one by her first husband and three by her second. The eldest was a great medicine man and his brothers were jealous and treated him harshly, never sharing their game or fish with him although he always shared with them.

After a time, he became tired of their unkindness and decided to punish them. One day, he entered their lodge and told them there was a very large seal close by, but he didn't tell them he had created the an-imal. The three brothers rushed to the shore and plunged their spears into the giant seal. To their surprise, they found they could not pull them out nor could they turn loose of the weapons.

The seal swam off to sea, dragging the three boys behind, and after traveling a long distance, deposited them on an island where they could at last free their hands. They hid in the bushes for they thought they were in enemy country and were afraid they would be killed.

After hiding for a good while without being disturbed, they cau-tiously began to survey this strange place. Before long they noticed a small canoe, paddled by a tiny man, coming near the island. The little fellow tossed out a stone for an anchor and began to fish. He dived out of the canoe and, after staying under the water a long time, came up with a very large fish. He repeated this operation several times and the brothers noticed that he counted the fish every time before he dived.

Since the brothers were hungry, one of them proposed that they swim out and steal a fish while the tiny man was under the water. Act-

* Read, American Friends Series Committee, *Uncommon Controversy: Fishing Rights of the Mucklehoof, Puyallup, and Nisqually Indians* (Seattle: University of Washington Press, 1970).

ing quickly, the brothers swam to the canoe and got the fish and made it back to the island before the diver surfaced. When the little man came up with another fish, he immediately discovered the theft. He pulled up the anchor, paddled to the island, and found the brothers as they hid.

Being very strong, he soon bound them, cast them in his canoe, and started home. Upon reaching his village, the brothers saw that everyone was very small and everything in the region was sized to fit them. They were thrown bound into a lodge and a council was called to decide their fate.

While the council was in session, a large flock of water birds flew over and began attacking people. These birds had the power of throwing quills, like porcupines, and although the people fought fiercely, they were completely overpowered by the birds. After their victory, the birds flew away and the brothers ran to the site and began pulling out the quills. As soon as they did this, the people were totally restored as if nothing had happened. They were very thankful and asked the boys what they could do to repay them for their help.

The boys asked that they be taken back to their own country and the council was again called to decide what mode of transportation to use to accomplish the trip. They concluded that a whale would be the best for this purpose and the three brothers were placed on the back of the monster and the trip was begun. When they were about half way home, the whale began to change his mind, and being a great magician, changed the boys into porpoises and told them to swim home. This was the creation of porpoises and, because the brothers had attacked the seal, porpoises and seals are still continually at war with each other.——Nisqually

SHOSHONE

The vast territory populated by the Shoshone people included Idaho, western Wyoming, Utah, central and northeastern Nevada, and a portion of southeastern California. The designation "Shoshone" is one of linquistic orientation rather than tribal for the most part. Today, the term refers generally to the group of Northern Shoshonean-speaking Indians living on the Fort Hall, Idaho Reservation and on the Wind River Reservation in Wyoming.

The Western Shoshone inhabited the Intermountane or Basin-Plateau area in the western United States. Generally they are identified today by their band or reservation titles such as Gosiute, Battle Mountain, Snake, etc. Never a cohesive people, each band of Shoshone was autonomous and extremely independent and lived in comparative isolation from their related groups.

Since both the Northern and Western Shoshone people were usually nonaggressive and settled on land which held no attraction for the white man, they were able to survive with less interference to their lifestyles than many of their counterparts. As a result of this isolation, much of the traditional ways of life were perpetuated. The Shoshone language is still spoken, the rituals and religious ceremonies are observed, and although acculturation pressures have increased in recent years, the people retain much of their cultural integrity.

Tribal stories are still remembered and passed from one generation to the next. A few examples of these are provided on the following pages.

Don't Be Greedy—Coyote Story

Coyote was always getting into trouble because he was so curious about what others were doing. Whenever he saw someone doing something, he tried to imitate it and this kept him in hot water most of the time.

One night as he was walking along the road all by himself, he came to a large oak tree where an owl was sitting. Coyote saw the owl doing something he had never seen before and he was fascinated. Owl put up his claws and pulled one of his eyes out of its socket and tossed it high in the air. He then held out his claws and tilted his head back. The eyeball fell back into its place in his head and his claws were filled with good, sweet, dried meat. He ate the meat and then pulled out his other eye and tossed it into the air. Again it fell back in place and his claws were again filled with meat.

Coyote stood and watched Owl for some time. Since he was always hungry and very greedy, he was very interested in what was happening. After a while his curiosity got the best of him and he asked, "Owl, what are you doing?"

"Oh," said Owl, "this is the way I get my food." This is true because

Owl gets his food by swooping down on smaller birds and animals like mice and rabbits and catching them in his claws.

Coyote asked if anyone could get their food by tossing their eyeballs into the air, but Owl warned him, "Just those with special powers can do this. Those without this power cannot do it."

As Coyote watched some more he thought, "That looks like an easy way to get food. Surely if a silly owl can do it, with all my brains, I can do it with no trouble." So he waited until Owl turned his head upward for an eye to fall in place. He pulled his right eye out and tossed it into the air and put his paw out to receive his meat. He turned his head back to catch his eye, but nothing happened. The eye caught on a branch of the oak tree and there was no meat in his hand. Old Coyote was sure mad.

"I'll get you down," he called out to his eye, "I'll make you sorry for what you did to me." He then pulled his left eye out of the socket and tossed it upward. "Go find your brother," he shouted, "and make him come home. And both of you bring me some dried meat right away."

But the left eye caught on the tree, also, and Coyote was left standing under the tree while Owl ate up his eyes. Then Old Coyote was left to crawl around and around the tree on the ground, yelling for his eyes to come back.

That is why today the Owl can see so well and why Coyote is always turning his head back and howling.——Shoshone

Coyote Steals the Pine Nuts

One day Coyote came to the Salmon River country and saw all the pine nuts growing very large. Since he was so greedy, he wanted to take them home with him to Nevada. However, the pine nuts belonged to Porcupine and he didn't want Coyote to take them away, but Coyote kept asking for them.

Now Porcupine was a great gambler and loved to bet on the hand game, so he told Coyote, "Let's play the hand game and, if you win, you can take some of the pine nuts back to Nevada with you."

So Coyote said, "Okay" and they began to play. Since both were excellent players and very smart, they played all day and all night. They played the second day and second night. Finally, in the end, Porcupine won and everyone was very tired and went to sleep. While everyone was asleep, Coyote stole the best pine nuts and went away to Nevada.

Today there are many pine nuts in Nevada, and they are the big, juicy ones. The pine nuts left in the Salmon River country are only the very small ones. They are the only ones left since Coyote stole the good ones from Porcupine.

That's the way Coyote is. Coyote always tricks everyone.——Shoshone

Why Cougars Have Long Tails

Long ago there was an Indian boy who lived with his family in a valley by a stream at the foot of a mountain. His father fished in the stream and hunted deer and elk in the hills. His mother dried the fish and meat for their winter food supply. One day while hunting, the father found a cougar cub and brought it home to his son. The boy and the cougar grew up together.

As the years passed, the boy became a man and it was time for him to seek the vision which would give him his name and his destiny. He went up to the mountain and after praying and fasting for three days, he received his vision as he slept. He saw a great red owl who told him he would be the hunter for his people and would always be the one to provide their food. After this time, the boy was known as Red Owl.

Meanwhile, the cougar was now full-grown and he hunted the deer and elk with Red Owl. They went everywhere together and brought home plenty of game for the women to prepare.

One day, Red Owl and the cougar were chasing a huge deer. It bounded up a rocky slope and over the top of a hill. The cougar and Red Owl were close behind and soon cornered the large buck at the foot of a cliff. Just as Red Owl was about to shoot his arrow, the deer gave a powerful leap and landed on top of the cliff. The cougar, likewise, leaped to the top but Red Owl could not jump that high and the cliff was too steep for him to climb. He called out for the cougar to wait until he could go around to the other side of the hill.

The cougar, however, turned and let his strong thick tail hang over the side of the cliff. Red Owl climbed the tail and reached the top of the cliff. In doing do, since he was quite a heavy man, his weight pulled Cougar's tail so hard that it stretched it, making it very long. Even now, all the cougar's children, grandchildren, and great-grandchildren have very long tails.——Shoshone

How Soda Springs Were Created

Long ago when the giant cottonwoods on Big River were no larger than arrows, all red men were at peace. The hatchet was buried everywhere, and hunter met hunter in the gamelands of one or the other with all hospitality and good-will. During this time, two chiefs, one of the Shoshone and the other of the Comanche nation, met one day at a certain spring. The Shoshone had been successful in the chase and the Comanche very unlucky, which put the latter in a rather ill humor.

In the course of conversation, a dispute arose as to the importance of their respective and related tribes. The Comanche made a treacherous and unprovoked attack on the Shoshone, striking him from behind as he stooped to drink of the water. The murdered man fell forward into the spring and immediately there was a great commotion there. Great bubbles and spurts of gas shot up from the bottom of the pool, and amid a cloud of vapor there arose an old, white-haired Indian, armed with a ponderous club of elk-horn.

The assassin knew who stood before him for the totem on the breast was that of Wankanaga, the father of both the Shoshone and the Comanche nations. He was a revered ancient one, famous for his brave deeds and celebrated in the hieroglyphic pictures of both peoples.

"Accursed of two nations!" cried the old man. "This day hast thou put death between the two greatest peoples under the sun. The blood of this Shoshone cries out to the Great Spirit for revenge." And he dashed out the brains of the Comanche with his great club and the murderer fell there beside his victim in the spring. After that the spring became foul and bitter and even to this day, no one can drink of its nauseous water. Then Wankanaga, seeing it had been defiled, took his club and smote a neighboring rock, and the rock burst forth into clear, bubbling water. Even today the water is so fresh and pleasing to the palate that no other water can even be compared to it. Both springs still pour forth from the same place; one sweet and pure and the other bitter and foul.——Shoshone

TLINGIT

The Tlingit Indians inhabited the entire southern coastal area of Alaska from Yakutat Bay southward. They are closely related to the Athapaskans and Haidas who were mentioned earlier in this section.

The first contact with the white world was in 1741 when Russian explorers discovered the Tlingit country. Explorers and traders from other countries soon came to the area, but the Russians had the most impact on the Indians.

In 1799, after decimating the Aleuts with horrendous treatment, the Russian fur traders moved down the Alaskan coast and built a fort near the present city of Sitka. The invaders' treatment was so harsh that the Sitka Indians rebelled in 1802 and drove the Russians out of the fort, killing a great many of them. Even after the recapture of Sitka two years later, the Indians did not surrender their independence without a fight, and frequent outbreaks among the natives continued until the United States bought Alaska.

Early estimates place the pre-white Tlingit population at about ten thousand. Current figures indicate that about one-half that number remain. Acculturation, warfare, and the white man's diseases have taken their toll.

Just as the Tlingits resisted Russian atrocities, they have to a great degree resisted the erosion of their culture by outside forces. In the cities, Tlingit life blends into the lifestyle of the community. That community spirit, however, displays a definite Tlingit flavor and the village life is strongly influenced by traditional Tlingit activities. The following stories are examples of oral tradition which is still being passed from generation to generation.

The Giant Worm

Once, a long time ago, a young girl had a woodworm for a pet. She fed it on her own milk and, as it grew too large to survive on her milk, she took food for it from the storeboxes of the villagers. The worm continued to grow until it was nearly fifteen feet long. The girl made up songs and sang them to the huge worm as if it were her own baby.

The villagers overheard these strange songs and wondered who the girl was singing to. Finally, one day the girl's mother peeped into the menstrual hut where the girl, according to custom, was staying. She saw the gigantic worm and heard her daughter singing to it. The people of the village were frightened by such strange happenings. They became angry also when they discovered their food supplies had been taken from their storeboxes, and they had nothing to keep them from going hungry during the oncoming winter days. They blamed the worm for their bad situation.

The father called out for his daughter to come out of the seclusion hut and, knowing she must obey, she changed her song into a mourning song for the worm and returned to her father's house.

As soon as she had gone, the villagers attacked the worm and chopped it into pieces. Soon they began to have good fortune and the fishing was so good that the village was saved from starvation. The girl explained that the village's success was caused by the worm and it should be honored by the people. From that time on, the worm has been regarded as a symbol of one of the totem clans of the Tlingit people.——Tlingit

The Beaver and the Porcupine

Long ago, the beaver and the porcupine were good friends and went everywhere together. They often visited each other's homes and, while they were friends, they often played tricks on each other.

One time, when the porcupine wanted to visit the beaver's home, Beaver agreed to take him across the water on his back. When they were partway across the lake, instead of Beaver taking Porcupine to his house, he dropped him off on a stump which was in the water. Porcupine was stranded and had to use his magic to get back to dry land. He caused the lake to freeze and walked to shore on the ice.

Some time later when the two friends were playing together, the porcupine decided to get even. He said, "Come on Beaver. It's your turn to ride on my back."

The beaver climbed on the porcupine's back and the porcupine took him to the top of the highest tree in the forest. He left the beaver stranded and he climbed down. Now beavers are not tree dwellers so he could not get out of the tree. He called and called, but nobody answered. He begged the porcupine for help, but the porcupine only laughed.

Finally, the beaver decided to slide down the tree. He hugged the trunk as tightly as he could and clung to the bark with his dull claws and slid down. And even to this day you can see the ridges and valleys in tree bark where Beaver slid down.——Tlingit

UTE

The Ute territory in pre-white time stretched from western Utah to eastern Colorado and from southern Wyoming to northern New Mexico. This warlike group, using the horse to patrol its territory, was never a cohesive tribal unit but rather, consisted of twelve or more autonomous bands, each claiming dominion over specific areas of land. Like most Indian nations, they referred to themselves as "The People," in their language "Noochee."

Large-scale buffalo hunting and improved transportation, made possible by the acquisition of the horse, led to grouping of related kin cliques into larger bands of loosely confederated families. The leadership of these bands was informal and limited to specific areas of activity.

Throughout their existence, the Utes have changed their cultural patterns because of influences of other groups. As their contact with Plains Indians increased after the horse became available, the Utes began to adopt both material and intellectual facets of Plains cultures and lose much of their original Basin culture. Some of these acquired cultural traits include beadwork, tipis, clothing, and spiritual practices such as the Sun Dance. However, not all of their tradition was diluted, and some of their stories are still told with little or no apparent outside influence. The stories "How Pike's Peak Was Made" and "The Creation" are examples of this fact.

How Pike's Peak Was Made

The Great Spirit made the chosen people and they lived in a gentle land on the slopes of the great mountain He had made and come to earth on. It was always summer and there was no cold snow or harsh winds and the animals were glad to be food for the Chosen Ones. There was no war or sorrow or discontent, and the man followed the laws given by the Great Spirit, and He watched over them.

One day, however, evil spirits came from the lowlands by the sea. They were too puny and weak to fight the Chosen Ones but were strong in deceit and in spreading discontent. They went all through the beautiful land and turned the men against each other. Things got so very bad that the Chosen Ones even turned against the Great Spirit and cursed Him. The sunshine went away and the snows came, and there was sorrow and war.

The Great Spirit saw what the evil ones had done and He became very angry. He stamped his foot and the rain came and covered the land. The Chosen Ones ran up the mountain to the Great Spirit's own land in the sky. They carried rocks and dirt in their hands with which to build another world. The Great Spirit, however, saw no good or remorse in them, only fear and evil, and He would not let them on His land.

So the waters took them, and as they died they cursed the Great Spirit and threw dirt and rocks toward Him in His sky land. A mountain was made, towering over the flooded land, so vast it shut out all sight of the Great Spirit. When the waters went away the huge mountain left a great shadow over all the land where it had once been summer. Today, that mountain lifts its snow-covered peak high above the clouds and shuts off the view of the land where the Great Spirit dwells. However, it does point the way to this happy land and where we will go if we follow the laws the Great Spirit has given us.——Ute

The Creation

At first, the Great Spirit lived alone in His beautiful home in the sky. After a while He became lonely and began to look around for new things to occupy His time. One day He took a stone and poked a hole in the floor of His land, which is our sky, and looked through at the vast nothingness below. He decided to create something to fill this great void of space.

First, He gathered up some dirt and rocks and mixed them with snow and rain. When the mixture was just right, He poured it through the hole to see what would happen. He left the whole mess settle for a few days, and then peeped through the hole to see what had taken place.

As He looked down He saw great snow-capped mountains of dirt and rocks and a large, flat plain stretching away beyond. The Great Spirit wanted to see what was down there so He made the hole in the sky bigger and crawled through to the top of the mountain. He saw that the new land was vast, but it was only bare rock and dirt. So He reached down and touched the land, and wherever His fingers touched there immediately appeared trees and forests and other green things. The sunshine came through the hole in the sky and warmed the land. The snow melted and the streams and rivers began to flow. Lakes and seas were formed and the grasses and flowers grew. The land was very pretty and the Great Spirit walked around and sat by the streams and was very pleased.

After a while, however, he became lonely again and wanted to share the beautiful world He had made. So He took his staff, and with the small end He made the fishes. He then breathed life on them and placed them in the streams, and they leaped joyously and swam away. Then the Great Spirit went into the forests and took handfuls of dry leaves from the ground and blew them into the air, and they grew wings and became birds. From the leaves of the mighty oak tree came the eagles and hawks; from the elm leaves came the ravens; and from the aspen leaves came the noisy jays. The birds sang and made music for the Great Spirit and He was pleased.

From the middle of His staff, the Great Spirit made animals. He created the antelope, deer, coyote, rabbit, buffalo, and all the other four-legged creatures. Different animals were made to live in different parts of the new world and to subsist on different foods which were provided. The Great Spirit looked at all He had made with pleasure and He sat down to rest. But pretty soon all the new life He had created began to fight and to kill each other.

When the Great Spirit saw what was happening His heart became sick. So with the large end of His staff, He made one more animal. He gave him great strength and wisdom and made him to rule all the other animals and establish the order necessary for the survival of the world. That new animal was the grizzly bear and he was the master of the land until the Great Spirit became angry with him one day and created man. However, that is another story.——Ute

YAKIMA

The first recorded contact with the Yakima people was in 1806 when the Lewis and Clark Expedition traversed their country. It is not known just how much of the true Yakima Nation they encountered but they estimated the population at 1200. In 1855, the United States entered into a treaty with the Yakima and thirteen other tribes, established the Yakima Reservation for them, and extended recognition of the conglomerate as the Yakima Nation. Therefore, in addition to destroying fourteen sovereign nations of people, the government forced the dilution of the Yakimas proper to the point that true identity of the tribes is now impossible.

A few vestiges of Yakima culture remain, being cherished and nurtured by succeeding generations in rather a "last straw" desperation. "How We Got Summer and Winter" is a tale which survives.

How We Got Summer and Winter

Many years ago when the world was first made, there were five brothers and a sister living in the warm southland. There was an abundance of sunshine and just enough warm, gentle rain to make everything grow well. The brothers, who were hunters, never failed to bring home plenty of meat for the family. While they hunted, the sister remained at home. She mended their clothes and made new garments from the hides of the animals the brothers brought home. She was always nicely dressed in buckskin that was ornamented with elk's teeth and beads of bone.

At the same time, in the cold northland, lived five brothers and their sister. Their home was just the opposite of the southern family for they lived in the land of ice and snow. These brothers were also hunters, but they were not very successful and many times they went hungry. One time when there was no game and they were about to starve, the northern brothers sent their sister to the home of the southern brothers to ask for some food.

She started out with her brothers following her. They had large icicles in their hands which they used as spears. As she approached, the southern brothers told their sister to dress in her finest buckskins and go to welcome her.

When she was ready, the southern girl walked out to meet the girl from the north. The girl from the south smiled and the air was warmed. The icicles which the northern boys planned to use as weapons melted and fell to the ground. The northern girl ran back and told her brothers what happened. They were very angry and said to each other, "Let's challenge the southern brothers to wrestle with us."

They sent their challenge and the southern brothers accepted. When it was almost autumn, the two families met halfway between their homes. The sisters each took along five buckets filled with water; the northern girl had cold water and the southern girl had warm. They planned to throw the contents at the feet of the wrestlers.

When everything was ready, the oldest brother from the north began wrestling with the oldest brother from the south. They were evenly matched and no one seemed able to get an advantage. Suddenly, the girl from the north threw one of her buckets of ice and water at the feet of her brother. This made him fight harder and he started to overcome his rival. Then the southern sister threw her warm water at the feet of the wrestlers. The ice melted and immediately the southern man beat the man from the north and killed him.

At once, the next oldest brother from the north attacked the victor. In a fierce fight he overcame the southern brother who soon lay on the ground dead. One by one, the brothers from each tribe wrestled with a brother from the other tribe. After a while only the youngest in each family was left alive.

These two wrestled for five days and neither was able to defeat the other. On the sixth day the boy from the South weakened and was almost beaten, but somehow rallied. They both agreed to stop and rest for a while, and the southern boy went to his home and stayed there five moons.

At the end of that time, he traveled north and met the northern boy where they had fought before. This time the northern boy was soundly defeated and driven far back into the cold land. For about six moons the southern brother had possession of the land of the northern family. At the end of six moons, the northern boy returned, and they wrested for a whole moon. This time the southern boy was defeated and driven home.

Even today, the two boys continue to wrestle for mastery of the land. When the southern boy defeats the northern one, we have summer. When the northern wrestler defeats the southern one, we have winter. Two battles are waged every year. Just before spring, the southern boy conquers the northern boy; in the autumn, the northern boy conquers the southern boy. Each rules the land for a few months.——Yakima

The California Indians

Because of its shape and the geographic variety, which includes areas of low hot deserts, high plateau country, coastal plains, and lofty mountains, the Indians of California represented cultures so diverse that they must be studied separately. Located with the boundaries of the state were desert tribes, coastal fishermen, salmon-oriented groups, mountain hunters, and flatland farmers.

In the Smithsonian Institution *Bureau of Ethnology Bulletin 145, Indian Tribes of North America,* John R. Swanton, noted ethnologist, lists sixty-two distinct Indian tribes native to the state of California. William F. Shipley, in "Native Languages of California," *Handbook of North American Indians, Volume 8—California,* states that there were at least sixty-four and perhaps as many as eighty, "mutually unintelligible tongues, further differentiated into an unknowably large number of dialects." With this extreme diversity of culture and language, it is obvious that a great many Indians lived in the Golden State before the invading forces of Europeans and, later, Americans, decimated their ranks.

In the previously mentioned *Handbook of North American Indians,* Sherburne F. Cook in his "Historical Demography" indicates that the native population in California in 1770 was approximately three hundred and ten thousand. Sad, indeed, is the fact that Mr. Cook estimates that less than twenty thousand descendants of these people were left by 1900, a decline of over ninety percent. This tremendous decrease in Indian population can be attributed to several sources and occurred in particular stages in time.

The first of these temporal divisions encompasses the period from 1770 to 1835 and can be titled the Mission Period. On July 16, 1769, Father Juniper Serra, a Franciscan, established the first Indian mission in California named San Diego de Alcala. Following this, a chain of missions was built about a day's journey apart along the coast. The last and northernmost, San Francisco de Solano, was dedicated in April, 1824, completing the twenty-one mission complex.*

By 1830 the Indian population had decreased to about two hundred forty-five thousand. Most of the decrease was among those crowded together in the mission compounds and exposed to many new diseases brought by the foreigners, against which they had no natural immunity. Many of these free spirits died simply of broken hearts due to the stringent restrictions imposed on them by the clergy and enforced by the military. Changes in diet, eating habits, and living in the company of strangers caused a drop in birth rate. Disruption of family and community life, so essential to Indian people, and the harassment, discipline, and regimentation also had a deleterious effect on the natives.

The second stage in the depopulation extended to the "Gold Rush" period in 1848. During this span of nearly two decades, diseases, military action with consequences of starvation and relocation, and slave-traders from the south decimated the aboriginal population. Cook estimates that by 1845 there were only one hundred and twenty-five to one hundred and fifty thousand Indians remaining within the limits of the state.

The third and final stage of genocide aimed at the native population was one of the most horrendous periods in American History.** Within the decade of 1845–55 an estimated one hundred thousand Indian people died from unnatural causes. Disease still claimed the lives of many, but brutality and barbarism perpetrated by the white popu-

* Read William E. Coffer, "Genocide of the California Indians," *The Indian* Historian (San Francisco: The American Indian Historical Society, Spring, 1977), pp.8–15.
** Read Robert F. Heizer, *The Destruction of California Indians,* (Salt Lake City: Peregrine Smith Inc., 1974), and Robert F. Heizer, *They Were Only Diggers,* (Socorro, N.M.: Ballena Press, 1974).

The Making of the Oceans
Acagchemem or Juaneños

lace brought death to most of those who perished during this time.

United States census reports of 1880 indicate that there were twenty thousand three hundred and eighty-five Indians in California, sixteen thousand six hundred and twenty-four in 1890 and fifteen thousand three hundred and thirty-seven in 1900.* These figures perhaps are not totally accurate, but by any measurement, and allowing for a liberal margin of error, the decrease in population ranged from eighty-five to ninety-five percent.

As the people and the tribes disappeared, so did the oral traditions which had given meaning and definition to their world. Men of learning and character such as H. H. Bancroft, Stephen Powers, and others attempted to record what they could for posterity. Most of their writings, however, are not available to the general reading public in a single publication. One must read many books, most of which are rather difficult to find without extensive search.

The following are tales of the California Indians, compiled by this author from some of these sources and, primarily from his own experiences with the few remaining elders of the tribes represented.

ACAGCHEMEM OR JUANEÑOS

The term Juaneños, or the Juaneño Band of Mission Indians, is generally used to designate the American Indians who were associated with and subservient to the Mission of San Juan Capistrano. Founded in 1776, this mission absorbed the many small bands of peaceful coastal natives living in the area. Heavily influenced by the Catholic Church and integrated with the Spanish, Mexican, and then American perspectives, the Acagchemem people have little of their tradition left. One of the few stories remaining is their version of how the oceans were formed.

The Making of the Oceans

Long ago an invisible, all-powerful being called Nocuma made the world. He also created all the things which grow and move upon the earth. Nocuma made this world round like a ball and rolled it in His

* Sherburne F. Cook, "Historical Demography" *Handbook of North American Indians*, (Washington: Smithsonian Institution, Volume 8–California, 1978).

hands to shape it. It was then steadied by sticking a heavy black rock in it as a sort of ballast. The sea, at this time, was only a small stream running around the world and was so crowded with fish that they had no room to even swim. There were so many of them that some of the younger ones proposed leaving the confining boundaries of the water and moving out onto dry land.

It was only with the utmost difficulty and strenuous argument that the elders prevented the foolish attempt. They explained to the younger ones that the air would kill them and even if they could survive that, the sun would be so hot that they would be dried out. And if that were not reason enough to prevent the venture, the elders pointed out that fish have no feet and that it would be impossible to live on land with no method of locomotion.

The old ones suggested that the proper plan was to improve and expand their present home. With the aid of two very large fish, this was accomplished. They broke open a huge granite rock and found a reservoir, like a giant bladder, inside the stone. It was filled with a bitter liquid, the taste of which pleased the fish. They emptied the substance into the stream of water in which they lived. Instantly the water became salty and swelled up and overflowed a great part of the earth. The new boundaries which were made are the seashores we know today.——Acagchemem or Juaneños

ACHOMAWI

The Pit River Indians consist of a number of tribes, one of the principal of which is the Achomawi. Located in the northeastern corner of California, today's membership of recognized Pit River Indians is only thirty-one.* Of course, many more than this number exist, but they are not acknowledged by the Bureau of Indian Affairs. This tribal unit suffered an extremely high mortality rate during the "gold rush" period and with the loss of population, much of the oral tradition disappeared. The following two stories are among the few which survived.

How Coyote Made People

After Coyote had made the world and designed the animals and other

* Bureau of Indian Affairs, Sacramento Area Office. *Tribal Information and Directory* (Sacramento: Bureau of Indian Affairs, October, 1977).

creatures to live on it, he decided the world should have people too. Old Coyote told his wife Pelican Woman, that if he made people that they would not be able to live with them but would have to go away. Pelican Woman agreed to leave for she wanted the people to live on the earth.

Coyote tried and tried to make people but had no luck. First, he carved them out of little oak sticks but there was no life in them. Next, he tried sticks of pine, but still nothing happened. He used sticks from all the different trees but they did not become people. He became very angry and scattered the many kinds of sticks all over the world. He cried, "When the fleas bite you, you will become people."

He then carved all kinds of people from sticks of the buckeye tree and placed them in his ceremonial house. He put some on the north side, some on the south, some on the east, and some on the west. He then cut some milkweed plants and poured the milk over the sticks and said, "You will now become people."

The next morning when Coyote entered the ceremonial house he heard the people talking and saw them walking around. He called them all together and gave each group a name and a language that was different from all others. He said, "The four lands, north, south, east, and west now have people who are different from each other. They will live in those places and be happy." Coyote then told the people that he and his wife were going away and that the people could not go with them.

He said to the people, "When you die you will come to my new home to live. Only dead people can come to my land; only dead people."

Before he left, Coyote gave names to all the trees and plants, and to all the birds and animals. He said, "From now on you will be called by the names I have given you." And he set everything in order as we know them today.

He then told his people, "When you die, after four days your spirit will come to my new home in the west, beyond the horizon, and there you will live with me."

He then called Pelican Woman and they left for their new land in the west. They went away to their new home beyond the ocean where they live today. When the people die, their spirits stay for four days and then go to the land beyond the western horizon to be with Coyote and Pelican Woman forever.——Achomawi

How the World Was Made

Long ago our earth was created by Coyote and Eagle. First, Coyote scratched it up with his paws out of the great void which was every-where. Eagle complained, however, that the world was flat and had no mountains for him to use for his home. Coyote attempted to remedy the situation and made some hills but they were not high enough. Eagle told Coyote that he would show him how to make mountains and set to work.

First he scratched up great ridges of dirt and rock with his long talons. Then as he flew over them he dropped some feathers which took root and became trees. He then loosed some down and pinfeath-ers which became bushes and plants.

The Coyote and the Fox* then set about to make the animals and man and to establish the rules of life. They quarreled as to whether they should let men live forever, the Coyote, being the evil spirit, against the Fox who was the good spirit. Coyote was in favor of man being allowed to live only a time and then he should die, while Fox argued that man should have the right to come back to life if he chose. Since nobody ever came back, it is evident that Coyote won the argu-ment.

Last of all, Coyote gave the Indians fire for everyone was freezing. He journeyed far to the west where the fire was kept, stole some of it, and carried it back in his ears. He built a great fire on the top of a high mountain and the Indians saw the smoke. They went up and got fire so they could be warm and comforted and have kept it ever since.——
Achomawi

CAHUILLA

A division of the southern California group of the Shoshonean division of the Uto-Aztecan linguistic stock, the Cahuilla occupied a large area of land prior to the European invasion of this hemisphere. Today, they are located on several small reservations and maintain, at least to some degree, a portion of their tradition. Although, like other California tribal units, their population has decreased dramatically, the Ca-

---

* It is not explained how Coyote, Eagle, and Fox happened to be in existence at the time of Creation. This is prevalent in stories in the oral tradition of many tribes.

huilla people are fiercely independent. But pressure from various outside cultures has left its mark. Few native speakers remain and many families have relocated in urban society for economic survival.

In recent years, as with many Indian groups, there has been a resurgence of the traditional way of life in the Cahuilla communities. Ceremonies, dances, songs, and stories which were nearly forgotten have been revived and are being taught to the youth of the tribe.

Currently there are fifteen hundred to two thousand Cahuilla enrolled in ten small reservations in southern California. Most of the people live off-reservation because of the shortage of water, lack of adequate job opportunities, and absence of health and other facilities. Most, however, would prefer to live on the reservations which provide them with an identity base.

The four stories which follow are part of the Cahuilla oral tradition that has survived and is being perpetuated by the tribe.

How the Mockingbird Got Its Song

A long time ago, before Man came to the desert, only the birds and the animals lived there. Everyone was very happy and enjoyed the hot, dry weather. Some years, however, there was no rain and the springs and rivers dried up. When these years came, the desert birds wished they could live in the mountains where the streams ran all the time and the air was cool.

They would not have known of the cool, wet mountains if it had not been for the ducks and geese who migrated every year. They would stop and rest and feed as they traveled north and south. There were thousands who would stop in the desert in the wet years and spend a lot of time before continuing their jounrney.

However, in dry years, only a few would come and they stayed only a short time. They would tell the desert birds of the land where they were heading, a land where everything was green and food and water was plentiful. They always urged the desert birds to accompany them but each dry year, after careful consideration, the desert birds would decide to stay in their arid homeland.

One year it was hotter and drier than ever and the desert birds suffered more than usual. After much hunger and thirst, they held a meeting and once again discussed moving to where it was cool and where the grass was green. The day birds and the night birds agreed to move to the mountains. Crow was elected as the leader of the day birds and Owl was selected for the night bird leader. The day they decided to leave, they all gathered together with much happy singing and talking.

As the appointed hour arrived, Crow gave the order and away they went. There were so many birds that they covered the whole sky. Away they went—all except one, Mockingbird.

Later, as night began to fall, the night birds gathered, and, at Owl's order, took off with a mighty flapping of wings. They were so numerous that they covered the entire sky. They flew all night and at dawn they arrived at the place the day birds had selected. The ducks and geese were right: this land was green and pleasant with an abundance of water. It was warm and very pleasant there.

Soon, however, the nights began to be cooler and gradually the days were colder, too. The bird people knew winter was on its way and began to prepare for it as they had every year in the desert. They put their heads under their wings, fluffed up their feathers and went to sleep, waiting for the warm sun.

As the days got colder and shorter, the bird people began to suffer. Many became ill and some died from the cold. As time went on, the whole area turned into ice and snow and there were no geese or ducks. They had left to go to the warm, desert country before winter came, and forgot to tell the desert birds to migrate. The bird people were in a terrible condition and had to do something.

Crow called a meeting and all the bird people decided to return to their warm desert homes. Away they went, flying west toward the setting sun. It was too late, however, for as they flew some became sick and died. Finally they came to the mountains which were so green and beautiful when they passed over them before. Now they were cold and white, and food and water could not be found. Heavy rains and snows with violent winds forced many to the ground where they froze.

Those who survived flew onward and soon felt the warm desert air. They were overjoyed at being home, but when they landed, there were only a few who had survived the ordeal. Although they knew they would have cold and dry years, it would not be as bad as the land where they had been.

The bird people began to build their nests and were happy to find that Mockingbird was there and had kept their land. All the bird people remembered what they had been through as a result of their foolish move. They remembered the cold, the snow and ice, the sickness and death. It was decided that each bird should make a song telling of their horrible experience so no other bird would ever make the same mistake.

Each bird family made their song and sang it every day so they would never forget. Mockingbird heard these songs over and over, day and night, until she began to forget her own song. She began to sing parts of the songs of the other birds and that is why, to this very day Mockingbird sings only parts of the songs of other birds and none of her own.——Cahuilla

How the Rattlesnake Got His Fangs

A long time ago, Moon Maiden was a fine growing young woman. She was a very beautiful and intelligent lady, such as all hope to be. She was teaching the People the right and wrong things of their tribal rules. She taught all the People, but took special care to instruct the girls so they would attract good husbands.

Moon Maiden took all the young people to a place of water and taught them to dance and run and jump and wrestle and play games. There were activities for the boys and different ones for the girls. She taught the girls and women to rise and bathe in the pool before the men awoke. She taught them how to care for their hair and keep it black and shiny. She taught them how to be happy and how to laugh and play.

She instructed them in all the songs of how the animals got to be like they were. The young people learned how Coyote got to be so comical and they sang about his long nose and tail and about his ragged fur. They learned about the many clans in their tribe, the Coyote, the Wild Cat, the Lion, and many others. They were also taught that they should never marry anyone from their own clan. If such a marriage took place the children would be afflicted and the people of their own clan would shun them.

One evening when the Moon Maiden led the young people home, singing and dancing, they danced all over a huge rattlesnake who liked to curl up in the doorway. They danced on his head and his nose and on his back and the snake felt he had been badly treated.

Mukat, the Creator, was lying in His lodge and saw how the poor old harmless snake had been mistreated, and he felt sorry for him. So He took two cactus thorns and placed them in the snake's mouth, so if someone tried to step on him they would be stung. When the young people came back that evening, they danced all over the snake again. He bit one, but nothing happened, no harm was done.

The next day Mukat got mesquite thorns and put them in the snake's mouth. The snake was ready for them this time and when the young people came home and started dancing on him, he bit the first one to stop on him. However, just as before, no harm was done.

Mukat decided to try again the next morning and took two hairs from His beard and put them in the mouth of the snake. He instructed the snake that if these fangs worked when he bit one of the dancers that he had better run and hide under the rocks or in the brush for the people would try to kill him.

Now that evening, the young people were happy and dancing, and they did it again; they started dancing on the snake, and the snake bit one of them and he became ill. Sure enough, the people became angry at the snake and tried to kill him, but he ran too fast and hid under some rocks, and the one he had bitten was the one who died.

Ever since that day, People have been trying to kill the rattlesnake and the snake has been hiding in brush or under rocks.——Cahuilla

What Happens After Death

When Mukat, the Creator of people, was on earth, He decided that to keep the world from becoming too crowded, every man must someday die. He then created a place in the east as a residence for the spirits of the dead. At the entrance to this place He made two large hills or mountains which were constantly moving. They would come together and then separate, over and over, and this movement never ceased.

Mukat then placed a watchman at the entrance to this land of spirits and when the spirits come to this place, the watchman questions them. After he gives them several tests, the spirits try to enter Telmikish, the spirit land. If they have lived a good life, been thoughtful and generous and kind to old people, and obeyed all Mukat's orders, they pass through the moving mountains with no trouble. If they have failed to do these things, the mountains come together and crush them. When this happens, they become bats, or butterflies, or rocks, or trees and live near the entrance.

The spirits who pass through live happily together and know each other. Often they gather and decide they want some living person to be with them. When they reach this decision, that person soon dies and goes to live with his friends in Telmikish.

Sometimes a man dies with no prior plans by the spirits. If the spirits do not want him there or have not prepared for him, he is sent back to the land of the living. We know this takes place when a person dies, and in a minute or two begins to breathe and comes back to life. When this occurs, the person who has died and come back to life must not tell what he saw while in the land of the spirits until three years have passed. If he tells before that, when he dies his spirit will be crushed between the moving mountains.

This was all done according to Mukat's plan. Many people today, especially the young people, do not pay any attention to Mukat's commands. Some day, when they die, they will be caught in the moving mountains and will never enter Telmikish, but will forever live outside.——Cahuilla

How the Stars Got in the Sky

Many years ago, the night sky was not as crowded as it is today. There was the moon and some stars, but some we now see were not there.

Living among the people there were three sisters who had great magical powers. One day they decided they did not want to stay with their families any more and that they wanted to live in the sky. They climbed the highest hill and made signs which are still there, and from them they went up in the sky where they became the Seven Sisters.

There were only three girls but the other four stars are the jewels they wore on their bodies. These seven bright stars appear only in June and during that time the desert people can see them in the dark sky.

Then there were two brothers. The older had been bitten by a snake when he was a young boy and it left one hand crippled. He was ashamed of his affliction and kept it hidden from everyone. He was so embarrassed that he wanted to go live someplace where no one could see his hand, but he didn't tell his brother of his desire to leave. One night as they lay sleeping in their hut, which had a hole in the roof, the crippled boy decided it was time for him to leave. He took a torch of plum wood, which burned with a red glow. He made his way through the hole in the roof and went to live in the sky.

In the morning the younger brother awoke and could not find his brother. For days he searched but to no avail, the boy was no place to be found. Then younger brother thought that if he slept in his brother's bed in the hut, he might have a dream which would reveal where the crippled one had gone.

That night as he lay in his brother's bed in the hut, he looked up at the hole in the roof and saw the red glowing star in the black sky. It was then he knew what had happened to his older brother. He got a stick from the smoke tree and lighted it. It burned with a white light and guided the younger boy as he made his way to join his brother. Today you can see the two brothers as they come out as stars in the winter months. The older brother comes out as a red glowing star in January and the younger brother appears as a white star each February.

Now the three sisters, before they went up into the sky as stars, used to tease an Indian girl because she had some of her front teeth missing. This caused her to be embarrassed all the time and she would never laugh and kept her mouth closed all the time. She was so unhappy that she left her family and went to live as a star in the night sky also. She became the most important of all stars, the one known as the North Star. Her necklace of jewels still hangs in the sky and she guides all the people of the world at night. But, because of her shame here on earth, she still keeps her face turned away from the three sisters.——— Cahuilla

CHUMASH

The Chumash Indians inhabit the coastal region north of Los Angeles in the Santa Barbara area. Most of the people disappeared in the same way as other California Indian groups: disease, military confrontations, missionization, and acculturation. From an estimated eight thousand in 1770, the Chumash population decreased tragically. By 1865 there were six hundred and fifty-nine people and in 1977 there were sixty-nine Chumash mixed-bloods living on the small Santa Ynez Reservation. There are undoubtedly many other descendants of this culture group living in various parts of California but most have no knowledge of their ancestors or their traditions.

In spite of the near demise of these Indians, there is still a rich cultural tradition practiced and their stories are very much alive.* One such tale is the astrological prophesy of personalities of people born during particular months of the year:

The Chumash Calendar

There was one old man in the Chumash Nation who was called the Astrologer. It was his duty to provide names for all babies born within the tribe according to the month of their birth. The Astrologer had lived many years and was extremely wise for he could forecast the destiny of each of the children of the tribe.

His prophecies were made according to the following pattern:

January (the month of the Toloache)—A person born in this month will have a large amount of self-respect. When they use their powers properly they always succeed.

February (the month when things begin to grow)—The winter rains soak into the earth and start the cycle of growth. Persons born during this month are uncertain and never sure of anything. It is very difficult for them to make decisions.

March (the month of Spring)—Persons born in March may be very strong, but others may be weak and sickly. It is a time of dichotomy. Seldom are the March people happy for very long. They may be joyous for a while, but sadness soon overtakes them.

April (the month of blooming flowers)—A person born in April is cheerful and works for the good of all. He is pleasant to the world for the flower season is pleasant.

May (the month of carrizo)—Persons born in May are full of knowledge, such as medicine, which will help their fellow humans.

June (the month when things are divided equally)—June is called this because it is the time for things to go out in different directions, to be reunited later. Persons born in this month are sensitive and serious. They are careful in all they do and are highly respected in the community.

July (the month when everything blows away)—Plants and trees begin to shed during July, and the wind blows their leaves away. A man born during this month is never at peace and is always agitating.

August (the month of fiesta)—Persons born in August are great ones for festivities. They are saving people and good to their neighbors.

September (the month when the dry things come down)—Leaves begin to fall more heavily and animals who do not like the cold start their descent to lower places. September people are cautious and watch for dangers.

October (the month of Sulupiauset)—Sulupiauset was the legendary grandfather who made canoes with pointed bows and used rods to construct the ribs. He instructed the people on how to build and use these crafts. A man born in October would become wealthy and would make beads for ornaments. He would be a drifter but wherever he traveled he would be protected.

November (the month of rain)—Persons born in November are never satisfied and keep seeking changes.

December (the month of brilliant sunshine)—Men born during this month tend to be childish for a long time. They finally leave this state and enter the life of activity. The sun also comes out of its lethargy and gives man the strength to comprehend his power as caretaker of the world.

GABRIELEÑO

This group of Shoshonean-speaking Indians inhabited the drainage area of the San Gabriel River, the territory around Los Angeles, and southward to include about half of Orange County, Santa Catalina Island, and probably San Clemente Island.* The name is derived from the Mission San Gabriel Archangel, established in 1771. This mission became the wealthiest and most prosperous of all and this "good fortune" was due primarily to the labor of the Indians recruited by the military and directed by the padres. As with the other "missionizing," the Indian population decreased rapidly, especially when the nearby pueblo Nuestra Señora la Reina de Los Angeles de Porciuncula (Los Angeles) began to grow. The secularization of the mission in 1834 added impetus to the decline of the Gabrieleno population.

* John R. Swanton, *The Indian Tribes of North America* (Washington: Smithsonian Institution Press, 1952), pp. 490–491.

From an estimated population in 1770 of five thousand, the Gabrieleno were so decimated by introduced diseases, dietary deficiencies, and homicide that by about 1900, they ceased to exist as a culturably identifiable group.* Descendants of these people, however, still are present and are identifiable as individual Gabrielenos.

Most of the oral tradition of this group of people has been lost or has been maintained in well-meaning but distorted recordings by popular "California" anthropologists who can only interpret the stories according to their own cultural perspectives. One of these is presented here.

Why Women Change Their Minds**

Two great Beings made the world, filled it with grass and trees, and gave form, life, and motion to the various animals that people land and sea. When this work was done the elder Creator went back up to heaven and left His younger brother alone on the earth. The solitary god left below made for himself men-children, so he would not be uttery companionless.

Fortunately, about this time, the Moon came to that neighborhood, and she was very fair in her delicate beauty. She was kind-hearted and filled the place of a mother to the men-children that the god had created. She watched over them and guarded them from all evil things of the night, standing at the door of their lodge. The children grew up very happily, laying great store by the love with which their guardians regarded them.

There came a day, however, when their hearts were saddened, a day when the men-children began to notice that neither their Creator nor the Moon gave them their undivided affection and care. Instead, the two Great Ones seemed to waste much precious love upon each other. The tall god began to steal out of His lodge at dusk and spend the night watches in the company of the white-haired Moon. The moon also on these occasions did not seem to pay much attention to her sentinel duty.

* Robert F. Heizer, Ed. *Handbook of North American Indians* (Washington: Smithsonian Institution Press, 1978), Volume 8, California, p. 540.
** Hubert Howe Bancroft, *The Works of Hubert Howe Bancroft* (San Francisco: A. L. Bancroft & Company, 1883), Vol. III, pp. 84–85.

The laxity by the two guardians was not the only problem facing the men-children for one night they were awakened by a weird wailing. When light came, they found a strange thing lying in the doorway which they afterward identified as a new-born baby.

The god and the Moon had eloped together and the Great One had returned to His place in the heavens. Before He left He appointed the moon a lodge in the sky where she can be seen today, with her gauzy robe and her shining silver hair, walking her celestial paths.

The child left on earth was a girl. She grew up very soft, very bright, very beautiful, like her mother the Moon. She was also like her mother in that she was fickle and frail. She was the first of womankind, and from her all other women descended, and from the moon. And as the moon changes, so do all women change.——Gabrieleno

KAROK

The Karok (upstream) people lived along the Klamath River in the northwestern portion of present-day California. Salmon played an important part in the lives of the Karok and many of their stories contain references to this food staple.

The tribe remained relatively unaffected by the influx of non-Indians into California until gold was discovered. Then their territory was overrun by the invading hordes of "gold-crazy" whites. In a period of about three years, the Karoks suffered approximately a sixty percent reduction in population. This loss was due to "military operations, social homicide, privation and disease, especially syphilis introduced by the whites," as described by William Bright. The 1972 figure issued by the Bureau of Indian Affairs indicates there are three thousand seven hundred and eighty-one individuals identified as having at least some Karok ancestry, some one thousand more than the 1848 estimate.

When the gold played out in their territory, the Karoks who survived were able to return to their traditional way of life and rebuild, undisturbed until recent times. Many of their stories are still told by the elders as they have been for centuries. A few of these have been included in this book.

How Coyote Stole Fire

In the beginning, after Chareya had created man and most of the other things in the world, He made fire and gave it into the custody of two old hags so the Karoks would not steal it. After exhausting every means to procure the treasure, the Karoks called on their old friend Coyote for help. Looking over the problem from every angle, Coyote came up with a plan and set about putting it into effect.

From the land of the Karoks to the home of the old women, he stationed a great numer of animals at convenient distances with the strongest and swiftest nearest the den of the old hags and the weakest further down the road. He then hid a Karok near the hut where the fire was kept with precise directions on how to act. Then Coyote trotted up to the door and asked to be let in out of the cold. Suspecting nothing, the old crones admitted him and he lay down in front of the fire and waited for his accomplice to do his part.

At the appointed time the man made a furious attack on the house and the old women rushed out to drive off the invader. Seeing his opportunity, Coyote immediately seized a burning piece of wood and took off down the trail as fast as he could run. The two hags, realizing they had been outwitted, turned after him in furious chase. Just as Coyote was beginning to tire and the women thought they were about to get their fire, Cougar took the firebrand and leaped away. Coyote laughed as the hags rushed by, gnashing their choppy gums as they took off after the great cat.

The Cougar passed to the Bear, the Bear to the Fox, and so on down the line. To the very end, the panting crones ran on their withered old bony legs in vain, and only two mishaps occurred among all the animals. The squirrel, well down toward the end of the file, burned his tail so badly that it curled up over his back as it is even today.

Last of all, poor Frog, who received the fire when it had burned down to a very small piece, hopped along so slowly that his pursuers gained on him. He gathered himself for every leap and strained every muscle but it was in vain for he was caught. His smoke-dimmed eyes stood out from his head and his heart thumped against the bony fingers which squeezed him so hard.

Frog was not through, however, and he gulped the fire down and gave a mighty jump which tore him out of the grasp of the old hags. He gave a mighty leap into the river and swam to the bottom where he was safe. He had paid an awful price though, for his handsome tail, which only the tadpole of his race would ever again wear, was gone.

Only the remnant of the Frog was left to spit out on some pieces of wood the precious embers he had saved at so great a cost. And it is because Frog spat out this fire on these pieces of wood that it can always be extracted again by rubbing them hard together.——Karok

How Coyote Stocked the River with Salmon

In the beginning Chareya, the Creator, had made salmon, but He had put them in the big-water. He made a great fishdam at the mouth of the Klamath River so that they could not go upstream. This dam was closed by something resembling a white man's key which was given to two old hags to guard. They were to watch over it day and night so none of the Indians could get near it.

Now the people loved fish and had a great hunger for them and men, women, and children cried out for food. Coyote, swore by the stool of Chareya that before another moon their lodges would be filled with salmon and even the dogs would be satisfied. So he traveled down the Klamath many days until he came to the mouth of the river and saw the big water and heard the thunder of the waves.

Up he went to the hut of the old women and rapped on the door. He asked for hospitality for the night and, since he was so polite and debonair, the old crones could find no reason to refuse him. He entered and lay down by the fire to get warm while they prepared salmon for supper, which they ate without giving him even one bite.

All night long he lay by the fire pretending to sleep, but thinking over his plans and waiting for something to happen so he could get the key. In the morning one of the old hags took the key and started off toward the dam to get some fish for breakfast. Like a flash, Coyote leaped at her, tripping her so she fell head over heels and the key was dislodged and fell on the ground. Before she knew what had hit her, Coyote had the key and was gone, running for the dam as fast as he could.

He inserted the key in the great lock and began to twist it with all his might. Finally the fastenings gave way and, with a great roar, the green water rushed through all ashine with salmon. The great wall of water

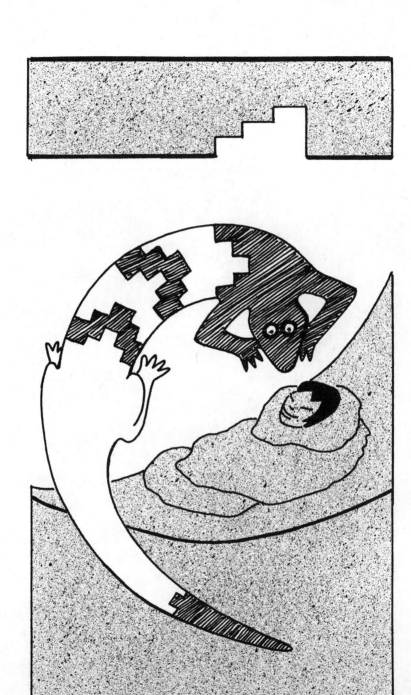

How Coyote and Lizard Made Children
Karok

utterly destroyed the dam so that ever after fish found free way up the
Klamath.——Karok

How Coyote and Lizard Made Children

Long ago it was Coyote who first made a baby and he ordained that
humans would make babies the same way he did.

The animals were talking in the sweathouse about what humans
were going to do and how woman would give birth to babies. One animal suggested that when she was ready to deliver, woman should have
her belly cut open and the baby removed. It was decided this would
destroy the mother though, and there would be too few women.

Someone suggested that since the baby was inside the woman and
had to have some way to come out, it should be born through the
mother's mouth. Coyote ruled this manner as unacceptable and suggested that the baby should come out behind. Lizard thought this an
excellent idea and the other animals concurred.

Then Coyote said, "One will be female and the next will be male."
Everyone agreed this was a good idea for this would make a mixture of
male and female. Lizard then said he was going to make the boys'
hands and feet, as well as the penis. He said the hands and feet would
develop while the baby was still in the mother.

It was then decided how large the baby should be when it was born.
If it grew too large, the mother would die and if it was too small, it
would not live. It was at this time the animals gave herbal medicine to
the humans. It was also at this time that the boys were instructed never
to kill Lizard and the girls were told that Lizard was their husband and
should be respected.

When the babies are small, it is Lizard who tells them when to sleep,
and when they are asleep it is Lizard who tells them funny stories
which makes them smile while they sleep. When babies cry in their
sleep, it is because Lizard is pinching them.

Lizard likes to stay around humans and likes to lay on top of the
sweathouses where it is warm, moving his chest up and down. It is too
bad for Lizard that the sweathouses are disappearing from California
and Lizard is being forced to lie on rocks in the sun to get warm. They
do not live around the Indian villages any more.——Karok

How Fire Was Obtained

A long time ago, Man had no fire for Fire-Owner kept it all for himself. He lived across the ocean and it was very difficult for Man to conceive how he could get some fire. Man, animals, and Sky-Owner talked for a long time about how they could get it.

Sky-Owner said he could not get it and it would be up to the others. Finally one of them suggested that they gamble with Fire-Owner and take the fire from him. It was decided that Bald Eagle would be the one to get the fire but he must have the help of the other animals. Bald Eagle would get the fire and give it to Coyote, for he was a swift runner. Beyond Coyote, on a ridge would be Deer who would receive the fire from Coyote. Beyond Deer would be Fisher, and then Duck. Each would carry the fire until he tired and then pass it to the next animal, until they finally got it to their land.

Then Eagle did as he said he would. He gambled and sang and blew some sparks from the fire. Coyote caught them and ran. Fire-Owner and his friends chased Coyote but could not catch him. When Coyote became tired, he passed the fire on to Deer who bounded away. Then Fisher ran with it, and then Duck. They had escaped with the fire.

When Duck arrived home, though, he had no fire; it had gone out. He then took two willow sticks and rubbed them together for a long time. Eventually, he got a little smoke and then some fire.

Now everyone was happy and they made fire in the sweathouse and fire in their homes. They all could now swim and, when they were cold from the water, they could warm themselves by the fire. The women were also glad for when they bathed in the cold stream every morning, they too could warm themselves by the fire. And so they do to this day. If they had not gotten the fire, no one could bathe or get shellfish from the ocean.——Karok

LUISEÑO

Luiseño is the name provided by the Spaniards and later used by the United States to designate those tribes of Indians who were associated with the Mission of San Luis Rey de Francia. They were also called Ghecham and occupied an area from the Pacific Ocean eastward to the mountains which extend south from Mount San Jacinto and bounded on the north by the Juaneños, Gabrielenos, and Serranos, and on the south by the Diegueño group.*

There were perhaps as many as fifty villages of these Shoshonean people scattered over a large area of land and many of these were never subjugated by being relocated in the mission or on reservations. The policy at San Luis Rey Mission differed somewhat from others by maintaining the Luiseño settlement pattern. The padres did visit the villages to perform religious services and supervise agricultural endeavors, but traditional methods of life and government were allowed to remain under the control of the natives.

These scattered villages, as well as the Indians brought under direct control of the mission, succumbed to the heavy influence of the Catholic Church and in the process lost much of their language, religion, and tradition.

Today there are approximately twelve hundred Luiseño Indians living on seven small reservations in southern California. These are the descendants of the five to ten thousand tribespeople who resided in the area prior to contact with the European invaders.

"The Making of Earth and the Moon" is one of the stories of this people's explanation of a natural phenomenon.

The Making of Earth and the Moon

In the beginning, everything was empty; Empty Quietness was the only being. Then came a whitish greyness and, from this, two whitish objects which were eggs. They lay there three days and then were made alive and recognized each other. From them came two beings which were Father Sky and Mother Earth. They conversed with each other in a very strange language which no one on earth could understand today.

"I am stretched," said Mother Earth. "I am extended. I shake, I resound, and I am earthquake."
Father Sky answered, "I am night. I am the arch of the heavens. I rise, I kill, I sever life."

* Swanton, *Indian Tribes of North America.*

These two married in the darkness and gave birth to children, who came in pairs. These were all sacred things used in ceremonies. Even the food which the people eat and the tools they use were born in this way and were once people. For instance, the sacred mortar in which the Jimsonweed root was ground for the boys' ceremony was the oldest child of all. Other children were the strings of shell money and the dancing stick with the crystal at the end; also the eagle and the bear, the palm tree, the cottonwood, and the acorns. The sun came forth at the same time and because he was so hot, his brothers and sisters sent him into the sky.

When all things had been born, the Earth Mother lay quiet with her feet to the north and her head to the south as she is today. The people wandered all over the earth and settled. One of them was a great hero called Wiyot who was wise and taught the people their games and art. Wiyot had a daughter, the frog, who became very angry with him. She was a woman and she knew magic, so she made him ill. Wiyot was ill for a long time and the people, one by one, tried to help him. During this time he sang death songs which are now sung at the mourning anniversary. As each month came, he described it and sang, "Shall I die this month?" The people carried him all over the country trying to make him better, but at last he died and became the moon. The people burned his body just as the have burned their dead ever since.

The people always hold a ceremony for the new moon. It is a form of greeting Wiyot and is thought to keep him strong and give them all health and good fortune.——Luiseño

MAIDU

This group of Penutian speaking people is generally divided into three distinct sections of land area in the northeastern portion of the state. The term Maidu refers to the tribal entity known as the Mountain or Northeastern Maidu, while the Southern Maidu are called Nisenan. They inhabited a series of river valleys in the mountains including the drainage areas of the American, Bear, Butte, and Feather Rivers.

From an estimated nine to ten thousand population in the early 1800s the Maidu people have decreased until there are now less than one thousand identifiable persons. Although Maidu life was little affected by white contacts until gold was discovered, the miners with their deadly diseases and their cruel treatment decimated them after 1848. Some of the most callous disregard for human life ever recorded occurred during the gold rush in this area.

The Maidu were a fiercely independent people and fought the interlopers in an attempt to retain their sacred homeland. Throughout the 1850s and 1860s skirmishes occurred between various groups of the Maidu and vigilantes and militia (supported and encouraged by the state in an effort to rid the territory of Indians); but by 1870 resistance by the Indians ceased as most had been killed or removed to Round Valley Reservation.

Conditions of present-day Maidu Indians are much the same as those of Indians all over America—low economic status, high unemployment, low quality housing and sanitary conditions, poor health, and inadequate educational achievement levels. There is a resurgence of cultural interest though, and the Maidu are manifesting this in the revival of ceremonies and oral tradition.

The next four stories are among those heard once again in the Maidu communities.

How World Maker Made People

When He had made the world from the small bits of dirt He scraped from beneath Turtle's fingernails, World Maker and Coyote walked around to see how things were. As they traveled, World Maker fashioned new beings from small pieces of earth He picked up, and gave them life. He made the bear, the cougar, the rabbits, and all other animals which inhabit the earth. As He walked He scattered seeds which grew and clothed the land with the many kinds of grasses, bushes, and trees. He waved His hands and all the different birds came into being.

At last World Maker and Coyote stood at the top of the highest mountain and looked out over the Creation and World Maker was very pleased. He then spoke to the spirits and forces which only He could see. He told them that He would make Man who would live on this beautiful earth and enjoy it and use all that had been created.

He returned to His hut and dug a large hole nearby which He filled with red dirt and seawater. From this mixture World Maker fashioned two figures, smooth and shiny, male and female. Coyote tried to get him to fashion their hands into paws like his, but World Maker made the human hands to look like His so the people could perform the tasks He assigned to them.

As He worked on modeling these new figures, He concentrated so hard that great drops of sweat fell from His brow. They gathered in large puddles on the floor of the lodge. Throughout the afternoon and into the night streams of sweat poured from World Maker's body, and at night when He had the two figures lay down to sleep, they floated in the salty water.

Man and Woman, already becoming more than mere earth and clay, drank in the sweat from World Maker through every pore. Each of the figures absorbed the moisture taking on something special of the Creator. They held this special gift forever thereafter and they became the parents of all people who followed. In those early days ever phase of life was as World Maker had planned it. No one worked, no one sickened, no one died.

The women would set their baskets beneath the great acorn tree at night and the next morning the baskets would be full of all the good foods necessary to sustain them and make them happy.

Coyote, being a sneaky, evil being, could not stand to see all this happiness. He went among the people, telling them evil stories and creating disunity among them. From that time on, man was marked with troubles, work, sickness, old age, tears, and death. In this way, the people were divided into tribes, each speaking their own languages, each different from the others.

So the people spread away in all directions and this is why there were Indians all over this part of the world, living in different ways and speaking different languages. It was all the fault of Coyote.——Maidu

World Maker's Gift to Man

Long ago in the time when legends were made, World Maker created people and gave them all the things for a happy life. Then along came Coyote and showed them Evil, the shady side of life, the earthen side of man. Although it was the people who broke the rules of World Maker, they always placed the blame on Coyote.

It was Coyote who the people saw and heard as he played tricks on them. It was he they saw lie and cheat to get what he wanted from others, and although he always lost in the end, the people never seemed to understand the lessons in his actions. No one profited by his mistakes and they kept emulating Coyote's ways. This gave them someone to blame when they did wrong.

From this time, the life of mankind has been marked by troubles, work, sickness, tears, and death. Everyone seemed to be two persons in one body; one following the mandates of World Maker and doing good, and the other following Coyote and his evil ways.

In the same manner, the people were divided into tribes, each speaking their own languages and living their different ways of life. First Man, receiving counsel from World Maker, instructed the various tribes on how to utilize all the things of the world.

First Man gave the tribes their laws and their stories, taught them how to hunt and fish, how to weave and make their baskets, and how to cook the foods which were in their areas. He then sent the people out in various directions. Some went to the north and became warriors, some to the south to be dancers, musicians went to the east, and singers to the west.

As each tribe left, First Man gave the women special instructions about the acorn. He explained how it was the first thing that was created and was intended to be the most important food for man and would be available as food until the end of time. He then showed them how to gather the acorns, how to shell them and make them into powder. First Man then showed the women how to bake acorns in the coals and how to boil them in their baskets and to make acorn biscuits.

So the people spread all over the world with the knowledge of the acorn, World Maker's gift to man.——Maidu

Why Bats See Poorly

At the beginning of time Coyote had created the world and its inhabitants but had left out one thing—fire. Away in the west where the Sun lived there was plenty but no one could get it for it was so far off and closely guarded. So the bat proposed that the lizard should go and steal some. Lizard did as he was requested but he had a difficult time bringing it back home for everyone wanted to steal it from him.

He had to travel by night to prevent thieves from robbing him and to keep from setting everything on fire. One night when he had nearly reached home he came upon a group of sandhill cranes who were sitting up all night gambling.* Lizard sneaked along the side of a log, as he does yet today, holding the fire in his hand. The cranes, however, spotted him and immediately gave chase. Now their legs were so long, poor Lizard had no chance to escape so he set fire to the grass and let it burn along behind him. Soon the fire was roaring and he had a difficult time staying ahead of it.

When Bat saw the fire coming, being unused to it, he was half-blinded and his eyes hurt terribly. He cried out to the lizard that his eyes would be destroyed and asked that they be covered with pitch. Lizard took the pitch and rubbed it over Bat's eyes so thick that he could see nothing. He flew wildly about this way and that, unable to see, just as he still does. He flew in and out of the fire and burned his head and his tail. Then he flew off to the west calling for the wind to blow the pitch off his eyes. The wind heard and blew but he could not get all the pitch off and that is why Bat sees so poorly. And because he was in the fire so long, even today he looks black and singed.——
Maidu (Konkow)

How the World Was Made

One day, long, long ago, Turtle was floating about in the darkness on a raft looking for some place to start a world. There was nothing but water and darkness and he was very discouraged. Spirit appeared from the sky and sat down on the raft beside Turtle. "Why don't you make me a world," said Turtle. "But I have no earth, nothing to build a world from," said Spirit. Turtle then agreed to dive to the bottom of the water and bring back the building material.

Poor Turtle had no idea how far it was to the bottom but he dived anyway. After a long time, he reached bottom and grabbed a large chunk of earth. By the time he got back to the surface, however, the dirt had all washed away. He began to moan and wail that he had failed, but Spirit looked under his fingernails and, sure enough, there was a small amount of earth there.

Spirit scraped the dirt from under Turtle's nails and began to roll it

* Gambling is a great recreation with Indians, especially tribes from Northern California. It has ritualistic significance in their tribal life even today and tournaments are held at many festivals.

in his hands. To Turtle's surprise, the piece of earth began to grow. It grew larger and larger until it was the size of the world today.

Now Spirit brought other things to make the world a better place. He brought the Sun, who was his sister, to provide light during the day, and he brought the Moon, who was his brother, to make the night brighter. Spirit next made the trees to grow, pine, juniper, ash, and the special oak which provided the acorns for the Indians to eat. Soon Coyote and Rattlesnake and the other animals had arrived, and finally came Man and Woman.

Man went around teaching everyone names and languages, what plants to eat, how to hunt and trap, the laws, and the ceremonies. When everyone knew what they needed, Man and Woman introduced Death. And since they were the oldest man and woman, they died first and went to live in the Spirit House.——Maidu

MODOC

The Moatokni (Modoc) people originally occupied a territory which today constitutes an area of south-central Oregon, extending across the northern border of California. They spoke a Lutuamian dialect of the Shapwailutan linguistic stock.

These natives came in contact with the whites later than most California groups so there was no long history of conflict. They did, however, prove to be quite a disturbing element when white immigrants finally began to invade their homeland. Many fights developed which gave the Modocs the reputation of fierce and uncompromising warriors. In 1864 the Modocs ceded their territory to the United States and moved to the Klamath Reservation, but they were never contented and persistently tried to regain their own country.

In 1870, a Modoc named Kintpuash, called Captain Jack by the whites, led the more militant element of the tribe back to northern California and refused to return to the reservation. The attempt by the government to force the Indians to return precipitated the Modoc War of 1872–73. Captain Jack led his people to the inaccessible lava beds of northern California and for several months resisted all attempts to dislodge them. Eventually they were overcome and Kintpuash and five other leaders were hanged, thus ending the short but violent revolution. Part of the tribe was sent to Oklahoma and placed on the Quapaw

Reservation and the remainder were returned to the Klamath Reservation. By splitting the people, further resistance by the Modocs was prevented.

After incarceration on reservations, the Modoc population decreased and by 1937 there were only three hundred and twenty-nine reported. Along with this reduction, the oral traditions and the cultural life of the Modoc people nearly disappeared. A few stories remain and two are related on the following pages.

Why the Bat Flies at Night

Once a long time ago, there was a war between the animals and the birds. Bat was on the birds' side, but in the first battle the birds were badly beaten by the animals. When Bat saw the fight was going against the birds, he sneaked away and hid in a hollow log until the fight was over. Then, as the animals were leaving, he slipped in among them.

When the animals noticed Bat in their midst, they asked him, "What are you doing here? You are one of the birds who fought against us."

"Oh, no! I'm one of you," Bat replied. "I don't belong with the birds. Did you ever see a bird who had double teeth like mine? Go look in their mouths and if you find one with teeth like mine, you can say I am a bird. But I am not a bird; I am one of you."

Convinced that Bat was telling the truth, the animals allowed Bat to remain with them.

Soon, there was another big battle and this time the birds were victorious. As soon as Bat saw his side beginning to lose, he slipped away and again hid in the hollow log until the fight was all over. As the birds were going home, happily chattering over the outcome of the fight, Bat sneaked out of the hollow log and in among the birds.

When they finally noticed him, they said, "What are you doing here? We saw you fighting on the animals' side; you are our enemy."

"Oh," said the bat, "you are mistaken! I am a bird, not an animal. Did you ever see one of them with wings? I am truly a bird."

They allowed Bat to remain with them and did not question him any more.

By this time Bat was getting pretty smug and he continued going back and forth between the birds and the animals as long as the fighting lasted. Finally, however, the birds and the animals called a truce and the war ended, and there was Bat, right in the middle. The two groups called a council to decide what to do with him. They pronounced their sentence, "From this time on, you will not belong with either the birds or the animals. You will fly around at night alone and will never have any friends either among those that fly or those that walk."

And so it is to this day. Bat is shunned by all other creatures and flies alone and only at night.——Modoc

How Kumush Made the World

One day Kumush was sitting on the east shore of Tule Lake resting. He looked around him and realized there was nothing anywhere except the lake; no land, no rocks, no trees, nothing but water. He then decided to make land all around the lake.

He reached down to the bottom of the water and drew up a handful of mud. He piled it up in front of him and started molding it into a hill. Next Kumush began to shape the mud with his hands and spread it all around the lake until it was surrounded by land.

After looking things over, Kumush was not satisfied so he began pushing up dirt here and there into mountains. He also drew his fingernails across parts of the land to make rivers and streams. Then he began to make the plants and the trees to decorate the earth. The birds and fish and animals were then made to live in the world and enjoy it. Everything was beauty and happiness.

Then Kumush began to be tired. It was a lot of work to make a world and the trees and birds and animals to live on it. It was almost winter and he decided he would do like the bear, go to sleep in a hole and rest all winter.

Kumush dug a hole under Tule Lake and left the hill he had made to mark the spot. As the hill dried out it became rock and is still there today.

Before Kumush went to sleep he took his fingernail and scratched a hole in the rock so he could see out if he wanted. The hole is still there and if a person climbs up the rock, he can look all over the country for the lake has dried up and the land is now farmland.

Someday Kumush will wake up and look out over the world he

made. He will be angry at how things have changed and will bring the water back to cover Tule Lake again. He will change the world to be like it was when he first made it.——Modoc

PATWIN

The Patwin Indians occupied the western portion of the Sacramento River Valley and held a large land area which extended from San Francisco Bay inland and northward. These Penutian-speaking people were plentiful prior to the coming of the whites, but after contact their population declined rapidly. Missionization, disease, military actions, vigilante raids, slavery, and loss of their will to survive soon eliminated the Patwin as a separate cultural entity. By 1923–24, Alfred Kroeber, famed anthropologist, could find no Patwin in the southern portion of their territory and only a few survivors in the north. In 1972, the Bureau of Indian Affairs listed only eleven Patwins scattered around California.*

As the Patwins disappeared from this earth, their traditions went with them. There have been attempts by leading anthropologists to reconstruct Patwin life, but these have had only limited success. Only about a dozen of their stories have been perpetuated and as the few remaining Patwins die, these tales also are in great danger of being lost or diluted by alien interpretations.

The following is this author's attempt to relate a Patwin story accurately.

When the Earth Burned

Once there was a man who fell in love with two sisters and wanted them both for his wives. The old man was very ugly and the women, who were magpies, laughed at him when he proposed. He became very angry and cursed the women and went away to the far north country. He was so angry that he set the world on fire and rowed out to sea in a tule boat and was never seen again.

The fire, however, was burning fiercely and ate its way southward,

---

* Patti Johnson, "Patwin" in *Handbook of North American Indians.*

consuming everything in its path. It burned people, animals, trees, rocks, water, and even the ground itself. Old Coyote saw the fire and smoke of the fire from his home away to the south and ran as fast as he could to put it out. He took with him two little boys, whom he put in a sack, and ran like the wind to the north. He ran so hard that, by the time he got to the fire, he was exhausted and dropped the sack which held the two boys.

Coyote finally mustered up enough strength to chew up some Indian sugar which he spat on the fire and put it out. Now there was no more danger from fire and Coyote was very thirsty but there was no water. He chewed some more Indian sugar, dug a hole in the bottom of the creek, and put the chewed sugar in it. This turned to water and filled all the streams so earth had water again.

Coyote next turned his attention to the two little boys who were sad because they were the only people on earth. Building a sweat lodge, Coyote split a number of little sticks and laid them out in a particular pattern over night. The next morning these sticks had all turned to people who were company for the boys. Coyote sent them out to the various areas of the world and, in this way, the earth was repeopled.
——Patwin

POMO

Pomo is not a tribal designation but rather refers to a group of seven northern California language groups which anthropologists have placed under the rubric Pomo. There are seven distinct tribes located north of San Francisco Bay which fall into this category. Therefore, there was no actual Pomo culture, except as an abstraction made by ethnographers. There were the seven tribes which carried on highly similar, but not identical, lifestyles.

It is estimated that eight thousand Pomo-speaking people inhabited the territory in 1770, but according to the 1930 census, there were only one thousand one hundred and forty-three remaining. According to the Bureau of Indian Affairs' *Tribal Directory*, in 1977 there were four hundred and one Pomo Indians residing on seven small reservations in northern California and a few more living on two others. Combined with two hundred and twenty identified but living off-reservation, the BIA rolls indicate perhaps seven hundred Pomos still in the state. It is undoubtedly true that there are many unidentified Pomo people of varying blood degree still in existence scattered around the country but most do not have cultural association with the reservation groups.

The northern Pomo, who call themselves Kashaya, first came in contact with whites, not with Spaniards or Americans, but with the Russian otter hunters who had moved down the Pacific coast from Alaska. This tribe suffered less acculturation and depredation than did their southern relatives primarily because of the short duration of the Russian occupancy and, since the invaders were interested only in the pelts of the sea otter, they disturbed the native lifeways much less than the missionaries or gold-seekers. According to McLendon and Oswalt in *Handbook of North American Indians,* p. 277, of the approximately two hundred or so identifiable Kashaya people, about half of them speak their native languages.

In maintaining a semblance of their culture, the Pomos have retained more of their oral tradition than have most other California Indians. Three of their stories are presented here.

How the Sun and Moon Were Made

In the beginning there was no light, but a thick darkness covered all the earth. Man stumbled blindly against man and against the animals, the birds clashed together in the air, and there was confusion everywhere.

The Hawk happened by chance to fly into the face of the Coyote. There followed mutual apologies and afterward a long discussion on the emergency of the situation. Determined to make some effort toward abating the public evil, the two set about a remedy. The Coyote gathered a heap of tules, rolled them into a ball, and gave it to the Hawk, together with some pieces of flint.

Gathering it all together as well as he could, Hawk flew straight up into the sky, where he struck fire with the flints, lit his ball of reeds, and left it there whirling along all in a fierce red glow as it continued until the present. It is the sun.

The moon was made in the same way, but because the tules of which it was constructed were rather damp, its light has always been somewhat uncertain and feeble.——Pomo

The Birth of Totokonula

Once, a long time ago, two boys lived in the Yosemite Valley in California. They were very happy for everything they needed was close at hand. One warm summer day they went down to the river for a swim. After paddling and splashing about to their hearts' content, they became tired and moved out on the shore to rest. They climbed up on a large rock by the stream and lay down in the sunshine to dry themselves. It was not long until they fell into a deep sleep and slept so soundly that they never awakened. Many days and months they slumbered on, through rain and snow, summer and winter.

During all this time, the great rock was growing, little by little, day and night, until it lifted the boys high in the air. They were so high that their friends could not see them though they looked for them everywhere. The rock continued to grow, up through the clouds, past the blue sky, until their faces touched the moon. Even to this day, it is possible to see the prints of their faces when the moon is full. Still the boys slept on, year after year.

Finally, a giant condor, soaring high in the sky to converse with Father Sun, saw the two sleeping boys. He returned to earth and called a conference with all the animals to figure out how to get the boys down from the top of the great rock. Every animal made a jump up the face of the rock as far as he could leap. The field mouse could only jump a little way, but he tried. The rat, the squirrel, the racoon, and others attempted but failed. The grizzly bear made a great leap but could not get to the top. His huge claws dug valleys and left ridges as he slid to the bottom. The cougar leaped farther than any of the other animals, but he too, failed to reach the top and fell back to the ground.

Then along came the tiny measuring worm who was the smallest of all the creatures. Little by little, step-by-step, he began to creep up the rock as he measured his way. Soon he was above the marks left by the cougar and other animals and out of sight of the animals below. They figured the little worm would tire out and never make it to the top but he continued day after day for about one whole snow. At last he reached the top and awakened the boys. The climb had made him very strong so he gathered up the two boys and began to descend the rock as he had climbed it. Eventually he got to the bottom with the boys and the animals had a great celebration. They decided to name the huge rock after the measuring worm, Totokonula, which the Indians call it today. The white men call it El Capitan.———Pomo

The Quest of Totokonula*

A certain Totokonula was once a great leader of his people. He was known far and wide as a great hunter and an excellent farmer, and his tribe never wanted for food as long as he attended to their welfare. However, one day an event happened which brought about a change in all this.

While out hunting Totokonula met a spirit-maid, the guardian of the beautiful valley where the tribe resided. She was not as the dusky beauties he had known among his people, but white and fair, with lovely yellow hair that fell over her shoulders like sunshine. Her blue eyes had a light in them like the sky where the sun goes down. White cloudlike wings were folded behind her shoulders, and her voice was sweeter than the songs of birds. It was no wonder that Totokonula fell so madly in love with her. He reached out to touch her but the snowy wings lifted her above his sight and he stood alone in the place she had been.

No more did Totokonula lead in the chase and no more did he tend the crops. He wandered here and there like a man in a dream, ever seeking that wonderful shining vision that had made all else stale and plain to his sight. The land began to languish with no one to care for it, and soon the gardens became a wilderness where drought laid waste and the wild beasts spoiled what was left.

One day the beautiful spirit returned at last to visit her valley and she wept to see the desolation, and she knelt and asked the Great Spirit to help her. The Creator heard her pleas and, stooping from His place, clove the dome of granite where she knelt from top to bottom, and the snow-water from the Sierra Nevadas rushed through the gorge, bringing fertility to the fields below. A beautiful lake was formed between the walls of the mountain and a river issued from it to feed the valley forever. Then sang the birds as of old, and the odor of flowers rose as if it were incense, and the trees put forth their buds, and the corn shot up

* Hubert Howe Bancroft, *The Works of Hubert Howe Bancroft* (San Francisco: A. L. Bancroft and Company, 1883), pp. 124–26 Vol. III.

to meet the sun and rustled when the breeze crept through the tall stalks.

The fair maiden moved away as she had come, but the people called the riven granite dome by her name, Tisayac, as it is known even today. After her departure Totokonula returned from his weary quest and, after hearing the spirit-maiden had visited the valley, the same madness as before seized him. He was even worse than before by at least seven times, and he turned his back on the lodges of his people.

He took out his hunting knife and cut the outline of his face in the granite cliffs so that, even if he never returned, his people would remember him and he would remain with them forever. He never did return from that hopeless search for the young maiden, but the graven rock was called Totokonula, after his name, and his likeness may still be seen, three thousand feet high, guarding the entrance to the beautiful valley.——Pomo

POTOYANTE

Very little is known of this group of California native people for they were obliterated by the pressures of the white man's invasion in the middle of the nineteenth century. Their language, customs, and most of their traditions have been lost. This author felt the following story should be included in honor of this nation which perished.

How Coyotes Turned into Men

There was an age when no men existed, nothing but coyotes. When one of these animals died, his body was the breeding place for a multitude of little animals. These little animals were in reality spirits, which, after crawling about for a time on the dead coyote and taking all kinds of shapes, ended by spreading wings and floating off to the moon.

This naturally would not do, for the earth was in danger of being depopulated. The old coyotes called a council to see if they could come up with a remedy for the problem. They issued a general order that all bodies should be incinerated immediately after death.*

* The custom of cremation was practiced by this group of Indians until about the 1850s, when as an identifiable group, they were wiped out during the "great genocide period" of California history. (See William E. Coffer, "Genocide of the California Indians" *The Indian Historian* (San Francisco: The American Indian Historical Society, Spring, 1977).

In time, little by little, these primeval coyotes began to assume the shape of men. At first there were many imperfections, but a toe, an ear, a hand, bit by bit, were gradually built into the perfect form of man walking upright and looking upward. For one thing, they still grieve, however, of all their lost estate—their tails are gone. The acquired habit of sitting upright has utterly erased and destroyed that beautiful member. Lost is indeed lost, and gone is gone forever. Yet, still in dance and festival, the men throw off the weary burden of utilitarian care, and attach as nearly as maybe in the ancient place, an artificial tail and forget for a short, happy time the degeneracy of the present in simulating the glory of the past.*——Potoyante

SAN PASQUAL

The San Pasqual Band of Mission Indians are native to a beautiful valley in southern California and speak a dialect of the Yuman language family. The present reservation is not on their ancestral ground but rather, lies about six miles north of their valley. When their reservation was established July 1, 1910, it was located through error at its present location—at least the Bureau of American Ethnology claims it was because of an "unexcusable error." Oddly though, the traditional land was in an extremely fertile, tillable valley, while the official reservation was established on three parcels of rocky, useless and barren hillsides. None of the San Pasqual Indians had ever lived on the reserved land for it was considered Shoshonean territory and, as stated above, the San Pasquals were Yuman. By the time the "error" was discovered, all the land fit to be occupied had been secured by white ranchers and farmers and the "mistake" was allowed to stand.

According to the Bureau of Indian Affairs' 1977 *Tribal Directory*, sixty-three San Pasqual Indians live on the reservation. Most of these residents work in the urban areas of San Diego, Los Angeles, or Orange County and either commute to the cities daily or spend the workweek there and return home on the weekends.

Many of the traditional ways have disappeared and life at San Pasqual is quite similar to the rural culture of their white neighbors. In recent years, a revival has begun to be evidenced, especially in tribal

* Hubert Howe Bancroft *The Works of Hubert Howe Bancroft* (San Francisco: A. L. Bancroft & Company, 1883), Vol III, pp. 87–88.

identity, as the Indians are moving back to the reservation. Some of the traditions have survived the acculturation processes of the Catholic Church, Spanish invaders, and Mexican and American settlers. Two stories which have withstood these forces are related here.

The Story of the Eagle Chief

Many years ago, in a tiny village in the southern portion of what is now California, there was a tiny village of the Inkepah Indians. The chief of the village was called Poltho, and he was a Quissie or Spirit Man who could change himself from a man to a bird or animal. When Poltho wanted to do this, he would go all alone to a high cliff above Brandy Canyon and there, while singing to the spirits, a transformation would take place. As his song reached its loudest pitch he would change into a great eagle. Then he would fly out over the valley and kill as many rabbits as he wished and carry them back to the cliff. He would then sing to the spirits again and change back to a man. Then he would return to the village with his load of rabbits where all would wonder at his prowess as a hunter.

Poltho had given stern orders that no one was ever to follow him when he went on these solitary hunting trips and threatened severe punishment to anyone who dared to disobey him. In spite of this, two of his tribesmen finally gave in to their curiosity and one day they followed him as he made his way to Brandy Cliff.

As they hid in the bushes near the top of the cliff, they heard the spirit songs and saw their chief turn from a man to an eagle. As soon as the great eagle soared away looking for rabbits, the frightened men rushed back to their village. That night all the hunters returned except Poltho who did not appear. There was much talk and worry and speculation concerning the absence of their leader.

Finally, the two guilty men could bear it no longer. They confessed their disobedience to Poltho's orders and told what they had seen on the cliff. A great wailing arose from the people for they feared they would never see their beloved chief again. Days passed and then one morning as they came from their caves, Poltho stood there to greet them. Their rejoicing was cut short when he told them he would only be with them a short time. He would stay until he trained his grandson to become their chief in his place.

The training began at once and every day Poltho took his grandson to the great rock cliff above the village. The awestruck villagers could hear them singing to the spirits all through the day and far into the night. Once the singing continued until the break of day and then came silence. The peoples of the village crowded close together and waited fearfully.

Suddenly, there came the sound of wings and looking up they saw a great eagle flying overhead. As it passed over them it gave a loud cry and they knew it was Poltho's farewell. Stretching their arms toward the sky, they called and called for Poltho to come back. Their chief, however, never came back, and to this day, the eagle's nest high among the clefts of that high cliff above Brandy Canyon is still there, but empty.——San Pasqual

The Great Spirit Blesses the Indian People

Away back in the beginning of time Ahmy-yaha, the Great Spirit, took clay from the earth and molded it into the form of a man. He stood the image up and it became Yohomat, the first man. He then took more clay and molded it in the form of a woman. "Lest man be lonely," He whispered. He stood the woman up but she fell down. He stood her up again and again she fell. Then Ahmy-yaha pulled a whisker from His chin and wrapped it around the woman. After that, she stood up beside the man and became Tuchipah, the first woman.

After the creation of Yohomat and Tuchipah the Great Spirit looked with His clear, all-seeing eyes deep into the heart of Yohomat, the Fatherman, and there He saw the spirits of all the future nations of earth striving for mastery.

He wondered to which nation He should give the highest place, the riches and honors of this earth life. He contemplated this while the red man, the brown, the black, and the white passed before His vision. Finally he spoke. "To the red man, the Lachappa, will I give my choicest gifts." The spirits all heard and understood and a great wailing arose. Especially did the Niku (white spirit) mourn and wail because it could not have first place. The spirit of the Lachappa was made very sad by the grief of the Niku spirit. He spoke softly to Ahmy-yaha and said, "Give the first place to Niku and stop his grieving; there will be many blessings left for my people." "It is done," announced the Great Spirit. And so to this day the riches and honors of the world belong to the white people, but Ahmy-yaha still loves the red man best and by His spirit still speaks words of comfort to him.——San Pasqual

TOLOWA

The Tolowa Indians of northwestern California are one of the few groups of Athapaskan-speaking people in the state. This language is spoken by the natives in the interior of Alaska and the Yukon Territory and by other Indians scattered along the Pacific coast north of the Tolowa. The Hoopa of inland California and the Navajo and Apache of Arizona, New Mexico, and Utah also speak dialects of the Athapaskan tongue indicating migrations from the northwest.

At the first white contact, the Tolowa lived in eight villages along the coast. Population estimates for these people vary, but there were probably close to two thousand Tolowa during the prewhite era. In 1910, according to a Federal census of northwestern California and southwestern Oregon, there were only one hundred and twenty-one Tolowa Indians remaining. As with other tribes, these people were decimated by new diseases for which they had no natural immunity. In this case, the killers were measles and cholera. By 1930, the "Oregon Athapaskans" including the Tolowa and other tribes, numbered five hundred and four.

Much of the Tolowa ritual activity was focused on ceremonies connected with the harvest of marine life. Two alien religious movements drastically affected these people, the Ghost Dance in the 1870s and the Shaker Religion in the 1920s. The latter assisted in the erosion of traditional religion among the Tolowa but, in spite of this influence, much of their oral tradition remains.

The following story of the Flood and the Fire is a typical example.

The Flood and the Fire

Once many years ago there were many Indians on earth and they were very happy. They had all they needed to sustain life, the weather was pleasant most of the time, and there was no fighting between the tribes. One day, however, it began to rain very hard. It lasted a long time and the water kept rising until the valleys were all filled. The Indians climbed the mountains to escape the water but finally even the mountains were covered and the people, along with the animals, perished.

There were two people, a man and a woman, who climbed to the highest peak and were the only two on earth who did not drown. They lived on fish, cooking them by placing them under their arms for everything on earth was covered by water and there was no fire. Finally the water began to subside and the earth was eventually back in the shape it was before the flood. From the pair who survived the great deluge all other people descended, as also did the animals, the birds, the insects and all other creatures which now inhabit the world. As the Indian people died, their spirits assumed the forms of deer, elk, bear, and other life as they desired during their lifetime. By this means the earth was once again peopled with all the life forms as before the flood.

The people, however, still had no fire to cook their food or to keep warm by. They looked enviously at the Moon for having fire while they had none. The Spider People formed a plan and secured the help of the Snake people in implementing it. The Spiders wove a balloon from their webs and started the perilous journey to get some fire from the Moon. They kept attached to the earth by playing out a spun rope as they went. In time they reached their destination but the Moon People were suspicious of them for they had an idea what the Spiders were after.

The Spider People convinced the Moon People that all they wanted was to gamble with them. Since the Moon People were quite fond of gambling, this pleased them very much, and the game quickly began. While the gambling was taking place by the fire, a Snake arrived, having climbed the rope, darted through the fire, grabbed some embers and made his escape before the Moon People recovered from the surprise.

When he arrived back on earth, it was necessary for him to travel all over the earth, touching every rock, tree, and stick so that from then on they would all contain fire. The hearts of all the people were glad and they welcomed the Snake warrior back into their midst. The Spider People were not so lucky, though, for they were kept prisoners by the Moon People for a long time before they were released and allowed to go home.

They were pleased with the appearance of the earth as it glowed brightly from the fires as it had before the flood. The Spiders returned thinking the other people would be grateful for what they had done, but they were gravely disappointed. Upon their arrival they were quickly put to death as a token peace offering to the Moon People. Since that time the Snake People have been hated by all others on earth, and the Spider People, fearing the same cruel treatment their ancestors received, remain shy and frightened to this day.——Tolowa

WINTU

The Wintu are the northernmost division of the Copehan (Powell, 1891) or Wintun (Kroeber, 1925) division of the Penutian language family. There were nine major groups of Wintu occupying the valleys of the upper Sacramento and Trinity Rivers in northwestern California. Prior to the coming of the white man, the Wintu people were quite a large group, having an estimated population of fourteen thousand two hundred and fifty. Soon after the first meeting with the European invaders in 1826, the depopulation began. A malaria epidemic in 1830–33 introduced from Oregon by fur trappers, took the lives of about three-quarters of the Sacramento Valley Indians. From 1846 until the 1880s, the Wintu suffered tremendous population losses due to extreme atrocities perpetrated by California vigilantes, gold seekers, State and Federal military forces, slave traders, farmers and ranchers, and railroad company employees.*

By 1910 there were only three hundred and ninety-five Wintu people enumerated and, according to the BIA *Tribal Directory* for 1977, there were forty Wintu living on three tiny rancherias with a few more scattered on three other areas of trust land in northern California.

With this drastic decrease in Wintu people it was natural that their oral traditions would also diminish. Some stories have remained though, and efforts are being made by numerous Indian-oriented organizations, as well as by the descendants themselves, to revive and perpetuate the Wintu culture. Two of their stories are provided here.

Bleeding Heart Lake

Once long, long ago an old man lived by a small lake with his only daughter. The old man's wife had died giving birth to the girl baby.

The little girl grew up to be very beautiful and was very good to her father. She kept his lodge clean, cooked good food for him, and kept

* Coffer, "Genocide of the California Indians."

his clothing mended. She also was an excellent maker of cooking baskets. She was very lonesome however, for there were no other people living near them, and the old man chased away any young men who came near. Sometimes the girl would see campfires across the lake but no one ever came near their camp.

One day, a young Indian man approached the old man's lodge. He had heard stories about the beautiful maiden and wanted to see her for himself. He had heard of how the old man chased everyone away who came near the camp. The young man, however, was determined not to be frightened away.

He put on his finest clothing, lots of beads, and even wore his otter-skin arrow bag. As he approached the old man's lodge, he was met by the fearsome old warrior who threatened to cut out his heart and throw it into the lake if he did not leave. The young man talked to the old man but he kept watching the young girl. He had never seen one so beautiful and he vowed he would have her for his wife.

The young man was brave, but not very wise for he decided to fight the old warrior for the girl. Although the boy was young and strong, he was no match for the experience and wisdom of his opponent. They fought for two days, and finally the old man killed the young warrior. He cut his heart out and after turning the young girl into a large, heart-shaped rock, smeared her with the blood. He then pronounced a curse on his daughter. He said she would always be a rock and would stand by the water's edge and be covered with the blood of her lover. He then threw the heart into the lake and announced that every spring the water close to the rock would turn blood-red.

Indians who are brave enough to venture into the area in the spring claim the big red heart-shaped rock still stands there and the water around it is red like blood.——Wintu

The Building of the Sierra Nevada

At the time when the world was covered with water, long before there was man, there existed three fowl, Hawk, Crow, and Duck. The latter, after diving to the bottom and bringing up a beakful of mud, died. Crow and Hawk each took half the mud that had been brought up and set to work to make the mountains. Starting in the south, each began to build a range of mountains stretching northward with Hawk working on the eastern range and Crow on the western. It was a long, weary job but finally the goal was reached when, at last, the workers laid the last peak, Mount Shasta.

Looking over their project, Hawk saw that there was something wrong, for the western range was much larger than his. He accused Crow of foul play, of stealing some of his mud. This did not bother Crow a bit. He just laughed and didn't even deny the theft. He seemed very proud of his success in outsmarting his partner.

The honest Hawk was quite upset over what happened and stood thinking for a long time with his head bent over to one side just as hawks still do. As he was thinking, he absent-mindedly picked up a leaf of Indian tobacco and began to idly chew on it and wisdom came with the chewing.

Strengthening himself mightily, Hawk fixed his claws in the mountains and turned the whole chain in the water like a great floating wheel. At last the range of his rival had changed places with his and the Sierra Nevada was on the east and the Coast Range on the west as they remain until this day.——Wintu

YOKUT

The Yokut tribes consisted of about forty tribal units inhabiting the southern portion of the San Joaquin Valley from Kings River to the Tehachapi Mountains. For many years the Yokut language was thought to be unique but in recent years, although not by concensus, it has been generally classified as a division of the Penutian linguistic family.

These people, unlike many of their neighbors, did not suffer extremely from the presence of the Spanish. They were too far inland for the missionary effort to affect them and their most turbulent period was during the time California was ruled by Mexico, 1822–46. Mexican influence was slight during this time except for an epidemic of malaria in 1833. Most of the contacts were the result of punitive Mexican raids to retaliate for lost cattle or for capturing Indian slaves to be sent south to Mexico.

Cultural and physical genocide in the northern San Joaquin Valley occurred after the annexation of California by the United States. Gold seekers decimated the tribes at that time. The southern Yokuts, due to the absence of gold in their lake country, received the depletion of their population a little later as settlers over-ran their land and turned it into privately owned farms and ranches.

From an estimated eighteen thousand Yokuts in 1770, their population decreased to five hundred and thirty-three in 1910. According to the 1977 BIA *Tribal Directory,* Yokut Indians are living in four areas of California. The Tule River Reservation had three hundred and fifteen Yokuts in residence; Table Mountain Rancheria had forty-two residents, but this trust land has been terminated and the Indians were given deeds to their allotted parcels; and a few Yokuts are mixed with members of other tribes on the Tuolumne and the Santa Rosa Rancherias.

Although there are few Yokuts remaining, they hold tenaciously to some of their oral traditions. The following story is told by the people from the southern portion of the San Joaquin Valley.

The Secret World of the Dead

Once, long ago, a man loved his wife so much that he attempted to bring her back after she died. After he buried her, he hid in a hole beside her grave. When she arose from the grave the second night, he tried to seize her, but she slipped through his hands.

He followed her to the Island of the Dead where he stayed for six days and watched the dead people dance. The man pleaded with the Chief of the Dead to allow his wife's soul to return to their home but the Chief refused. He did, however, allow the man to go back and instructed him to hide in his lodge for six days. He was told to come out on the sixth day and dance.

The man returned to his lodge and did as he was instructed. He was so anxious to tell his people of the Island of the Dead though, that he came out of his lodge on the fifth day. He danced for the people and told them his amazing story. When he stopped dancing, a rattlesnake bit him. He died and went to join his wife. Thus the people came to know where the souls of the dead go.——Yokut

YUROK

The Yurok people before 1850 lived in scattered villages along the coast in the extreme northwestern corner of California and inland for about forty-five miles along the Klamath River. They were called by their present name by the Karok people and it differentiates the two groups, Karok meaning "upstream" and Yurok meaning "downstream."

A controversy exists among linguists today as to the Yurok language. One theory espoused by many linguists is that the language is of the Algonquian family generally associated with the northeastern portion of the United States and southeastern Canada. The Cheyenne are usually considered the westernmost Algonquian speakers.

The Yuroks, as other California Indian groups, have suffered tremendous losses in population. In 1770 there were an estimated two thousand five hundred tribesmen but the population decreased rapidly after white exposure in 1826. The census of 1910 enumerated six hundred and sixty-eight, and that of 1930, four hundred and seventy-one. The Bureau of Indian Affairs identifies three hundred and thirteen Yuroks living on two California reservations and a few living among other tribes on another small rancheria.

Many of the stories of these people are centered around "Coyote" who played many roles in Indian oral tradition. The story of how he acquired his ragged tail is one which casts him in the role of the devious trickster who eventually loses out.

How Coyote Got His Ragged Tail

One day Coyote came walking down a stream and he came on a group of animals and birds which was quite upset. A great eagle had come among them and had taken all the fur and tails from the animals and all the feathers from the birds. He had them all and he sat on the top of a high mountain overlooking the Klamath River. Everyone came from all over the world to try to get the feathers, fur, and tails. They were very embarrassed to be seen without any covering.

Each of them shot their arrows at the eagle but none of them reached him for the mountain was too high. Even Coyote, who thought he could do anything was unable to shoot the eagle. He told everyone to watch, and he fired his arrow straight at the great bird but alas, it fell far short. Being a stubborn creature, Coyote kept shooting all day until his quiver was empty.

As soon as the sun came up the next day, all the animals began shooting again. Finally the little owl proved to be the best marksman and one of his arrows hit the eagle. He fell off the mountain peak and rolled almost to the river. It was then decided that the next morning everyone would go together and get their skin coverings. No one was to go before the others for if anyone went first, he would take the best and whoever was last would get the poorest.

Coyote, the devious one, devised a scheme which would get him there first so he would get the finest fur and the most luxurious tail. As everyone began to settle down for the night and go to sleep, Coyote took a sharp stick and placed it under his head so he would stay awake. But he slept nevertheless, in spite of the stick piercing him, and when he awoke, everyone was gone. They distributed the feathers and hair and only one old ragged tail, which no one would have, remained. They decided to leave this for Coyote.

By the time he had reached the dead eagle, Coyote found everyone had gone, and there was only one old tail left. He took that and stuck it on his rear end and today, what sticks out from this mangled mess is Coyote's part.——Yurok

Seven
Miscellaneous

This section contains stories and bits and pieces of Indian folklore that do not fit into the major divisions of this book. Because the author feels they are relevant to the general content and are also in danger of being lost, they are listed under the rubric "Miscellaneous."

Included are stories from Mexico and other Latin American countries, poetry which cannot be assigned to any particular Indian entity, and numerous "old sayings" which are still heard in conversation with traditional Indian people.

It is hoped they will furnish enjoyment to the reader as they did to the author as he collected them.

Yakoke cha imola (Thanks and good fortune)!

Koi Hosh

Ixtlaccihuatl and Popocatépetl

Many years ago there was a powerful leader of the Aztec people who had a very beautiful daughter named Ixtlaccihuatl. The ruler loved her for she was his only child and therefore would succeed him as leader of the great Aztec Empire. The old man ruled his people with kindness because of his feelings for his daughter. This benevolence caused many of his own people, as well as many from conquered nations, to dislike him, and, as age began to have its effect on him, these enemies began to make war against him.

He called to his aid the bravest of the young warriors of his tribes and offered his throne and the hand of his daughter to the one who could overcome his enemies. Among the soldiers who went out to fight was a stalwart young warrior called Popocatépetl. He had been in love with Ixtlaccihuatl for years and she felt the same about him.

The war was long and cruel and many were killed on both sides. When the fighting was over and Popocatépetl was about ready to return home to claim the throne and the hand of his love, his rivals sent word back that he had been killed in battle. The young maiden was so shocked and saddened that a strange illness befell her. Neither the priests nor the medicine men could cure her of this malady and she soon died.

When Popocatépetl returned and found her dead, nothing could lessen his grief. He did not want to go on living so he built a large pyramid upon which he placed his loved one. Next to it he constructed another for himself, where he stands today holding a torch to light her eternal sleep.

During the many years that followed, the snows covered the bodies of the young warrior and his beloved, but it never extinguished the torch which continues to burn, warm and everlasting, like the love of Popocatépetl for his beautiful Ixtlaccihuatl.*——Aztec

Repopulating the Earth

In the Age of Water a great flood covered all the earth and all the people who lived at that time were turned into fishes. Only one man and one woman escaped, saving themselves by crawling into the hollow trunk of a large cypress tree.

For many days they floated on the water and had little food with which to sustain themselves. Finally the waters receded and they went aground on the top of a high mountain which was called Colhuacan. As the waters continued to dry up, the man and the woman began to establish a lifestyle to meet their immediate need.

* Popocatépetl and Ixtlaccihuatl are two of Mexico's famous volcanoes.

They built a house and harvested the natural plants which grew abundantly in the soaked earth. Here they increased and multiplied and their children began to gather about them. All the children however were born dumb and had no languages with which to communicate. One day a dove came to them and gave them languages, the many different ones we hear today.

Fifteen of the descendants of Coxcox, as the man was called, spoke the same language and were able to understand each other. These fifteen were the founders of the great nations of the Toltecs, the Aztecs, and the Acolhuas.——Aztec

Quetzalcoatl

The chief divinity of the Nahuatl nations was Quetzalcoatl, the gentle god, ruler of the air, controller of the sun and rain, and source of all prosperity. In the glorious days of the Toltecs, he had been their king, the creator of their golden age. He gave them metals, improved their government, taught them to live in harmony, and how to love. Replacing cruelty with human dignity he made them a prosperous people. He was their god, with his chief shrine at Cholula where all the people, even those who lived apart from that city, came to worship him and built temples in his honor in their own cities.

Quetzalcoatl had come to them from toward the rising sun, and he was white. He had large eyes, long black hair, and a heavy beard. After he had ruled for twenty years and the nations were peaceful and prosperous, Quetzalcoatl informed the people it was time for him to leave.

Traveling eastward he came to the seashore and sailed to the east on a raft of snakes. His last words to his people were that one day bearded white men, brethren of his, and perhaps even he himself, would come by way of the sea in which the sun rises, and would enter in and rule the land. He then sailed away.

From that day, with the faith of the Hebrews awaiting the coming of their Messiah, the Mexican people watched for the fulfillment of this promise made by Quetzalcoatl, the prophecy which told of a gentle rule, free from bloody sacrifices and oppression.

Thus it was that the tidings of strange sails and of bearded white men on their eastern shore were received at the capital with great joy. The Mexicans thought they had received the brethren of their god, but

they had instead welcomed Cortez and his murderous Spaniards.——
Aztec

The Origin of Peyote

A young prince named Jiculi was out one day hunting for deer. As he
walked through the woods, he was suddenly surrounded by witches.
They were ugly and cruel and evil, and they wanted to harm him. He
attempted to fight them but it was not long before they overpowered
him. They tied him up and threw him in a cage.

Jiculi tried vainly to break his bonds but was tied too well. A plumed
lion approached his cage and invited him to pull out one of his feathers
which he said could be used to loosen his ropes. The prince recognized
that this was a trick and the lion was a sorcerer trying to tempt him. He
knew that if he took the feather, great troubles would befall him. The
sorcerer became very angry and roared off into the forest.

Some of the singing birds, seeing the difficulty the young prince had,
began to whistle and sing, calling the forest animals to come and help.
A group of mice heard and entered the cage and began to gnaw at the
bonds. Others worked on the bars of the cage and destroyed them.

Gaining his freedom, the prince began to flee, but the witches chased
him. The gods changed him into a deer but the evil witches transformed themselves into fierce dogs and began to gain on Jiculi. When
they had caught up and surrounded him and it seemed as though the
ferocious dogs were about to devour the poor deer, it disappeared. In
place of the frightened deer was a tiny knoblike cactus buried in the
earth. It was peyote.

Thus the gods mocked the witches, and the prince, who was good to
his people, never took human form again. He continues living as the
peyote, which does so much good for its people.——Huichol

The Great Flood*

Once long ago, a shepherd was tending his llamas as they fed on the
mountain slopes. He noticed his animals seemed oppressed with sad-

* The account of this South American tribe's version of the flood is included to illustrate
the widespread distribution of this phenomenon and how the stories correlate in diverse
geographic and cultural settings.

ness and passed the entire night attentively watching the course of the stars. Filled with amazement, the shepherd questioned the llamas as to the cause of their concern. Directing his attention to a group of six stars massed closely together, they told him this was a sign that the world would soon be destroyed by water, and instructed him if he wished to escape the flood, to take refuge with his family and flocks on the top of a neighboring mountain.

Acting on this advice, the shepherd quickly collected his llamas and proceeded with them to the top of the mountain, where a crowd of other animals had already sought safety. The warning had not come a moment too soon, for they had hardly reached the summit when the sea burst its bounds and, with a terrible roaring, rushed over the land. But as the waters rose higher and higher, filling the valleys and covering the plains, the mountain of refuge rose with it, floating upon the surface like a ship upon the waves.

This flood lasted five days, during which time the sun hid itself and the earth was wrapped in darkness. On the fifth day, the waters began to subside and the stars shone down on the desolate world, which was eventually repeopled by the descendants of the shepherd.——Inca*

The Creation

The first humans, one man and one woman, were created by God to take care of an apple called "The Prince." God called the man "Adam" and the woman "Eve." They were told to care for the apple but not to eat it.

At first they were faithful in carrying out their orders even though Eve wanted to eat the fruit and kept telling Adams how good it smelled. Adam resisted the temptation but after three days he gave in and they ate the apple.

Shortly afterward the couple noted with surprise that in the process of digesting the apple, their bodies were changing drastically. One piece stuck in Adam's throat becoming the little bone which is seen in the throats of men only. Another piece of the apple went down and formed his male organs.

* Hubert Howe Bancroft, *The Works of Hubert Howe Bancroft* (San Francisco: The History Company, 1886) Vol. V, pp. 14–15.

It was different with Eve and her changes were not the same as Adam's. One part of the apple made her breasts, and another made her female organs.

Now seeing the extreme differences in their bodies, Adam and Eve became very curious about the possible use of these new organs. After much experimenting they found a good use for them and they fell into sin. Since this time humanity has been multiplied through intercourse.*——Maya

How Life Began on Earth

Long, long ago before there were days or years, the world was in great darkness and there was no light. The earth was covered with water and there was nothing but mud and slime all over it. Out of this darkness one day a god became visible and his name was the Deer, and his surname was the Lion-Snake. At the same time there appeared a very beautiful goddess called Deer, and her surname was Tiger-Snake.

When these two deities became visible in the world, they came together and made a great rock, upon which they built a beautiful palace in which to live. On the very top of this building there was a large ax made of copper with the blade turned uppermost. Upon the thin edge of this copper ax rested the heavens.

The rock itself was called The Place of Heaven and this was the first home of the gods on earth. They lived there for many years in peace and contentment although the world around them was still in darkness.

Two sons were born to these first gods of the earth and they were very handsome and very learned in all wisdom and arts. These young men were endowed with special and unusual skills. When the elder wanted to amuse himself, he took the form of an eagle and would fly far and wide, soaring over the whole world. The younger would turn himself into a snakelike creature but having wings also which he used in such a way that he could become invisible and could fly through rocks and walls as easily as through the air.

They lived in great peace with their parents and worshipped them

* This story is undoubtedly mixed with native tradition, Christian missionary influence, and typical Indian humor.

and made offerings to them. The sons built a beautiful garden in which they placed all the trees and flowers which gave fruit and beauty to their surroundings. They then gathered the waters in certain places so the earth was exposed and dried out. They then lifted the darkness from the earth and gave it light and made it ready for mankind. They then placed man in the world to enjoy their creation.

Man developed and became evil so a great deluge came to cleanse the earth. All that survived the flood were those who were worthy to carry out the work of the two boys. After the deluge had passed, the human kingdom was restored as at the first, and the Mixtec kingdom was populated, and the heavens and the earth were established.——— Mixtec

The Sacred Bird

Once long ago in the land at the tip of South America lived a group of people called Yamana. Every year, their sacred Ibis birds would arrive to spend the short summer living with the people. One day a man walked out of his house as Spring approached and saw an Ibis flying overhead. He became so excited that he shouted loudly, "Spring has come. The Ibis has returned." Everyone came running out and created much noise and excitement. The whole tribe shouted and danced and raised such a racket that the Ibis, being a very cranky bird by nature, became extremely angry.

She called down a great storm of snow and wind and ice and cold upon the noisy people. The storm lasted for about a month and the humans were forced to remain in their lodges all that time. At last the snow stopped and the sun came out. It shone so hot that all the trees were scorched off the mountains. The melted snow flowed in great floods down the slopes. Even then the sun did not melt the snow on the mountains and some in the deep canyons. Some even lasted out on the ocean and still floats around in the form of icebergs. The land remained barren and unfriendly to people and the forests never grew back. The great snows and hot scorching sun still keep this a hostile place. It became the custom for the parents to keep their children quiet at the time of the Ibis and, when this great sensitive bird came near, they walked about silently, treating her with great respect. They did

not want to offend her and risk making their land an even worse place
to live.——Yamana

Why Night Hawk Has a Crooked Bill*

> Once the OLD MAN of the Indians
> Got caught fast beneath a stone.
> There he lay from morn to nightfall.
> No one heard him scream or moan—
> Or if anyone did hear him, no one
> Cared to give him aid
> For he often acted cruelly,
> Many friends he had betrayed.
> Night Hawk on this evening's hunting
> Spied OLD MAN in his sad plight,
> And felt sorry thus to see him
> All alone and filled with fright.
> So the bird dashed at the boulder
> Like an arrow towards its mark.
> With his bill he tried to smash it,
> Working fiercely through the dark.
> Finally he, with one last effort,
> Using all his strength and heart,
> Struck the stone a blow so mighty
> That it crumbled all apart.
> OLD MAN felt, for once, real grateful
> To this bird who set him free.
> So he spoke to Night Hawk, saying:
> "Ho, Night Hawk, come here by me.
> On your back I'll sprinkle stardust
> To give you a speckled coat—

* This poem appeared in a Los Angeles newspaper about January 1935. A newspaper
clipping was found in an old book and this much information was ascertained by printing
on the reverse side. The author is not known by this writer, nor was it possible to determine the tribe from which the story came. It is worthy however, of space in this publication.

It will make you very pretty.
Here's a ring, too, for your throat.
You shall be forever graceful—
As you soar into the night.
There shall be no bird your equal
In his speed or skill or flight."
Thus OLD MAN rewarded Night Hawk,
But forgot to mend his bill
Which was bent against the boulder—
So he wears it that way still.

——Har Har Aitch

Indian Folklore

Owls are the bodies taken over by dead warriors who wish to visit their people.——Papago

One's teeth will fall out if he eats food over which caterpillars have crawled.——Pima/Papago

The jack rabbit causes open sores.——Pima

The ground squirrel of the mesas causes nosebleeds.——Pima

The eagle causes hemorrhaging.——Pima

The bear causes the body to swell.——Pima/Papago

The buzzard causes eye sores on a baby.——Pima

To kill a horned toad brings on sickness.——Pima/Papago

If the wind blows three consecutive days from the east, it will rain.——Many tribes

Kill a snake and leave it lay with its stomach to the sun and rain will come.——Pueblo

If a redheaded woodpecker pecks on a house or a tree near a house, danger threatens that house.——Choctaw

If you have a nightmare, put a fork under your pillow before going back to sleep.——Many tribes

If you drop a fork, someone hungry is coming.——Cherokee

Never try to kill a snake with a freshly cut stick; you will be bitten.——Choctaw

When there is a ringing in your ear, someone is talking about you.——Choctaw

When your nose itches, someone is coming.——Choctaw

When your palm itches, you will receive money.——Choctaw

If you walk with only one shoe on, you must retrace your steps exactly or suffer bad luck.——Choctaw

If you count the stars and don't finish, you will die.——Choctaw

If you dream of fish, you will receive money.——Choctaw

If a pregnant woman drives a wagon across a stream, she leaves the spirit of her baby on the far side and his life will be short.——Choctaw

A newborn child should be plunged into water just after birth to temper it, like metal.——Choctaw

If you don't eat hog meat on New Year's Day you won't have enough food for the rest of the year.——Choctaw

Cousins who marry will have deformed children.——Choctaw

If you see two rabbits that look like they are talking to one another, someone will die.——Choctaw

If a rabbit crosses the road in front of you, spit or you will have bad luck.——Choctaw

If a young maiden drops a dishcloth, she won't be able to find a suitor.——Choctaw

Do not give a knife as a present to a friend for it will sever the friendship.——Osage

If you fight over a girl before you marry her, she will be unfaithful after marriage.——Choctaw

If you point at a rainbow, your finger will rot.——Choctaw

If you handle a toad, you will get warts.——Choctaw

If you point at a watermelon, it will rot.——Choctaw

Mexican Indian Tradition

A piece of peyote boiled or chewed or put into food or a drink will cause the person who takes it to fall madly in love.——Huichol

One can get rid of an enemy by touching his hand with peyote hairs or by throwing the hairs over the shoulder in the direction in which the enemy is walking.——Huichol

The peyote plant has four faces and therefore sees everything and is very powerful.——Tarahumara

Anyone who steals peyote goes crazy.——Tarahumara

Peyote plants are very modest so they are kept in a jar or basket in a separate storehouse. If they were in the house they would be shocked at immodest things they might see.——Tarahumara

The earth is in the form of a giant crocodile set down in the waters by the gods. The mountains and valleys are the scales on the great beast's back.——Aztec

A hair or two of a woman who died in childbirth is a good luck charm for a warrior.——Aztec

When the sun and moon set in the west, they enter an underground passage that allows them to pass through the earth to the point at which the started.——Maya

When the world comes to an end by being eaten up by a giant jaguar, everyone will go up to the sky to live as gods.——Lacandon

If you burn the biscuits, it will rain.——Many tribes

Do not look a mole in the eye or you will go blind.——Cherokee

Look your mother-in-law in the eye and you go blind or crazy.—— Many tribes

Fires must be kindled on a still day so the smoke goes straight up and prayers sent to the Great Spirit go in the smoke.——Many tribes

To see a ghost is a certain percursor to death.——Choctaw

To dream of ghosts causes sickness and even death.——Choctaw

When a person touches a dead body, he purifies himself by taking "ghost medicine," throwing it on the fire, making smoke from it, and sitting in the smoke.——Apache

Dead person's names are never mentioned.——Many tribes

After a death, no one wears red for several days.——Apache

If a pregnant woman looks at a corpse or helps her husband dress an animal, her child will be born dead or disfigured.——Zuñi

If the husband of a pregnant woman maims an animal, the child will be born similarly maimed, or deformed, or perhaps blind.——Zuñi

Taking a nap during labor will bring forth a male child. If a female child is desired, all men must leave the room when the child is about to be born.——Zuñi

If a pregnant woman views a corpse, she must look straight at it. If she looks slantingly, the child will be cross-eyed.——Mesquakie

A nightmare is caused by a restless ghost and it is necessary for incantations to drive it away.——Many tribes

Barking foxes or screeching owls are omens of death.——Many tribes

A dead person, since he has become a ghost, should be buried as soon as possible. Otherwise, his spirit will linger near the body and might take the spirit of someone living with it, especially the spirits of little children.——Cheyenne

Those performing a burial must brush off their own bodies with green grass and then put it on the corpse in the shape of a cross. Then they will not dream of the deceased.——Apache

Burials must take place quickly and the relatives and friends leave as soon as they can. Only witches are seen fooling around graves.——Apache

Pregnant women who touch crawfish will have their babies born feet first.——Mesquakie

Do not feed a baby tongue meat before he can speak or his tongue will grow too big and he won't speak well.——Jicarilla Apache

To relieve the soreness in the gums of a teething baby, rub them with rabbit brains.——Choctaw

If while traveling at night a coyote crosses your trail, you must turn back to avoid bad luck.——Navajo

Do not kill quail for they are the spirits of dead children.——Papago

If a hunter inhales the breath of a dying deer, it will make him sweat and immediately become sick.——Navajo

A man's hat falling off is considered an ill omen.——Cahuilla

Pregnant women should not eat the legs of game or their children will be born feet first.——Cahuilla

If a pregnant woman eats fruit which a bird has pecked at, her child will have sores.——Cahuilla

A small amount of wild sage carried on a deer hunt brings good luck.——Wintu

If a child touches a mole, the child might go blind.——Cherokee

If a menstruating woman accidentally touches a man, he will have nosebleed, headaches, and leg pains.——Creek

A warrior who killed an enemy in his own land was entitled to wear at his heels, a fox-skin fastened to each moccasin.——Blood

He who killed a grizzly bear could wear a necklace of bears' claws.——Blood

Eagle tail-feathers will ward off disease if worn on the person.——Blackfeet

Index